SOCIAL INDICATORS

Social Indicators

The EU and Social Inclusion

Tony Atkinson, Bea Cantillon,
Eric Marlier, and Brian Nolan

With a Foreword by Frank Vandenbroucke

OXFORD
UNIVERSITY PRESS

OXFORD
UNIVERSITY PRESS

Great Clarendon Street, Oxford OX2 6DP

Oxford University Press is a department of the University of Oxford.
It furthers the University's objective of excellence in research, scholarship,
and education by publishing worldwide in

Oxford New York

Auckland Bangkok Buenos Aires Cape Town Chennai
Dar es Salaam Delhi Hong Kong Istanbul Karachi Kolkata
Kuala Lumpur Madrid Melbourne Mexico City Mumbai Nairobi
São Paulo Shanghai Singapore Taipei Tokyo Toronto

with an associated company in Berlin

Oxford is a registered trade mark of Oxford University Press
in the UK and in certain other countries

Published in the United States
by Oxford University Press Inc., New York

British Library Cataloguing in Publication Data

Data available

Library of Congress Cataloging in Publication Data

Data available

ISBN 0-19-925349-8 (Pbk)
ISBN 0-19-925249-1 (Hbk)

1 3 5 7 9 10 8 6 4 2

Typeset by Newgen Imaging Systems (P) Ltd., Chennai, India
Printed in Great Britain
on acid-free paper by
Biddles Ltd., www.biddles.co.uk

Foreword

Social policy was explicitly introduced as a distinct focus of attention for European cooperation at the special European Summit in Lisbon in March 2000. The Lisbon Council concluded that 'Steps must be taken to make a decisive impact on the eradication of poverty by setting adequate targets to be agreed by the Council by the end of the year'. Objectives to fight against poverty and social exclusion were then agreed at the European Council in Nice in December 2000. Since it is impossible to monitor progress in the EU member states with regard to social inclusion in the absence of comparable, quantitative indicators, the Belgian government decided to make the establishment of common European social indicators a priority for its presidency of the Council of the European Union during the second half of 2001. To underpin this political ambition, my colleague Johan Vande Lanotte (Deputy Prime Minister and Minister for Budget, Social Integration and Social Economy) and I organized a conference on 'Indicators for Social Inclusion: Making Common EU Objectives Work' in Antwerp in September 2001. This book is based on the excellent report written for that conference by Tony Atkinson, Bea Cantillon, Eric Marlier, and Brian Nolan.

It was agreed at Nice that the promotion of social inclusion within the overall strategy of the EU would be best achieved by an open method of coordination. This method involves setting common objectives at European level, designing appropriate national policies to achieve the objectives, and reporting national policy developments and outcomes. The open method of coordination is designed to help member states develop their own policies, reflecting their individual national situations, to share their experience, and to review their outcomes in a transparent and comparable environment.

I know there is some scepticism about the open method of coordination given its character of 'soft law'. Yet I am convinced that an effective open method of coordination in the field of social inclusion can play a crucial political role at this stage in European politics. It will create a common understanding of our core social values that goes beyond solemn declarations at the level of heads of state and government, and so should enable us to define in a more precise way the substance of the European Social Model. It has, then, the potential to be a powerful driver to improve the quality of social protection in Europe. However, all this requires one condition to be fulfilled: we have to move beyond generalities about the unacceptability of poverty in our societies. This is why indicators are of fundamental importance. In order to be able to fight social exclusion effectively, we need to be able to measure it accurately.

The European Employment Strategy has shown that the open method of coordination works. The discussion of the National Action Plans on Employment and the elaboration of European Guidelines for Employment Policies turned out to be a substantive exercise in which not only the quantity, but also the quality, of employment is taking an increasingly important place.

Just as with the European Employment Strategy, a common European strategy on social inclusion should be a process whereby explicit, clear, and mutually agreed objectives are defined, after which *peer reviews* will enable member states to examine and learn from the best practices in Europe. Our objectives should be realistic yet ambitious. What Europe needs is an exercise in ambition in the social policy area, the establishment of 'standards of excellence' rather than standards of mediocrity. The commitment to excellence in social policy is a basic common value of the European social framework. But there is not a single best practice: there are different ways to reach excellence, and there is no end in sight for this process, since we can always do better.

Indicators can also fulfil a normative function when they are related to targets, such as in the European Employment Strategy, or—to take another example in the field of anti-poverty policy to which all EU member states signed up—the Policy Framework for the eradication of poverty adopted at the Social Summit in Copenhagen in 1995. Five years later, at the United Nations Millennium Conference in September 2000, the international community committed itself to halving extreme poverty in the world by 2015. On the basis of commonly agreed indicators, the EU can play a leading role in the Copenhagen process, by showing that this commitment is taken very seriously within the EU, and is subject to coordination at EU level.

Developing quantitative indicators to measure social and economic progress is not a new endeavour. For a long time GDP per head has been used as an indicator of economic progress. The development of quantitative social indicators is certainly a more complex and sensitive issue; but, as the report by Atkinson *et al.* shows, it is feasible. The discussion of the Report during the Antwerp Conference confirmed that, notwithstanding many problems of data and interpretation, extensively discussed in the Report, we do have sufficient scientific knowledge to define social indicators conceptually, to apply them empirically, and to use them in politics. There might be political arguments for not engaging in this process (unconvincing arguments, in my opinion), but there cannot be scientific arguments.

From the outset of the political discussion in the EU on the construction of these indicators, the Belgian government insisted that my colleague Johan Vande Lanotte and I should find agreement on a multidimensional set of indicators, as social exclusion is a multidimensional problem. Let me expand on this crucial point. If we work with a 'line' of 60% of median income, that line cannot be a 'poverty line': it indicates something else. Clearly, someone with less than 60% of median income has a low income. But it is the combination of low income with other factors that leads to poverty. These additional factors may differ from country to country. For example, in Belgium we have a fee-based health insurance system; although there is rather generous reimbursement per individual medical act (i.e. per fee), there is currently no adequate protection against the accumulation of fees and personal co-payments. Hence low income combined with chronic illness may be a cause of financial hardship and even poverty, even though our general health care system performs well. What a '60% line' indicates, therefore, is the number of people who are 'at risk of poverty'. Whether or not that risk materializes depends on other factors, such as the cost of chronic illness, which have to be monitored closely by social policy-makers. Delineating the group of people for whom such monitoring and practical measures are most relevant by using the 60% line can render policy-making and policy more efficient.

During the conference, some criticized the Atkinson *et al.* report for not justifying the choice of 60% as a cut-off point—as opposed to 50%, for instance. I agree that we cannot say that the choice of the cut-off point is purely 'arbitrary'. Yet, I believe it is fair to say that at this stage we do not know enough to decide whether the most appropriate cut-off point is 60% or 50%, if the line is meant to delineate those who are 'at risk of poverty' when confronted with other problems. The policy error, when choosing the larger group, might be less worrisome than the opposite error.

In order to arrive at an adequate and politically acceptable set of indicators, we have been able to build on different valuable sources. In September 2000 the European Commission made the first contribution at EU level with a Communication on structural indicators. This first step has been built upon by the Social Protection Committee and its sub-group on Indicators, chaired by David Stanton. The Atkinson *et al.* report on *Indicators for Social Inclusion in Europe* and the deliberations of the Conference on Indicators for Social Inclusion in Antwerp were useful inputs for the sub-group on Indicators when it prepared its final report for the council meeting of 3 December 2001.

Reaching a consensus by the end of 2001 was a major ambition of the Belgian presidency of the Council. The set of statistical concepts and definitions included in this *Indicators* report represents in effect a *toolbox* of instruments that will allow member states to use a common language for assessment in the area of poverty and social exclusion. Although member states will be expected to make use of these common indicators, they will, of course, be encouraged to complement the EU indicators with their own choice of country-specific indicators, which will allow them to highlight their national specificities. This will enable policy-making to be more transparent for the citizens of Europe. No doubt, it will also serve as a major source of ideas about new indicators to be adopted by the EU as a whole.

We have to make it clear that the purpose of the establishment of a common set of indicators is not a naming and shaming exercise. Emula-tion through peer review in what some have labelled a social policy 'tournament' does not make winners and losers: on the contrary, we can only win together, because we can all do better, and learn from each other. Some member states perform better in one area, and others in a different area, so that there is a great deal of scope for mutual learning. If there is a 'rank order tournament' at some stage of the process, it should serve the exclusive purpose of improving the *overall* record of *all* European welfare states through the identification and shar-ing of best practices. The peer review process supports this mutual learning.

The indicators are not a vehicle for defining any pecking order among Europe's nations, but are a tool to preserve and rejuvenate Europe's hall-mark of social protection for all its citizens. Indeed, a credible commit-ment to combat poverty and social exclusion presupposes a firm commitment to the establishment of an efficient and productive welfare state, and its continuous adaptation to new social needs and risks. The set of indicators combines national information on specific challenges and solutions, with a key supranational goal that is fundamentally the same for everyone: progress towards more social inclusion and social quality.

I fully endorse the structure of the indicators proposed by Atkinson *et al.* They propose three distinct levels of indicator:

Level 1 is to consist of a small number of lead indicators for the main fields that we believe should be covered.

Level 2 would support these lead indicators and describe other dimensions of the challenge. Both these levels would be commonly agreed and defined indicators, used by member states in their National Action Plans (inclusion) and by the Commission in its Reports. It is crucially important that the portfolio of EU indicators should command general support as a balanced representation of Europe's social concerns.

In addition, there are *Level 3* indicators: those that member states themselves decide to include in their National Action Plans on Social Inclusion, to highlight specificities in particular areas, and to help interpret the Level 1 and 2 indicators. The importance of these Level 3 indicators must not be underestimated. They provide a key element in the process whereby member states can learn from each other. A positive approach to such country-specific indicators will also aid acceptance of the overall process in member states.

It is clear that the indicators should cover the living conditions of the poorest, which means that all reasonable investments should be made to include hard-to-reach groups (such as ethnic minorities, travellers, the homeless, and those living in institutions) in the samples. Involving non-governmental organizations as critical partners in the statistical process may be seen as an additional guarantee that the poorest will definitely be included in the statistics. Another mission of these organizations is to give a *voice* to those living in poverty, which should allow them to participate in the further development of the indicators. Indeed, it is essential that the victims of social exclusion can co-determine how exclusion and inclusion should be measured—not only in terms of degree of deprivation, but also in terms of participation, social power, etc.

One of the most important contributions made by the present report is to have brought out the principles one would want to see underpinning the choice of appropriate common indicators (see Chapter 2). Articulating these principles provides a powerful framework within which to address the choice of the most satisfactory set of indicators for social progress in the Union. One is, of course, constrained by the availability of data, and the Report recommends—and I fully agree—that a high priority should be given to the building of statistical capacity in this area. This is an essential investment if Europe is to become a successful socially inclusive and knowledge-based economy.

The development of indicators is necessarily a dynamic process. Indeed, this report is part of such a dynamic. While indicators should have a reasonable degree of stability in order to fulfil their function of monitoring progress over time, it is essential that the choice of indicators not be regarded as fixed in stone, for at least three reasons. First, as we gain experience in their operation, we will no doubt be able to refine the definition and implementation of indicators. Second, the social and economic situation is constantly changing, generating new issues and new challenges: the Union should concern itself with today's and tomorrow's problems, not with yesterday's. Third, discussion of indicators needs to be broadened, responding to the views of social partners, non-governmental organizations, those experiencing social exclusion—indeed, all of Europe's citizens.

One further important way in which the European process is dynamic is that the EU is in the process of enlargement. Consideration needs to be given to the implications of the entry of a new group of member states, such as regarding any request to the accession countries to draw up National Action Plans for inclusion. Promoting Europe's social model also sends a clear signal to prospective member states that this is an achieved model, that it is part and parcel of European civilization, and that it must be endorsed as an ambition by all those applying for membership. We must now make European social policy strong and enduring. That is exactly what we must do before we invite other countries to endorse the European project.

Adoption by the European Union of a set of commonly agreed and defined social indicators will represent a major step towards achieving the social objectives of Europe. The social indicators will provide a framework within which member states can develop social and labour market policy in a way that both reflects national circumstances and embodies the EU goal of social cohesion. Indicators will be important not just for national governments, but also for local and regional communities, for the social partners, for non-governmental organizations, for social analysts, for civil societies, and for individual citizens of Europe.

Last but not least, the social indicators must themselves reflect our sense of democracy through a dialogue with socially excluded groups about the conceptual and methodological frameworks to be used, and through explicit measurement of poor people's own experience of participation, freedom, and social inclusion.

Social indicators are not of course a miracle cure for the social problems of the EU, but they constitute a key instrument for defining and monitoring policies that are put in place to deal with these problems. The ultimate effectiveness of social indicators depends on there being the political will to exploit them fully and put into effect the necessary policies. Truly effective indicators need therefore to be followed not only in the letter, but above all in the spirit. Implementation depends on the political support of member state governments. Hard decisions have been taken in the field of economic and monetary policy to introduce the common currency; the same level of commitment is required to ensure the success of the social agenda. The process we have embarked on clearly signals to Europe's citizens that European policy is now willing to fight for what really matters.

FRANK VANDENBROUCKE
Minister of Social Affairs and Pensions
Belgian Federal Government

Preface

This book is based on a report prepared at the request of the Belgian government, as part of the Belgian presidency of the Council of the European Union (EU) in the second half of 2001. It was commissioned by Mr Johan Vande Lanotte, Deputy Prime Minister and Minister for Budget, Social Integration, and Social Economy, and Mr Frank Vandenbroucke, Minister of Social Affairs and Pensions. We are most grateful to them for their support, both material and intellectual.

The Report was presented at a conference on 'Indicators for Social Inclusion: Making Common EU Objectives Work' at Antwerp on 14–15 September 2001. This conference brought together renowned EU academic researchers from the various fields linked to poverty and social exclusion in its multidimensionality, experts from statistical offices, those in member states concerned with constructing the National Action Plans for Social Inclusion, and members of the staff of the European Commission. Experts from non-EU countries, especially Central and Eastern European countries (Hungary, Latvia, Lithuania, Poland, Romania, Slovenia, Czech Republic) but also from Iceland, Norway, and Switzerland as well as New Zealand, were also present. The Conference included the social partners, representatives of NGOs, and people for whom social indicators provide an essential means of monitoring social development in Europe. In total, 270 participants coming from 26 countries were present. We have benefited from the constructive comments made by the invited commentators and conference participants, which have led to significant revisions.

The book was prepared within a period of eight months, and this was possible only as a result of the assistance we received from many people. The Report enjoyed the support of a Scientific Steering Committee and an Institutional Steering Committee,[1] members of whom made many valuable comments on two earlier drafts, which led to considerable improvements. We would like to thank members of the Indicators sub-group of the Social Protection Committee for their comments on national social reporting and their assistance. Helpful contributions and remarks were also made by Peter Abrahamson, Judith Atkinson, Luis

---

[1] Their membership is listed at the end of the book.

Ayala, Josef Bauernberger, Andrea Brandolini, Alfredo Bruto da Costa, Nick Burkitt, Lieve De Lathouwer, Robert Erikson, Michael Förster, Liana Georgiou, Michel Glaude, David Gordon, Anne-Catherine Guio, Hans Hansen, Richard Hauser, Markus Jäntti, Christine Mainguet, Magda Mercader-Prats, Danièle Meulders, John Micklewright, Lucile Olier, Spyros Pilos, Peter Robinson, Carlos Rodrigues, Javier Ruiz-Castillo, Chiara Saraceno, Wolf Scott, Hilary Steedman, Holly Sutherland, Adam Szulc, Peter Townsend, Karel Van den Bosch, Eddy Van Doorslaer, Klaas de Vos, Terry Ward, Chris Whelan, and Marie-Françoise Wilkinson.

We had valuable discussions with Heinz-Herbert Noll of the EuReporting Project at ZUMA, Mannheim; with members of the Italian Poverty Commission chaired by Chiara Saraceno; and with Federico Giammusso, Raffaele Tangorra, and Francesca Utili regarding the Italian National Action Plan. We thank members of the Analytical Services Division at the UK Department of Work and Pensions for their helpful comments. None of these people should however be held responsible in any way for the contents of the book.

T.A.
B.C.
E.M.
B.N.

Contents

1

Setting the Scene

The purpose of this book is to make a scientific contribution to the development of social indicators as part of the social agenda in the European Union. It assesses the strengths and weaknesses of different indicators relevant to social inclusion in Europe, and their usefulness in promoting good practice by member state governments and allowing comparable assessment of social outcomes. It is hoped that the book will play a role in widening public debate about the social dimension of Europe, and that it will be of value to the social partners, to non-governmental and grass-roots organizations, and to the socially disadvantaged. It seeks to provide both a constructive background document at a crucial stage in the evolution of the social dimension of the European Union and a reference work of continuing value.

In this chapter we set the scene, providing background about social indicators and about the development of the social agenda in the European Union. In particular, it seeks to make clear both what the book tries to achieve and what it is not intended to provide.

1.1. SOCIAL INDICATORS

Social indicators are an important tool for evaluating a country's level of social development and for assessing the impact of policy. Such indicators are already in use in several member states of the European Union (EU) and have begun to play a significant role in advancing the social dimension of Europe. This has been underpinned by the work carried out by the European Commission on the construction of indicators. Publications such as *The Social Situation in Europe*, *Social Protection in Europe*, and the *Social Portrait of Europe* have disseminated the social monitoring of the EU. On a wider geographical scale, international agencies such as OECD, WHO, UNICEF, and UNDP have contributed to the development of social indicators.

There is an extensive literature on social indicators, stemming from what is sometimes called the 'social indicator movement' of the 1960s.

At that time, a number of factors combined to generate interest in social indicators, including the ambition to add a system of social accounts to the System of National Accounts, and interest (in a number of countries) in constructing 'a parsimonious set of specific indices covering a broad range of social concerns' (Vogel 1997*b*: 105). These countries included the United States, as in the work of Bauer (1966) and in the publication of the US government of *Toward a Social Report* (US Department of Health, Education, and Welfare 1969). For Europe, reference should be made to Delors (1971).

A number of texts were prepared on the construction and use of indicators, such as Carley (1981), as well as studies of their impact on policy (e.g. De Neufville 1975; MacRae 1985). In Scandinavia the desire to move beyond purely monetary indicators of well-being led to a broader concept of social welfare. In 1968, for example, Sweden launched its *Level of Living Survey* (see Johansson 1973; Erikson and Åberg 1987; Erikson and Uusitalo 1987; Erikson 1993). The Nordic countries have since the 1980s coordinated such surveys and have published common social reports. These have drawn on the work in the early 1980s by the OECD, which published a list of social indicators (OECD 1982) and, subsequently, a compendium of indicators (OECD 1986). The OECD has just returned to this subject and has published an extensive report entitled *Society at a Glance: OECD Social Indicators* (2001*b*). On a world scale, the World Bank publishes *Social Indicators of Development* (the last print version is World Bank 1996) and the *World Development Report* (e.g. World Bank 2001). Since 1990 the UNDP has published the *Human Development Report* (UNDP 2000), which contains a great deal of information by country about the level of social development. The UNDP constructs the Human Development Index, which is a composite of three basic components: longevity, knowledge, and standard of living, and the Human Poverty Index 2, which combines longevity, illiteracy, poverty rate, and long-term unemployment. (For a review of social reporting, see Berger-Schmitt and Jankowitsch 1999.)

In this literature on social indicators, much consideration has been given to their relation with concepts of social welfare. Important work has been undertaken on 'the Social Quality of Europe' as part of an initiative during the Netherlands presidency, reported in Beck *et al.* (1997); and this is now being taken further in a network on social quality that forms part of the Fifth Framework Programme. The Eu-Reporting Project, coordinated by ZUMA at Mannheim, has been concerned with the conceptual basis for social reporting (see e.g. Berger-Schmitt 2000).

Berger-Schmitt and Noll (2000) provide a very clear account of the relation between concepts of quality of life, social cohesion, social capital, and social exclusion. In seeking to establish analytical foundations, one can draw on academic research in statistics, sociology, social policy, geography, welfare economics, and political science.

It is not our purpose to cover the same field here. Our aim is more pragmatic: to take forward the development of indicators for social inclusion at this crucial stage for the European social agenda. (In some respects we cover similar ground to the report of the Observatoire Social Européen, 2001.) We do not, therefore, discuss social indicators in general. We concentrate on their use for a specific—very important—purpose. The focus on social inclusion in the European Union gives a particular direction to our recommendations, notably our emphasis on measuring social outcomes, rather than the means by which they are achieved.

Equally, we do not attempt to provide a thorough grounding for the terms 'social exclusion' or 'social inclusion'—even though the latter appears in our title. These terms are employed in a wide variety of different ways. While this is part of their (political) appeal, it can undermine their value in an analytical context. Ideally, we would have considered more thoroughly the precise distinctions of meaning, and the relation between 'intermediate' indicators and more fundamental social goals. However, in line with our pragmatic objective of contributing to the policy-making process, we simply accept here the use of the terms as *shorthand* for a range of concerns considered to be important in setting the European social agenda. There is, we believe, broad agreement about the list of such concerns, which encompass poverty, deprivation, low educational qualifications, labour market disadvantage, joblessness, poor health, poor housing or homelessness, illiteracy and innumeracy, precariousness, and incapacity to participate in society. These are the fields that people have in mind when they talk about the social rights of EU citizens. As we argue in Chapter 3, while member states differ in their emphases, there is considerable common ground in the fifteen countries about the issues that they include under the heading of 'social inclusion'.

1.2. SOCIAL EUROPE

In the early days of the European Communities, social policy received little attention, and the Community organizations were provided with very limited powers in the social field. Social policy was, to a large extent, a means of achieving other objectives. The restructuring of the coal and steel industries, through the European Coal and Steel Community, involved social measures in aid of training, and financing the necessary adjustments. There was concern with removing barriers to labour mobility and ensuring that differences in the costs of social protection did not prevent competition in the supply of goods. Later, in the 1970s, the social dimension of the Community began to play a more important role. The Commission produced a Social Action Programme, accepted in 1974, which recognized that the Communities had an independent role to play in the formation of social policy and agreed on the implementation, in cooperation with member states, of specific measures to combat poverty.

In terms of concrete action, the achievements were limited in scale and scope. The Regional Development Fund was put in place. The Social Fund was increased in size, with an emphasis on the education, training, and insertion into the labour market of young persons, and on regional redistribution. Policy to combat poverty led in July 1975 to the first European Action Programme covering the period 1975–80. In December 1981 the Commission made an evaluation report, containing an estimate of 36.8 million poor people in the Community (of 12 countries) in 1975. This was based on a poverty line drawn at half the average income of the member state, which was the concrete implementation of the definition adopted by the Council of Ministers of the poor as 'individuals or families whose resources are so small as to exclude them from the minimal acceptable way of life of the member state in which they live' (Council Decision, 22 July 1975: see European Commission, 1985; also used in the second poverty programme—see European Commission, 1989: 11).

The social dimension increasingly received more attention in the European Communities. In 1989 the Commission put forward a draft of the 'Community Charter of Fundamental Social Rights', and this was adopted in modified form by 11 of the 12 then member states. The opposition of the United Kingdom (UK) at the time led to the Social Chapter as such being excluded from the final Treaty on European Union, but there was an attached Social Protocol, in which the other members expressed their wish to continue along the path laid down in the 1989 Social Charter. Since the election of the Labour Government in the UK in May 1997, the 'opt-out' by that member state has ended, and the Social Protocol has been incorporated.

Central to progress in European social policy has been the principle of subsidiarity, according to which the European Union can take action only if, and in so far as, the objectives of the proposed action cannot be sufficiently achieved by the member states. This means that policy to combat poverty and social exclusion is first and foremost the responsibility of member states.

1.3. **LISBON AND POST-LISBON**

New urgency has been given to the development of the European social agenda by the agreement reached at the Lisbon European Council. In March 2000, the Council decided that the Union should adopt the strategic goal for the next decade of becoming 'the most competitive and dynamic knowledge-based economy . . . with more and better jobs and greater social cohesion'. It is with the social wing of this goal that this book is concerned. The incorporation of the promotion of social inclusion within the overall strategy of the EU, and the agreement at the Nice Summit in December 2000 to advance social policy on the basis of an open method of coordination at Union level, represented a major step, and gave an express role for social indicators.

The open method of coordination, which is designed to help member states progressively to develop their own policies, involves fixing guidelines for the Union, establishing quantitative and qualitative indicators to be applied in each member state, and periodic monitoring. At Lisbon, the Council called on the Commission to report annually on the structural indicators of progress in member states towards the Union's strategic goal (*Synthesis Report*), and at Feira in June 2000 it requested the Commission to ensure the necessary coherence and standard presentation. In the field of social inclusion, in particular, an important role has been given to the Social Protection Committee (formerly the High Level Group on Social Protection), which has established a sub-group on Social Indicators. (The Social Protection Committee consists of senior representatives of member states who are charged with preparing the business for the Council of Ministers of Social Affairs.)

Policy to promote social inclusion is—under subsidiarity—the responsibility of member states. At the Nice Summit it was agreed that by June 2001 member states should implement a national two-year action plan for combating poverty and social exclusion, setting specific targets and taking into account national, regional, and local differences. These National Action Plans on Social Inclusion—referred to as NAPincl, to distinguish them from the National Action Plans on employment—are to state the progress aimed for by national policies and to list the indicators used to assess progress. The Commission is requested to monitor the implementation of the social agenda and to prepare an annual scoreboard of progress. It is invited to identify good practice and to promote its common acceptance. Once the set of indicators has been adopted by the European Council, it will be important to set the quality standards for the construction of indicators and to ensure comparability across member states.

At the Stockholm Summit in March 2001, the Commission in its *Synthesis Report* presented initial data on indicators, building on its September 2000 Communication on 'Structural Indicators' (European Commission 2000*a*). In the field of social inclusion, it proposed seven indicators:

1. distribution of income (ratio of share of top 20% to share of bottom 20%);
2. share of population below the poverty line before and after social transfers (defined as 60% of national median equivalized income);
3. persistence of poverty (share of population below the poverty line for three consecutive years);
4. proportion of jobless households;
5. regional disparities (coefficient of variation of regional unemployment rates);
6. low education (proportion of people aged 18–24 who are not in education or training and have only lower secondary education);
7. long-term unemployment rate.

Figures 1.1–1.7 show the values of these indicators for the EU member states, and in some cases for the whole EU15 (or those member states available), drawing on the indicators presented at Stockholm (European Commission 2001*a*) and on Eurostat (2000*a*). In each case member states are ordered, not alphabetically, but in increasing size of the indicator in question. The position of different member states is interesting. To take just one example, Portugal has the highest values for income inequality, persistent poverty, and low education, but is in the middle for long-term unemployment and has the second lowest values for jobless households and variation in the unemployment rate. Seeing the patterns revealed by these figures, one is immediately challenged to explain the differences between member states. How are they related to the policies pursued in different countries? How far are variations in poverty, unemployment, educational attainment, and inequality the product of different historical

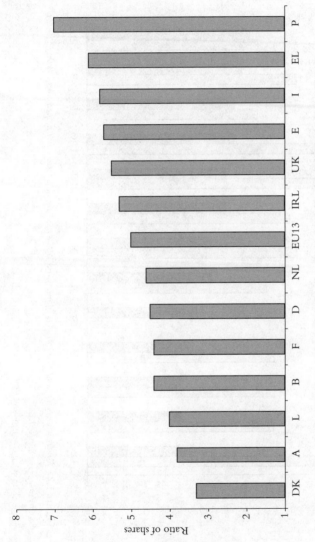

Figure 1.1. *Distribution of income (share of top 20% divided by share of bottom 20%), 1996*

Country codes: B, Belgium; DK, Denmark; D, Germany; EL, Greece; E, Spain; F, France; IRL, Ireland; I, Italy; L, Luxembourg; NL, Netherlands; A, Austria; P, Portugal; FIN, Finland; S, Sweden; UK, United Kingdom.

Source: Eurostat (2000*b*: table 2.1).

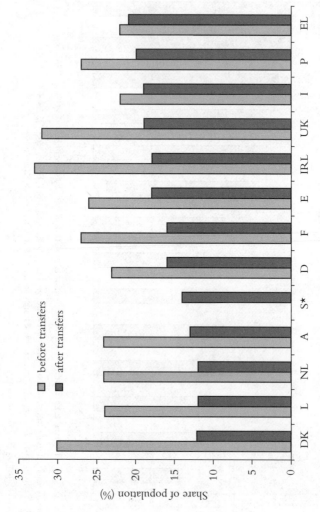

Figure 1.2. *Poverty rate before and after transfers (poverty line 60% median, transfers excluding pensions), 1996 (*1997)*

Country codes: see Figure 1.1.

Source: European Commission (2001a: 51).

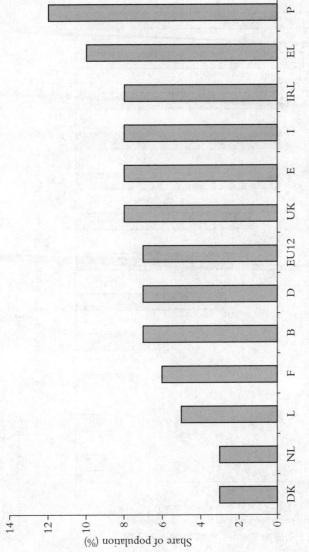

Figure 1.3. Persistence of poverty (share of population consistently below poverty line for three years), 1994–6

Country codes: see Figure 1.1.

Source: Eurostat (2000b: table A2.5.1).

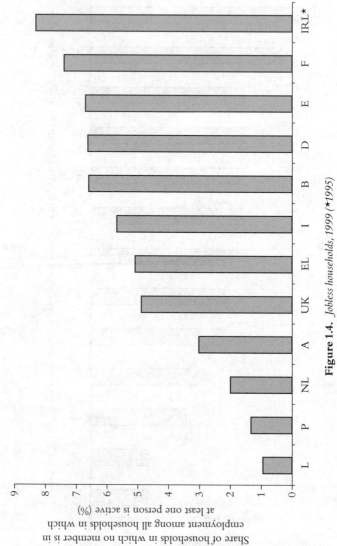

Figure 1.4. *Jobless households, 1999 (*1995)*

Country codes: see Figure 1.1.

Source: European Commission (2001a: 53).

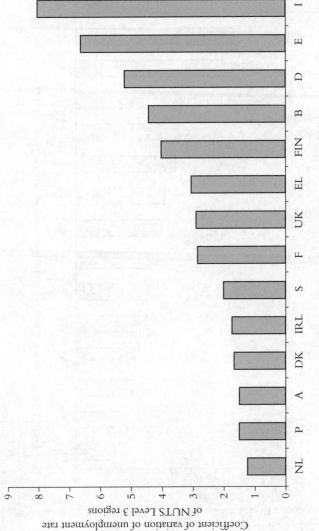

Figure 1.5. *Variation in unemployment rate across regions, 1999*

Country codes: see Figure 1.1.

Source: European Commission (2001a: 54).

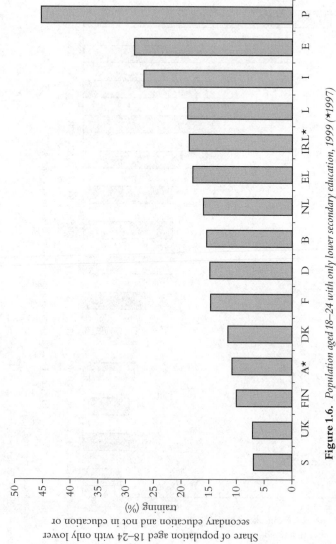

Figure 1.6. *Population aged 18–24 with only lower secondary education, 1999 (*1997)*

Country codes: see Figure 1.1.

Source: European Commission (2001a: 55).

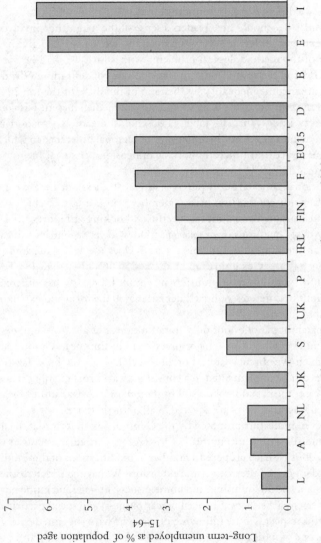

Figure 1.7. *Long-term unemployment rate, 2000*

Country codes: see Figure 1.1.

Source: European Commission (2001*a*: 56).

paths? These are fascinating questions, but they are not the issues we seek to address here. We intend these figures to be illustrative, rather than to contribute to a substantive analysis of the state of social Europe, and therefore we do not discuss the findings in depth.

Figures 1.1–1.7 should give readers a sense of the magnitude involved and the extent of differences between member states. They also give us a foretaste of the methodological problems with which we shall be confronted. Behind each of the indicators lie questions of definition. Why do we measure income inequality by the ratio of the share of the top 20% to that of the bottom 20%? Why should 60% of median income be taken as a poverty line? What do 'jobless households' mean? Is variation in unemployment rates the only dimension of regional difference in which we are interested? Are there important dimensions of social inclusion that are missing?

Definitional issues arise in purely national studies, but here we are concerned with comparison across member states, each of which has its own institutional and cultural specificity. Looking at Figures 1.1–1.7 instantly raises questions of *comparability*. Does 'lower secondary education' mean the same in all member states? Does the UK score highly because it has a key examination at the age of 16 rather than 18? The exclusion of pensions from transfers in Figure 1.2 clearly has different implications in different countries, depending on the form and extent of pension provision.

Comparability applies not only to definitions but also to the underlying data. There has been a major investment in European Union statistics, which we discuss later; but one still has to ask how far the indicators can be implemented in a consistent way across member states. In some cases the data do not exist. Limitations of data availability mean that not all member states are covered in all of these figures.

The seven indicators proposed by the Commission in its initial documents, and illustrated in Figures 1.1–1.7, receive particular attention in this book, but we have proposed a number of modifications of these indicators and suggested alternatives and extensions. We have considered other fields, notably health, housing, and homelessness; literacy and numeracy; access to essential services; financial precariousness; and social participation. In this respect, we are following others who have suggested enlarging the scope of indicators. The Observatoire Social Européen (2001), in its report on monetary and non-monetary indicators, proposed adding housing, health, information and communication, mobility, security and justice, leisure and culture. In their National Action Plans, member state governments have suggested a variety of indicators in addition to the seven proposed by the Commission.

1.4. **STRUCTURE OF THE BOOK**

In this book we aim to provide an analytic framework for the construction of indicators of social inclusion and to examine their implementation in the European Union. In particular, we consider:

- principles underlying the construction of policy-relevant indicators and the properties of indicators;
- experience with the use of indicators in the field of social inclusion in member states of the European Union;
- definition of indicators;
- issues that arise in their implementation;
- role of social indicators in the future development of the EU social agenda.

In Chapter 2 we begin with an examination of the principles underlying the construction of indicators to be used for the express purpose of assessing performance in achieving the social agenda of the European Union. The end product in the present context is a portfolio of common indicators applied across the European Union. The principles involved in its construction may concern the single indicators or the portfolio as a whole. Indicators can take different forms, and in the second part of Chapter 2 we consider the properties of indicators. Since any portfolio of indicators involves selecting from a range of competing alternatives, it is essential to understand the full set of possibilities. Choice of indicators involves compromise over objectives, but will also be constrained by data limitations and by institutional differences across countries. These are the subjects of the third part of Chapter 2.

In designing indicators for use in the EU monitoring process, a great deal can be learned from the experience of member states in their national policies to combat social exclusion. In Chapter 3 we review, country by country, social indicators from a member state perspective. In doing so, our aim is to illustrate the range of current practice in the use of social indicators in the field of social inclusion, not to provide a comprehensive assessment. Member states differ in the degree to which they have embarked on strategies aimed at promoting social inclusion that already include explicit targets and indicators against which to measure the effectiveness of policy. For this reason, the amount of space allocated to each country varies. In each case, however, we discuss the National Action Plan on Social Inclusion (NAPincl) submitted to the European Commission in June 2001. Our concern here is not with the policies proposed but with the method by which the plans were produced, their relation with previous policy formation, the use made of the seven indicators proposed by the Commission, and other indicators employed by member states which seem of wider interest, particularly where they relate to fields not covered by the Commission's indicators.

In Chapter 4 we commence our analysis of social indicators for use in the EU monitoring process, starting with the portfolio as a whole. We envisage a three-tier structure of indicators. There would be a small set of lead 'headline' indicators (Level 1), supported by a wider range of indicators at Level 2, where both levels would be common across member states. To these, member states would be encouraged to add their choice of Level 3 indicators, to highlight specificities in particular areas, and to help interpret the Level 1 and 2 indicators. The Level 1 and 2 indicators would be disaggregated in a number of ways, and we highlight the importance of giving separate indicators for women and men, and for examining the regional dimension wherever possible.

In Chapters 5–8 we examine individual indicators. We begin with a single field: the risk of financial poverty. We devote a whole chapter to this one indicator for two reasons. Poverty is intrinsically important, and, as described above, estimates of the extent of poverty in Europe have played a major role in the evolution of European social policy. Moreover, the design of poverty indicators serves to illustrate the issues that arise with indicators in general. The chapter reviews the many different approaches that have been adopted to the measurement of poverty, and sets out the choices that have to be made in arriving at a concrete implementation.

The indicators of financial poverty described in Chapter 5 provide a measure of the degree to which people face the risk of serious deprivation in terms of their standard of living or to which they fall below a specified minimum level of resources. To measure the seriousness of the risk people face, or the depth of their poverty, we have to associate further indicators. In Chapter 6 we consider the persistence of poverty, measures of the poverty gap, and the extent to which those with low financial resources are suffering enforced deprivation. In the final section of this chapter we turn to the broader issue of the overall distribution of income.

The twin aims of creating a dynamic knowledge-based economy and of ensuring social inclusion meet in the labour market. In Chapter 7 we examine the fields of education, unemployment, and employment. We start from the social indicators on low education, joblessness, and long-term unemployment proposed by the Commission, but we go beyond these, covering access to education, employment activation, and the working poor.

In Chapter 8 we consider indicators of health, housing and home-lessness, functional illiteracy and innumeracy, access to essential services, financial precariousness, and social participation. These are all potentially important fields that are not covered by the Commission's original pro-posals. In each case, our interest is in indicators relevant to social inclu-sion. Homelessness, for example, is clearly a major reason for concern about social exclusion. In the case of health, however, it is not mortality as such that concerns us, but differential mortality according to socio-economic or other characteristics, and the impact that poor health or disability has in exacerbating social exclusion. We are concerned, for example, that the disadvantage of those with low incomes may be compounded by a lack of adequate medical facilities.

The end result of our investigation is a list of 33 recommendations. These are printed in bold type, and are summarized at the end of the book, preceding a list of the proposed indicators. The recommendations and proposed indicators are intended as a contribution to the debate about European Union policy-making, and in Chapter 9 we consider the future policy process.

Our coverage has necessarily been selective. We draw attention in the course of the book to areas that need further investigation, but here we should note that a serious form of social exclusion not considered here is that associated with ethnicity or immigration. Discrimination against particular ethnic groups may be a causal factor in the dimensions we examine, such as poverty or unemployment. Social disadvantage in terms of housing or access to public services may be greater for ethnic minorities. Moreover, there are undoubtedly people who are not deprived according to the indicators covered here and yet are excluded from full participation in the society in which they are living. These are important concerns, but we cannot do them justice in this book.

Environmental issues impinge on a number of fields, such as the environmental quality of housing (Chapter 8), but we do not consider explicitly indicators relating to the environment. Again, this does not reflect any wish to downplay its importance.

Finally, we make no attempt to stand back and analyse the process by which European social policy is being formed, not least because this book is, in a small way, part of that process. The book should be seen as the response of scientific researchers to the request to contribute, to a tight timetable, a background paper to be used in the formation of policy. In writing the report we have taken as given the objectives to which Member States have collectively subscribed, such as the target of raising employment rates, and have not subjected them to critical scrutiny. Study as to how the European social agenda has evolved following the Lisbon Council, and evaluation of the significant decisions made collectively by member states, are important topics for future social science research.

2

Indicators in Principle

In this book we are concerned not with social indicators in general, but with social indicators as performance indicators, playing a political role in the development of the social agenda of the European Union. It is not enough, therefore, that they capture a significant aspect of social conditions: they must have a clear normative connotation. As such, they cannot be properly constructed in a purely ad hoc manner. There should be certain underlying principles. These principles may be implicit rather than explicit, but they are important. In this chapter we begin by spelling out a number of principles that could form the basis for indicator construction for this purpose. Making these principles explicit will undoubtedly expose differences of view and of emphasis across and within member states, but such differences will otherwise emerge in conflict over the definition and choice of indicators. By setting out the principles in this way, we hope to engage in public debate the different actors who should be involved, including the social partners and non-governmental organizations.

Indicators can take different forms, and in the second part of this chapter we consider the properties of indicators. Are they individual or household-based? Are they territorial? Are they relative or absolute? Are they static or dynamic? Since any portfolio of indicators involves selecting from a range of competing alternatives, it is essential to understand the full set of possibilities. Choice of a portfolio of indicators will be constrained by data limitations and by institutional differences across countries. What data should be used to implement the indicators? What, for example, is the relation between EU-wide data sources and national data? These are the subjects of the third part of this chapter.

It should be stressed at the outset that 'indicators' are precisely that. Potentially they have great value in pointing to significant social problems, and, taken together, a portfolio of indicators allows us to draw conclusions about social progress. But we cannot expect them to be a complete representation of the state of society. They are simply an indication. The nature of that indication will depend on the choices made with regard to definitions and with regard to data. Different indicators highlight different features of social problems, and suggest different priorities for policy intervention.

2.1. **PRINCIPLES OF INDICATOR CONSTRUCTION**

As we have stressed, our concern is with indicators for a particular purpose at a particular stage in the development of the European Union, and it is an important feature of this process that the policies to achieve social inclusion are the responsibility of member states, under the subsidiarity principle. Social inclusion is to be promoted through the method of open coordination, as described above. Member states are to agree on the objectives of policy, but they will be free to choose the methods by which these objectives are realized. One member state may achieve low poverty rates by active labour market policy; another may place greater reliance on social transfers. In one member state transfers may be provided by the state, in another transfers may be private. In one member state training may be associated with apprenticeships; in another, it may be part of the school system. This we have taken to mean that, for the present purpose, the social performance indicators should in principle be concerned with *outputs* rather than *inputs*. The aim is to measure social outcomes, not the means by which they are achieved.

The focus on outputs is stressed since statistics on inputs are more readily available than those on outputs. As was noted in the US *Toward a Social Report* over thirty years ago, the annual statistics on education contained over a hundred pages, 'yet has virtually no information on how much children have learned' (U.S. Department of Health, Education, and Welfare 1969: 66). At the same time, there may be differences of view as to what constitutes an 'output', and we would not want to be rigid in its interpretation. While we regard total spending on education, for example, as a measure of the resources being put into education, and hence would prefer a measure of educational attainment, we recognize that the availability of teachers may be an index of educational opportunities. If our concerns are forward-looking, then we may take into account the possibility that one can benefit from a service in the future. Confidence in the future can be improved by the existence of services; they have an option value that is a form of current output. A sense of exclusion may be generated by the absence of educational or health facilities. A person may be over school age but still feel that the absence of a secondary school in his or her town is a factor in social exclusion.

The end product in the present context is a portfolio of common indicators applied across the European Union. The principles involved in its construction may concern the single indicators or the portfolio as a whole. We begin with the principles that apply to single indicators.

Principles applied to single indicators

The first principle is that *an indicator should identify the essence of the problem and have a clear and accepted normative interpretation*. Translation of policy goals into quantitative measures inevitably means that we have to focus on certain aspects of the problem to the exclusion of others, but this should be done in such a way that it encapsulates the central concern and is not misleading. The indicator should be recognized as meaningful by users of all kinds. Indicators must be acceptable to the general public. This implies that the general principles of the method used must be understandable. For this reason, we believe that it is important to adopt a participatory approach to the construction of performance indicators, involving those at risk of social exclusion and organizations that represent their views. Overall, the indicators must have intuitive validity. They should produce results that seem 'reasonable' to Europe's citizens. A poverty indicator that showed over half the EU population to be poor would be regarded as grossly inflated. Moreover, for the purposes of this book, concerned with social inclusion in Europe, the indicators should be selected to have a clear normative interpretation. There should be general agreement that a movement in a particular direction represents an improvement. This would not necessarily apply to all indicators. The Commission cites the example of labour productivity; another example would be fertility, where countries may be neutral with regard to higher or lower levels of fertility. We should emphasize that our aim is to propose indicators *for a particular purpose*. The social inclusion indicators should be in a form such that national targets can be set, and performance assessed.

The second principle is that *an indicator should be robust and statistically validated*. It should be measurable in a way that commands general support. The data employed should be regarded as statistically reliable and should avoid arbitrary adjustments. Where data are derived from sample surveys, these surveys should comply with the best practices and highest standards of survey research methodology. The methods adopted should minimize errors arising from ambiguous questions, misleading definitions, bias resulting from non-response, and interviewer or coder mistakes. Indicators should as far as possible be validated by reference to other evidence. Indicators derived at the European level should be cross-checked against information available at the level of individual member states. Any indicator will necessarily involve some error, but it should not be systematically biased. It must also be statistically reliable over time in the sense that results must not be liable to unpredictable or inexplicable fluctuations. We should avoid measures, for instance, that are highly sensitive to weather conditions (affecting agricultural incomes) or that vary seasonally. We should be careful in the use of indicators that are liable to change for reasons unrelated to social policy, such as those that are sensitive to the economic cycle. This applies both to the values of the indicators themselves and to the yardsticks being applied, for example a poverty line set as a percentage of the median. Throughout the analysis, we have to bear in mind that the circumstances of those suffering social disadvantage (for example at the bottom of the income distribution, and/or unemployed, and/or living in institutions, and/or homeless) are among the most difficult to measure statistically. (See the discussion below on building statistical capacity.)

The third principle is that *an indicator should be responsive to effective policy interventions but not subject to manipulation*. Indicators must reflect the successful intervention of policy. It is misleading, and politically unacceptable, to have a poverty measure that records no change despite genuine improvements in the circumstances of the poor. Moreover, the indicators must be of a form that can be linked to policy initiatives. At the same time, the indicators should not be easily manipulable. There should be no temptation to member states to improve their score by artificial policy changes. An indicator based on the proportion of the unemployed receiving transfers, for example, could be manipulated by paying everyone 1 euro a month.

The fourth principle is that *an indicator should be measurable in a sufficiently comparable way across member states, and comparable as far as practicable with the standards applied internationally by the UN and the OECD*. Full comparability is an ideal that cannot normally be attained, since, even where data are harmonized across member states, variations in institutional and social structure mean that there may be differences in the interpretation of the data. The aim should be to reach an acceptable standard of comparability. Two considerations seem particularly important. The first is development at the statistical level. Where possible, member states should be encouraged to develop their statistical information to improve the degree of comparability; and consideration of the design of social indicators should influence the plans for new statistical instruments mounted at the European level. Cooperation with OECD and other international agencies is also important in extending the range of comparability. The second important consideration concerns the choice of indicators. Some indicators are more sensitive than others to differences across member states in their social structure. For example, an indicator of poverty should be equitable between countries with differing sizes of rural populations and hence differing degrees of production for home consumption. Imputed rent on owner-occupied housing (i.e. the rent owners save by owning their own houses or apartments) is another example. Differences in the extent of owner-occupation across countries mean that its omission has a differential effect. We should avoid indicators that are over-sensitive to these structural differences or raise specific problems of interpretation for particular member states.

The fifth principle is that *an indicator should be timely and susceptible to revision*. In the macroeconomic field, politicians have become accustomed to receiving highly current information. In the field of social inclusion, it is much more difficult to obtain up-to-date data (see some of the social indicators proposed in the 2001 *Synthesis Report* of the Commission: European Commission 2001*a*). The Portuguese National Action Plan on Social Inclusion of June 2001 (Government of Portugal 2001: 3) noted that the most recent data on poverty (relating to 1995) pre-dated important changes in labour market and social policy that were believed to have had a significant impact. Revision not only of data but also of the underlying concepts is equally important where advances are made in understanding and where there are changes in policy concerns. Ideally, it should be possible to chain the indicators before and after revision.

The sixth principle is that *the measurement of an indicator should not impose too large a burden on member states, on enterprises, or on the Union's citizens*. Provision of the information required to construct social indicators will be the responsibility of member states, whose statistical services are already under great pressure. The design of social indicators should, wherever possible, make use of information already supplied to Eurostat (the statistical office of the European Communities) or else information that the majority of member states already prepare for their own use. Where new information is needed, then as far as feasible it should be obtained using existing instruments, for example by adding questions to existing surveys.

Important among such instruments is the successor, as from 2003, to the European Community Household Panel (ECHP),[1] which is known as the EU-Statistics on Income and Living Conditions (EU-SILC). It is planned that the EU-SILC will become the EU reference source for income and social exclusion statistics. One characteristic of the instrument is that it will allow member states to separate the cross-sectional element (data collected at one specific point in time) from the longitudinal, panel element (data collected about the same set of people over several points in time). The objective is to anchor EU-SILC in the different national statistical systems. A consequence of this is that EU-SILC cross-sectional and longitudinal datasets may come from one single source (as for the current ECHP), but may also come from two or more different sources such as survey(s) and administrative register(s). In the latter case, the degree of integration—across dimensions and across time—is crucial. In this book we emphasize the multidimensionality of social disadvantage, and for this reason it is essential that we can link for an individual the information about different dimensions. Over time, one of the requirements of EU-SILC longitudinal information is that data on the same people should be collected for at least four consecutive years. An option for those countries planning to launch a new, single survey in this context is therefore a four-year rotational panel (in which a quarter of the sample is replaced every year).

Principles applied to the whole portfolio of indicators

We turn now to the principles to be applied to the composition of the whole portfolio of indicators.

The first principle is that *the portfolio of indicators should be balanced across different dimensions*. No set of indicators can be exhaustive, and there are costs in terms of lost transparency from having too extensive a range of indicators. Too large a set of indicators risks losing credibility, if member states can simply pick and choose. A selection has therefore to be made. This selection should ensure that all main areas of concern are covered and should take account of differences across member states in the importance they attach to different areas. Some countries may be particularly concerned about precariousness in the labour market; others may

---

[1] The ECHP is a panel survey based on a standardized questionnaire which involves interviewing a representative sample of households in each country, covering a wide range of topics, including income, health, education, housing, and employment. The first wave was conducted in 1994 in the then 12 EU member states; since then, Austria (1995) and Finland (1996) have joined the project. Sweden is not participating. See Eurostat (1999).

have attached national importance to the reduction of child poverty. While member states will be encouraged to complement the EU indicators with their own choice of indicators, it is important that the portfolio of EU indicators should command general support as a balanced representation of Europe's social concerns.

The second principle is that *the indicators should be mutually consistent and that the weight of single indicators in the portfolio should be proportionate*. Mutual consistency is an evident requirement. The term 'proportionate' refers to the fact that the interpretation of the set of indicators is greatly eased where the individual components have degrees of importance that, while not necessarily exactly equal, are not grossly different. It would be hard to make sense of a set of indicators that lumped together measures of central importance, such as national poverty rates, with indicators that would generally be regarded as of a more specialized or more local interest.

The final principle is that *the portfolio of indicators should be as transparent and accessible as possible to the citizens of the European Union*. At present there is a great deal of public confusion about the form and purposes of social indicators. It is therefore important that, as the Commission has stated, indicators should be 'easy to read and understand' (European Commission 2000*a*: 9). This applies to the individual indicators and to the set as a whole. We have also to be aware of the temptation to aggregate indicators. Journalists writing about trends will tend to count pluses and minuses. These considerations may well affect the range of indicators and the total number included. Too large a number of indicators would mean that the exercise would have lost both transparency and credibility. There has been extensive discussion at the European level of the number of indicators and of the case for a multi-level approach, and we explore this further in Chapter 4. We also have to recognize that the recent developments in the European social agenda are not well known among the general public. There has been only limited coverage in newspapers, television, and radio. Dissemination of the results of indicators, and of information about their methods of construction, is therefore an important task. In this process a key role will be played by non-governmental organizations and by the scientific community.

The above list of principles is open to debate, but we believe that making them explicit will aid the development of social indicators in the EU and help ensure their long-term durability. When we come to examine different areas, we consider how far different indicators, including the seven proposed by the Commission, both individually and as a portfolio, match up to these principles.

Recommendation 1. The nine principles listed above should form the basis for constructing indicators for social inclusion in the European Union.

Gender mainstreaming

As embodied in the Treaty of Amsterdam, equality of treatment between women and men is a prominent part of the EU agenda. Member states have agreed that a gender equality perspective should be integrated into all policy areas, an approach referred to as 'gender mainstreaming'. It is clear that all indicators of social inclusion should, where possible and meaningful, be disaggregated by gender. As expressed by the European Commission (1998), 'differences [may] cause apparently neutral policies to impact differently on women and men and reinforce existing inequalities and vulnerabilities arising from other structural differences, such as race/ethnicity, class, age, disability, etc. Therefore it is important that statistics and data are broken down by sex (men–women–total).' Comparisons can be made across member states of the male–female differences in social indicator values. The rate of low pay, for example, among women relative to men (i.e. the 'gender pay gap') would be compared across countries.

The issue of gender is important not only in terms of disaggregation but also in the definition of indicators. Choices made with regard to definitions may not be neutral with regard to gender, and we indicate a number of cases where this is evidently important. An example is provided by the distribution of resources within the household. In the present state of knowledge, we have, when considering income, to treat the household as the income-sharing unit; but this conceals significant inequalities between women and men in control over resources. Similarly, a focus on paid employment in defining joblessness, rather than on a wider concept of productive contribution, is not gender-neutral.

2.2. PROPERTIES OF INDICATORS

A great deal of information is now made available about the state of *Social Europe* (for a valuable survey, see Rothenbacher 1998). Governments at national, regional, and local levels publish compendia of social statistics; at the European level, the Commission publishes *inter alia* its regular report on *The Social Situation in the European Union*. There are publications from research institutes such as the Mannheim Centre for European

Social Research; there are regular EU-wide surveys providing such information, for instance the European Community Household Panel, the Labour Force Surveys, and the Eurobarometer. In considering this growing volume of information, it is helpful to begin with a number of conceptual points. Social indicators can be of different types and can have different properties.

Individual versus household

A natural starting point for construction of a social indicator for a country is the position of its individual citizens. If our concern is with health status, then we may sample households, but we wish to know about the health of each individual member, from the newly born baby daughter to the great-grandmother. For some purposes however we wish to look at the position of a wider unit than the individual. It would not make sense to consider the baby's income without regard to that of her parents and others. Once we aggregate, however, a range of possible definitions opens up for the unit of analysis, making use of criteria such as the following:

- common dwelling, with a *household* comprising those resident in a dwelling, sharing some degree of common housekeeping, but not necessarily related by family ties;
- common spending, where the *spending unit* is defined as those taking spending decisions to a considerable degree in common, where this may cover people who have no family relationship;
- blood or marital relationship, where members of the *family unit* are related by marriage/cohabitation or by blood relations;
- dependence, where the unit is defined to include a single person or couple plus any dependent children, this constituting the *inner family*.

In the case of a single person living alone, these criteria would all lead to the same unit of analysis. But where there is more than one person, we may have to make a choice. If we were to start with the household as the unit, then it could be argued that this is too wide, since it would include people who are not part of the economic unit, or people who are not related, or people who are not dependent. On the other hand, it could be argued that the unit is too narrow, in that there are people not resident in the dwelling who are part of the economic unit or who are dependent. The grandmother may live round the corner but eat all her meals with the family; the son may be a student with a room in the city but bring his laundry home each weekend; the breadwinner may have been seconded to Brussels.

The implications of different choices of unit depend on the variable in question. In the case of financial poverty, the use of a wider definition tends to involve a reduction in the measured poverty rate, since more income-sharing is assumed to be taking place. The student son may be below the poverty line if considered as a unit on his own, but when his income is added to that of his parents, the total may be enough to keep all of them out of poverty.[2] The Swedish National Action Plan on Social Inclusion notes that 'children over the age of 18 who live at home used to be counted as independent households, which resulted in an over-estimation of the number of poor people in the age group 18–29' (Government of Sweden 2001: 2). A switch to a household definition reduced the measured poverty percentage.

The choice between different units involves assumptions about factual matters, such as the extent of support offered by other family members. The great-grandmother would probably share the household's standard of living, but a group of students living together could not be treated as a unit. It involves value judgements about the extent to which people should be dependent. A policy change that discouraged people in their twenties from leaving home might reduce measured poverty but would not necessarily be regarded as a social improvement. The choice as far as European-wide indicators are concerned may also be influenced by the differences across member states in household composition. It should also be recognized that we may be interested in individual status interpreted in a household context. For example, we may wish to establish the number of individuals who are unemployed but who are living in a household with no one in paid work. This is in effect a combination of individual and household characteristics, and places particular demands on data collection.

The fact that we may wish to consider the position of a household as a whole does not imply that we should then count the number of households. The method of counting, or weighting, is distinct from the choice of the unit of analysis. Suppose that we are considering a variable that is defined at the household level, such as poor housing; then we have the

---

[2] Logically, the effect could go the other way. Suppose Mr X has an income below the poverty line and Ms Y has an income above the poverty line. Living separately, they lead to one person being in measured poverty; living together, it is possible that both are below the poverty line. This reflects the particular features of the headcount as a measure of poverty—see Atkinson (1998: 49).

issue as to whether to count households or individuals. Does a couple and two children in bad housing count once or four times? In our view, the fundamental concern when measuring social inclusion is with the position of Europe's citizens, and this points to counting persons. We recognize that the circumstances of the households in which people live are major determinants of the level of well-being of individuals, and that households may be socially excluded as a whole. We are not suggesting that individuals should be considered in isolation; but each person should count for one. The couple and two children are four of Europe's citizens who are in poor housing. Weighting households by the number of people leads to certain problems when measuring poverty, to which we return in Chapters 5 and 6, but in general we recommend the following procedure.

Recommendation 2. The fundamental concern when measuring social inclusion as part of the EU monitoring process is with the position of individual citizens, and in general statistics should be presented in terms of counting individuals or their circumstances (rather than households).

We should draw attention here to the definition of the total population. In referring to households, we are not suggesting that we should be concerned only with the household population. Our starting point is that we should be concerned with *all* those living in the European Union. This should be emphasized, since a number of statistical sources leave out important groups. Surveys are often limited to the household population. This leaves out those living in institutions, such as students and the military, and those living in hostels or shelters or reception centres. It leaves out the elderly living in residential accommodation and children taken into care by public authorities. It leaves out those living on the streets. Surveys may also exclude by their design other groups, such as non-nationals, or those whose accommodation is not bricks and mortar, such as those living on boats or in caravans. Whatever the limits imposed by data collection, it is imperative when considering social exclusion not to lose sight of these groups.

Relative versus absolute

There is much debate about 'absolute' versus 'relative' criteria. This distinction is misleading, since any indicator has to be interpreted relative to a standard. The essential question is the choice of standard and of the method of updating the standard over time. A poverty measure may be defined relative to mean or median incomes, for example, and this is the usual way the term 'relative' is employed. It contains its own updating mechanism: the poverty threshold will move over time in line with mean or median income, whether that is rising slowly or rapidly—or, indeed, falling—in terms of purchasing power. A contrast is often drawn with measures of poverty based on ability to afford a given bundle of goods and services. These are sometimes referred to as 'absolute', but in reality they do not represent a level of consumption that is in any sense 'absolutely' necessary for survival, as is demonstrated by the fact that when employed they also tend to be updated over time to reflect changing consumption patterns—if only at irregular intervals. The experience of the United States in this respect is described by Fisher (1992), who shows how in practice the basket of goods has been linked to general living standards. The more valid contrast, then, is between measures designed to move over time in line with the general standard of living in the society, and those that are regularly up-rated only by the increase in prices and are intended to represent a fixed level of purchasing power.

EU-wide indicators

EU-wide indicators are of interest for a number of reasons, not least as a comparison of EU performance with that of the United States or other OECD countries. Within the EU, the appeal may increase as the Union becomes more integrated. As it has been put by the Commission, 'the on-going European integration starts to blur the differences between individual member states. It could be argued that the EU is becoming more and more one society. In this light a uniform poverty line may be considered' (Eurostat 2000b: 20). Using the 1996 data of the European Community Household Panel, a line set at 60% of the median equivalized household income of the EU as a whole amounted to 6,000 PPS.[3] Related poverty rates did vary greatly: from one in twenty in Denmark and Austria to nearly one in two in Portugal.

But the construction of EU-wide indicators raises a number of issues. To begin with, a poverty line calculated for the EU as a whole may be

[3] Purchasing power standard. At that time, the conversion rate was 1 unit of PPS = 7.274 French francs, 42.13 Belgian francs, 9.740 Danish kronor, 2.148 Deutschmarks, 236.5 Spanish pesetas, 0.7032 Irish pounds, 1696 Italian lira, 40.79 Luxembourg francs, 2.25 Netherlands guilders, 15.19 Austrian schilling, 142.7 Portuguese escudo, and 0.7305 UK pounds sterling.

perceived as unrealistically high in some countries (i.e. too close to median income) and unacceptably low in others (i.e. far below the statutory minimum). A measure that concentrates poverty in a small number of member states may not be regarded as appealing. It may pay too little attention to the genuine problems of poverty within richer member states.

The second issue concerns the weighting of member states. Implicitly, many EU-wide numbers weight countries according to their size. Gross national product for the EU is formed by adding across member states. This does however mean that the experience of small countries has little influence on the EU-wide figure. For the purpose of economic management this may be acceptable, but for other purposes, notably social inclusion, we do want to ensure that each member state has a perceptible influence on the aggregate indicator, just as the voting system is not strictly proportional to population.

The third issue concerns the treatment of within-member-state differences. The use, for example, of regional variation of unemployment as an indicator for a member state takes no account of the relation with contiguous regions in other member states. Policy by the French government to aid the Pas de Calais may reduce regional disparities in France but increase the contrast with the South-East of the United Kingdom. It is possible that a national policy to reduce regional disparities has the effect of *increasing* disparities between regions in the EU as a whole. Whether it does so depends on the form of the overall indicator and the decomposition of Europe-wide variation into its between- and within-member-state components.

In this book we concentrate on indicators applied at the level of the member state, and do not consider national disparities between member states. We return however to this important issue at the end of the book.

Static and dynamic

Certain indicators are based on a person or household's current status. A person is unemployed at the current date, or the household's income is below the poverty line at the interview date. This has traditionally been the main concern of social indicators. Increasingly, however, we have become interested in dynamic indicators. As it is put by Bradbury *et al.* (2001), a child poverty rate of 10% 'could mean that every tenth child is always poor, or that all children are in poverty for one month in ten. Knowing where reality lies between these extremes is vital.'

Indicators may be dynamic in several senses. One sense is that we are concerned with changes, or a lack of change, over time for an individual. We may be concerned that a person was unemployed, or in poverty, both at date t and at date $(t+1)$. As this example brings out, the introduction of dynamic considerations complicates measurement. We have to distinguish a situation where the person was unemployed continuously from the interview in year t to the interview in year $(t+1)$ from a situation where he had a job in between which lasted less than a year. In other words, we are extending the period of observation, and the employment history can be summarized in many different ways. An indicator of how many people have been persistently unemployed is different from an indicator as to whether a person has been unemployed at any time in the past x years.

Social indicators may be forward-looking. People are excluded not just because they are currently without a job or income, but also because they have little prospects for the future. Social exclusion is a matter not only of *ex post* trajectories but also of *ex ante* expectations. In this case, we are seeking to measure current variables that are predictors of future developments. An indicator such as low school attainment, or truancy, may be important not only in its own right, but also because it increases the risk of poverty and social disadvantage in later life.

Stock and flow indicators

Related to dynamics, but different, is the distinction between stock and flow indicators. An example is provided by education, where we may be interested in the qualifications of those entering the labour force (a flow measure) or in the qualifications of all those in the existing labour force (a stock measure). The flow measure, in this case, is one of the determinants of the changes in the stock. (The other is the qualification level of those leaving the stock.) Flow measures are more subject to policy influence. It may take a decade for the effects of changed educational policies to be observed in the stock measure. Equally, flow measures may be more variable over time, reflecting the experience of individual school cohorts.

In the case of economic resources, the distinction between stock and flow may be seen as the difference between a stock of assets and a flow of income. Income is the main variable that has been considered when measuring poverty, although, if one applies a standard based on eligibility for minimum income schemes, then in some member states this involves an asset test as well as an income test. We may however want to consider a separate indicator based on the lack of wealth. This may take the form of an index of 'precariousness', measured for example by the absence of liquid funds on which a person could draw in the case of emergency. It may take the form of an index of indebtedness, where the person owes money or is in arrears on payment for utilities or for rent or for mortgage payments.

Levels versus changes

A third, and again related, use of the term 'dynamic' is the distinction between indicators of the current social conditions in member states and indicators of the changes in those conditions. Here we are referring not to changes for a particular individual, but to changes for the population. As just discussed, there may be no improvement in the educational level of those already in the labour force, but the inflow of new workers may be better qualified than the outflow of workers retiring. The overall level of educational qualifications is improving.

There are two different arguments for focusing on changes, rather than levels. The first is statistical. If it were the case that the indicators could not be compared across member states but that the errors were constant over time (or changed equally in all member states), then the first differences would allow comparisons to be made. The second is that, from a policy viewpoint, it is the direction of movement that is of most concern. The government of a member state may be fully aware that their country's performance, in one particular dimension, is inferior to that of other EU members, but may reasonably wish to emphasize progress towards closing the gap.

Multidimensional indicators

The European Union has consistently sought to broaden the concept of social exclusion, stressing its multidimensional nature and drawing a contrast with sole reliance on a monetary poverty indicator. In its 1992 submission on 'intensifying the fight against social exclusion', the Commission stated of social exclusion that, 'more clearly than the concept of poverty, understood far too often as referring exclusively to income, it also states out the multidimensional nature of the mechanisms whereby individuals and groups are excluded from taking part in the social exchanges, from the component practices and rights of social integration' (European Commission 1992: 8). According to the

October 2000 statement on 'The Fight against Poverty and Social Exclusion', 'poverty and social exclusion take complex and multidimensional forms which require the mobilisation of a wide range of policies under that general strategy. Alongside employment policy, social protection has a pre-eminent role to play, while the importance of other factors such as housing, education, health, information and communications, mobility, security and justice, leisure and culture should also be acknowledged' (European Commission, 2000*b*).

The portfolio of social indicators is by definition multidimensional, covering a range of fields as indicated in these quotations; but individual components may themselves have multiple dimensions. For poverty, for example, we may have two indicators: current household income, and a measure of deprivation in terms of life-style. These may be complementary sources of information in trying to identify those experiencing exclusion because of a lack of resources. Life-style deprivation levels depend on command over resources and experiences over a long period, not just on the flow of income into the household this week, month, or even year.

The main conceptual issue with such multiple dimensioned indicators concerns the relation between different dimensions. Do we assume that the different dimensions are non-comparable and that they have therefore to be presented separately? If so, then this leads to a proliferation of indicators, reducing their transparency and acceptability. Or do we assume that we can aggregate them? If so, how is this to be done? Do we take the cases of overlap? Are we concerned with the proportion of the population who fall below on both measures? Or is our concern with those below on either one or other indicator? Multiple measures enrich our knowledge but also pose questions.

Subjective and objective indicators

The indicators proposed by the European Commission may be described as 'objective' in the sense that the status of individuals or households can be verified by documentary evidence and is not based on a subjective judgement by the respondent. There is however a risk that sole reliance on objective indicators could be seen as reducing the legitimacy of the exercise. Why should we totally disregard the views of those suffering social exclusion?

There are three distinct senses in which indicators could incorporate subjective elements. The first is where the standard or target is set on the basis of citizens' responses to survey questions. This standard is then applied to the incomes of all households to count the poor. An example is the question the Gallup Poll has regularly asked in the United States: 'What is the smallest amount of money a family of four needs each week to get along in this community?' An analysis of the responses over the period 1950–86 showed that they tended to rise about 0.8% for each 1% rise in household income, adjusting for price changes (Van den Bosch 2001). Thus, over time a poverty line based on those answers would rise strongly in real terms. Another example is the 'Leyden approach' discussed in Chapter 5 (see Van Praag *et al.* 1982), where persons are asked about the minimum income they need for their own household in order to make ends meet (or to reach some other target, such as not being poor).

A second subjective approach is to ask people 'what income is needed to keep a family such as yours out of poverty' and whether their income is above or below this level. This approach is adopted in Britain for example by Gordon *et al.* (2000: 30), who distinguish between 'absolute', 'general', and 'overall' poverty. A third use of the term 'subjective' is where people are asked to make a subjective evaluation of their own situation and the indicator is directly based on those responses (i.e. not mediated through questions on the definition of a poverty line). An example is the question in the ECHP which asks respondents to assess whether they are themselves having difficulties in making ends meet. The answers to such questions depend not only on the living standards of respondents, but also on their expectations, which are influenced by past experiences and by their reference groups. It should be stressed that this is a different use of subjectivity compared with the first approach, as no overall poverty line or standard is derived, common to all households. Both second and third interpretations of the subjective approach imply that the situation of different persons is evaluated by different standards, raising important issues of equity in a policy context.

Territorial indicators

Indicators may have an important territorial dimension, as was explicitly recognized by the Commission in its June 2000 submission, which referred to the need to take account of regional and local differences. We are likely to be interested in how poverty rates differ across regions, or whether low education is a feature of some localities but not others. Furthermore, whereas poverty or low education are characteristics of individual households, there are other types of indicator which—it may be hypothesized—relate to a population rather than the individual. Disadvantage may be located in a community and not a property of the particular individuals who live there. The crime rate may be a property of a specified locality. Life expectancy, for example, may depend—at least in part—on the local environment, so that a person moving to another area could thereby modify his or her life expectancy. Deprivation indices are constructed for local government units.[4] Such territorial indicators have been particularly adopted by national governments that have targeted policy geographically. Area-based anti-exclusion policy is based on a set of hypotheses about the location of exclusion, and this points to the collection of area-based data. But for the same reason, the collection of household-based indicators is necessary to evaluate the hypotheses on which this policy is based.

One important reason why territorial indicators need to be considered is that a number of member states have decentralized significant elements of social policy to regional, provincial, or local governments. In this respect, the construction of National Action Plans on Social Inclusion involves not only central governments but also lower-level governments. (The same applies to the National Action Plans on Employment.) The National Action Plan on Social Inclusion for Belgium begins by explaining that the fight against social exclusion is a responsibility divided between the federal Belgian government and the governments of the communities and regions. The plan therefore brings together the actions undertaken at different levels of government. In Spain, the National Action Plan on Social Inclusion has been produced as a result of collaboration between the government, the autonomous communities, and local authorities. The National Action Plan on Social Inclusion for Germany describes how strategies for combating poverty and social exclusion tend to differ regionally on account of the country's federal structure (Government of the Federal Republic of Germany 2001: 5). The United Kingdom (UK) National Action Plan noted that 'the UK is no longer a unitary state. . . . many of the key areas of policy responsibility in the field of poverty and social exclusion rest with the devolved administrations (Government of the United Kingdom 2001: 1). These devolved and local governments may set their own targets and may

---

[4] In the UK such indicators have been constructed by the Social Disadvantage Research Group at the University of Oxford. See their website http://www.apsoc.ox.ac.uk/sdrgdocs/ and Noble and Smith (1996) for a study of two contrasting areas (Oldham and Oxford).

adopt their own performance indicators. There may for instance be different poverty lines by region. What is more, regions within countries may differ in their powers. (For example, the Scottish and Welsh Assemblies in the UK have different powers.)

2.3. DATA FOR SOCIAL INDICATOR CONSTRUCTION

The construction of social indicators is necessarily a compromise between the theoretical definition and the empirically possible. Data may not be available, or the available data may not be comparable across countries (or even within countries) or across time. The collection of data may be too expensive, too burdensome on persons or enterprises, or may face constraints in terms of public acceptability. At the same time, it should be an ambition of a knowledge-based economy to improve the information base on which policy is debated and assessed. New technology allows powerful new uses of data, for example in policy simulation, where European researchers have made major contributions. The European Union should seek to pioneer new advances in the acquisition and use of data on social inclusion.

The goals both of timeliness and of minimizing the external burden mean that the Commission should look first to information provided by the European Statistical System. In our view, the further development of this system is a major priority. National governments will make their own choices, but in their National Action Plans they should be encouraged to implement social indicators as far as possible using data common in source across the European Union, or available in EU databases (such as the harmonized household budget surveys).

The social inclusion indicators proposed by the Commission in its 2001 *Synthesis Report* drew on three main European sources: the European Labour Force Survey (LFS), the European Community Household Panel (ECHP), and the regional statistics. Each of these is a most important source. The ECHP is an excellent example of the return to foresight. The use made of ECHP data in today's policy discussion must exceed even the most optimistic assumptions of the designers of the Panel nearly a decade ago. Setting the Panel in place was a farsighted investment. At the same time, experience with the Panel has revealed some of the problems, notably of technical difficulties and poor timeliness, and this has delayed or limited the extent of the application of its results. The development of the new instrument, the EU-SILC, to replace ECHP from 2003 will build on this experience, and its design is reflecting the needs of social indicator construction.

In the same way, the LFS needs to be examined from the perspective of its role in providing employment indicators and of how individual employment status can be related to a harmonized definition of the household and the characteristics of those households. Reference should also be made to the harmonized household budget surveys (HBS). Eurostat has invested considerable resources in establishing this valuable dataset, and it is important that it be fully exploited. Work that requires data on household expenditure have the possibility of making full use of these surveys, which have traditionally been a major source of information (for example the studies in the UK inspired by Abel-Smith and Townsend 1965). At present the access arrangements limit the effective use of LFS and HBS datasets. While we appreciate that the data have been obtained by a different process, we recommend that the access conditions approximate as closely as possible those for the ECHP. Use of the ECHP by the scientific community has led to significant improvement of the data and documentation; the data access issue is therefore linked with quality improvements.

Use of sample surveys

Results of different surveys may diverge simply because of *sample fluctuations*. Sampling merely allows one to draw conclusions about a characteristic of the population with a certain degree of (un)reliability. The accuracy and reliability of sample-based estimates depend primarily on the sample size and design. There are, however, other elements that may cause survey results to vary.

Another important aspect of surveys is the degree of non-response. Almost inevitably, a number of interviewees will refuse to participate in the survey, or they may be either unreachable or untraceable. First and foremost, this implies fewer available cases, and therefore less efficient sample-based estimates. Moreover, to the extent that *non-response* is selective, i.e. that its occurrence within a specific category is more than proportional, it will provide biased estimates. This problem is particularly apparent in panel surveys, as with each wave there is inevitably some attrition. In order to correct for non-response biases, weighting factors are to be incorporated. (Each respondent is allocated a certain weight which is inversely proportional to the probability that the respondent will be included in the sample.) Certainly in the case of panel surveys, these factors can be estimated fairly accurately, as the previous wave will always provide a great deal of information about both the respondents who participated and those who did not (except for the first wave). The degree of (selectivity in) attrition and the adequacy of the *weighting procedure* may influence the survey results.

It is invariably the case in surveys that a number of respondents fail to answer certain questions. Situations where respondents either refuse or are unable to answer certain questions that apply to them are referred to as *item non-response*. Questions that respondents experience as sensitive or difficult to answer tend to generate greater item non-response. This is often the case with questions about income. Item non-response reduces the number of cases that can be included in the analysis. Moreover, if item non-response is selective, it can give rise to biased estimates. If item non-response is systematically greater within specific population segments (e.g. large households, self-employed, high-income households), it may cause biased income and poverty figures. For this reason, it is usual in surveys to correct by means of so-called *imputation procedures* for item non-response. In such imputation procedures, a respondent with non-response on a variable is attributed a value on the basis of (similar) respondents who have responded to that item. There are various imputation procedures of varying quality. The higher is item non-response, the more important is the quality of the imputation procedure.

A further problem is that survey results may be disproportionately affected by outliers, for example very high or low (negative) values for income or other variables. These outliers may arise simply on account of sampling variability, but they may also suggest shortcomings in the data. An independent worker, for instance, may record a large loss in a particular period, but this may reflect the particular accounting practice. Large incomes or large losses may be purely transitory. For these reasons, it is a common practice to apply top-coding or bottom-coding to income and other data. (The former means that all incomes above X euro are entered as X euro, and bottom-coding applies the same procedure in reverse at the bottom of the distribution.) The research objectives, the design of the fieldwork, the expertise and supervision of the interviewers, the length and adequacy of the questionnaire, and the processing of the data may also affect the quality of the measurement or the representativeness of the sample, and thus can also give rise to divergent results.

Given the complexity of survey statistics and the level of error or uncertainty of the results, information about the sample and question design and about weighting and imputation procedures should be made available. To this end, in the case of income distribution, the Expert Group on Household Income Statistics (known as the Canberra Group) (2001) developed a Robustness Assessment Report (RAR) which encapsulates the information needed to ensure that comparable and consistent information is available on each statistical output from which the user can judge their fitness for purpose. It is important for users to bear always in mind that 'even where "good" survey data do exist, serious and often quite subtle issues of comparability and measurement still abound' (Strauss and Thomas 1996: 30).

Use of ECHP and EU-SILC

To elaborate on these points, we believe that the needs of social indicator construction can be divided into two main steps: (i) the use of ECHP for the first stage of indicator development, and (ii) the use of EU-SILC data when they come on stream. The ECHP is the key source on income and living conditions used by the Commission, but it has to be qualified by the fact that the question design predated the present interest in social indicators, so that data availability is already predetermined, and by the—inevitable—concerns expressed by some member states about some of the findings for their own countries. The latter may mean that national governments agree to a particular indicator but argue that it should be measured *also* according to national sources. This raises a key question that needs to be addressed: the relationship between data derived from European statistical instruments and data available from national sources. In our view, the best procedure at this stage is a pragmatic one.

The ECHP will undoubtedly be the main source for indicators on social inclusion used by the European Commission (for example in the Joint report on Social Inclusion) and by several member states, but some member states may want to qualify the conclusions reached in the light of information from national sources, where such national sources exist. The two proceed in parallel. This may of course lead to conflicting conclusions. The ECHP, by its panel sample design, may show a movement in one direction, whereas national cross-sectional surveys may show a movement in the opposite direction. It is therefore important that Eurostat, in consort with the national statistical agencies and other organizations that are engaged in relevant research, further investigate the reasons for these divergences, along the lines of the very valuable work already conducted. In our view, Eurostat should continue to invest resources in comparing the national surveys and other information (including registers) used by member states, since in the present state of knowledge we cannot afford to neglect any source of evidence.

The second stage, in terms of application, is the use of the new EU-SILC. Of particular importance are the sample size and the areas of coverage. Sample size is especially significant, since many of the social indicators under consideration relate to sub-groups of the population, such as those aged 65 and over. With a rotating panel or cross-sectional survey design, it is possible to increase sample size if this becomes necessary, but the lags in the production of data mean that this issue should be addressed sooner rather than later. As far as question design is concerned, the detailed discussion of indicators in Chapters 5–8 will provide an input into this process.

The move to EU-SILC, with its priority on a cross-sectional dimension, will no doubt make the results more directly comparable with those from national sources. This does not, of course, remove the need for a reconciliation of the findings with those in national data. In the case of income poverty, there have already been tests of the external validity of the ECHP. In June 1999 a questionnaire on national measurement of poverty was sent to national statistical institutes, who were asked to provide estimates of poverty based on national sources and national definitions. For three countries (France, Netherlands, and the UK) the differences arising from definitions and from population coverage were investigated. This seems to us an excellent model, which should be developed further. The same applies to the ECHP Quality Reports that Eurostat has already twice produced. We recommend that each of the social indicators adopted which has been calculated using a European instrument should, wherever possible, be validated by reference to national sources. The validation can take a number of different forms, and need not depend on there being equivalent national sources. It may be a comparison of the underlying aggregates. For instance, if the poverty indicators are calculated before and after transfers, then a comparison should be made of the total transfers recorded in the survey with the known administrative totals. The required validation will differ from indicator to indicator.

On data quality, we therefore make the third recommendation.

Recommendation 3. A systematic validation procedure should be associated with each agreed social indicator, assessing its reliability in the light of all available sources.

Broadening the field

There are further features of European data collection that we believe to be relevant to the construction of social indicators, which may take us beyond the range of data currently employed. One is the salience of contextual data. An important trend in the study of social inclusion is the consideration of people in their context. The example has just been given of interpreting individual unemployment in the context of the household in which the person lives, but this goes much wider. We may wish to interpret a person's situation in the light of the community in which they live. A person who is unemployed in a town in which unemployment is very rare is in a different position from that of a person whose neighbours are all unemployed. There would be considerable value, for example, in associating the national surveys with studies of particular cities, matched across the European Union.

Secondly, we need to pay particular attention to the position of people who are not part of the household population: those living in institutions, those in the armed forces or in prison, and those who are homeless. This is a heterogeneous group, but includes some of those most at risk of social exclusion. Statistics based on household surveys miss this group, and we need to consider ways in which its members can be covered. This will require a significant investment, but it is of great importance.

These concerns point to the use of data in addition to those from household surveys. We may wish to relate the person's situation to the employment context, linking data on households and employers. Such linking is becoming increasingly possible as new techniques are developed for handling very large datasets. Reference should be made here to national register systems. In a number of member states, especially the Nordic ones, there are national registers where a great deal of information can be assembled from the administration of income taxation, social security records, employment services, local government, etc. In the case of Belgium, for example, the scope for using administrative data in the study of social exclusion has been extensively discussed by Vranken *et al.* (1998*a*) and by Levecque and Vranken (2000). In a project funded under the TSER Programme, Saraceno (2002) and colleagues (see Voges 2001) have shown how administrative data on social assistance can be used in a comparative way for six EU member states. Register sources have the advantages of relatively low cost and of reduced burden on respondents. In the present context, a further important advantage of register data is that of speed. The need for timeliness is one of the major constraints on the choice of social indicators. The use of such sources may encounter major legal problems as well as difficulties in terms of public acceptability, but they offer a potential way forward, as has been recognized in the preparation for the EU-SILC. And it should be remembered that new technology offers the possibility of new safeguards as well as new data linkages. At the same time, we should note that, even for those countries making extensive use of register information, household surveys will be required in order to obtain qualitative information. They will also be necessary to ensure that a EU-harmonized concept of household can be implemented, which would be based not simply on common residence, but also on the sharing of expenditure. The survey is necessary to identify people in the register and their relation to other household members.

Building statistical capacity

In considering the development of social indicators in Europe, consideration has to be given not only to the data themselves but also to statistical capacity-building. The construction of social indicators in the European Union, and their maintenance on a regular basis, depends on there being a highly qualified staff of statisticians and computer specialists in each member state. Past experience has shown that data weaknesses arise when there are problems of communication between data producers and data users. Apparent differences in results can often be traced to differences in procedures and definitions, and attainment of a high level of comparability depends on close cooperation, which in turn depends on the available manpower in national statistical agencies and government departments. Equally there is a need for adequate resources, human and material, to be made available to Eurostat. To this, we would add the need for wider diffusion of quantitative skills in the research community (academic, private research institutions, enterprises). In short, we stress that the building of statistical capacity is an essential investment if the EU is indeed to become a knowledge-based economy.

Recommendation 4. High priority should be given to the building of statistical capacity.

3

Social Indicators from a Member State Perspective

Since key contributors to the development of social indicators at Community level are member-state perspectives and practices, in this chapter we review the situation in this regard. In doing so, our aim is to illustrate the range of current practice in the use of social indicators, not to provide a comprehensive assessment on a country-by-country basis. For a valuable review of both European and national initiatives, pre-dating the National Action Plans on Social Inclusion, readers are referred to Vranken *et al.* (2001). These authors compare the conceptual frameworks adopted in different countries, the databases employed, and the indicators used, summarizing national reports on poverty and social exclusion that have been produced by official and academic researchers.

Member states differ in the degree to which they have set explicit targets for combating social exclusion. In some cases there are strategies aimed at promoting social inclusion that already include explicit targets and indicators against which to measure the effectiveness of policy. Some countries, such as Ireland, have set a national objective for the reduction of financial poverty; others have adopted a set of progress indicators by which performance is to be evaluated; and still others monitor the trends in poverty and social exclusion in a less structured manner and without pre-commitment to identified targets. For this reason, the amount of space allocated to each country varies. In each case, however, a National Action Plan on Social Inclusion (NAPincl) was submitted to the Commission in June 2001. The NAPincls were requested to state the progress aimed for by national policies and to list the indicators used to assess progress, and the European Union is to move from that base towards commonly agreed and defined indicators. Thus, the National Plans provided an opportunity for member states to crystallize both their broad perspectives on social indicators and the specifics of how to formulate targets and monitor progress. We do not attempt a detailed review of the policies proposed under these Action Plans. Our concern here is not with the policies, but with the use of performance indicators.

The main elements on which we comment are (i) the method by which the Plans were produced and their relation with previous policy formation, (ii) the use made of the seven indicators proposed by the Commission, and (iii) other indicators employed by member states which seem of wider interest, particularly where they relate to fields not covered by the Commission's indicators. In describing the indicators proposed by member states, we adopt a classification that corresponds broadly to the order of our discussion here:

1. Financial
2. Education
3. Employment
4. Health
5. Housing
6. Social participation

For each member state, we present below a brief summary of the social reporting in place prior to the National Action Plans and then describe the main features of the NAPincl. As will be clear, our treatment here does not do justice to the National Action Plans, many of which are substantial documents. (The plans run in total to some 1,200 pages.) Many of the Plans include examples of 'Good Practices', to which we do not refer, but which are most valuable sources of ideas for cross-country fertilization. We also take for granted the fact that member states have set targets and indicators for the labour market in the context of National Action Plans on Employment, and do not document these employment plans.

3.1. **BELGIUM**

Belgium has at present no official targets in the area of poverty. Official indicators are not explicitly adopted to monitor progress in this area. There has however been a great deal of relevant research. Since 1980, the Center for Social Policy at the Antwerp University produces on a regular base 'Social Indicators-Reports' (Deleeck *et al.* 1986*a,b*, 1991*a,b*; Cantillon *et al.* 1999*a,b*). In these reports, which are broadly discussed and used by political parties, social organizations, and governments, estimates are presented on the extent of poverty (based on the socioeconomic panel (SEP)) and the adequacy of social policies (mainly social security, tax expenditure, housing, education). As far as benefits are concerned, indicators include the amount of social benefits as a percentage of GDP per capita and as a percentage of the poverty line. There is also consider-able emphasis on regional aspects.

In 1994 a General Report on Poverty and Social Exclusion was sub-mitted to the Belgian government (Koning Boudewijnstichting 1994; Fondation Roi Baudouin 1994). On the basis of this report, which heavily relied on the experiences of people living in poverty, anti-poverty initi-atives were subsequently developed. These include the adoption in 2000 of a programme aiming, notably via measures for insertion in the labour market, to reduce by one-third in five years the number of people depend-ent on the social minimum. In addition, since the mid-1990s, yearbooks on poverty and social inclusion in the different regions have been pro-duced (Vranken *et al.* 1992–2000; Gemeenschappelijke Gemeenschaps-commissie voor Brussel-Hoofdstad 1993–2000; Ministère de la Région Wallonne 2001). These reports include a broad range of indicators in the field of income, education, housing, and health. Since 1998, an observa-tory on poverty and social exclusion has been in charge of the coordina-tion of a dialogue between organizations in which the poor participate, together with governments, departments, and social organizations. The results of this structural dialogue are published in a biannual publication of a *Report on Poverty*.

Following the model of the earlier General Report on Poverty, the development of the National Action Plan on Social Inclusion for Belgium built on a dialogue with the excluded and organizations that speak for the poor, an approach which it is hoped will be developed fur-ther: 'the participation of the target group of socially excluded is an essen-tial element in the design of indicators' (Government of Belgium 2001: 8). As already noted, the preparation of the Report posed a particular chal-lenge for the Belgian team, because the responsibility for policies to com-bat social exclusion is divided between the federal government and the governments of the Communities and the Regions. The Plan therefore re-quired an assembly of all the various policies currently in effect at different levels, and a 60-page summary of measures is appended to the NAPincl.

The NAPincl describes the evolution from a purely monetary indi-cator of poverty to a multidimensioned set of indicators that treat a net-work of exclusions. The Report begins with the structural indicators proposed by the Commission and then presents a number of other key indicators:

• *Financial*: thresholds of 40, 50, 60, and 70% median income, 50% of mean income, and continuous graph of intermediate thresholds;

efficiency of social transfers; percentage of adult population with recorded debts

- *Education*: educational spending per child; relation between education of parents and children
- *Employment*: percentage of employees below poverty line (the 'working poor'); degree of activation of the unemployed
- *Health*: percentage unable to obtain medical treatment for financial reasons; percentage of the adult population whose daily activities are seriously restricted by state of health
- *Housing*: percentage lacking specified amenities; number of homeless; unmet demand for social housing
- *Social participation*: percentage not going away on holiday; experiencing social isolation; percentage with access to Internet; functional illiteracy; reintegration of ex-prisoners; legal assistance

Calculations have been made for these indicators, drawing on a range of data sources, including the European Community Household Panel, the Labour Force Survey, the health survey, and the national bank. The Report also refers to the future development of an index of multi-dimensional deprivation.

3.2. DENMARK

In Denmark, strategies aimed at promoting social inclusion place a great deal of emphasis on employment and active labour market policies; since 1998, those in receipt of social protection cash transfers have both the right and the obligation (after a year of receipt, in the case of those aged 30 and over) to take up active work or take part in activation programmes. Indicators of labour market success are thus given prominence, but other indicators are also important. The Ministry of Economic Affairs (2000) has produced analyses of low-income families and the persistence of low income over time (see also Pedersen and Smith 2000). The most recent report set a low-income threshold of half the median and found only 3.1% of the population below that threshold. These statistics are based on administrative records, which may differ from those based on household surveys. Various indicators are also available in the areas of health, housing, education, etc., based on administrative data. The Institute for Social Research (SFI), which is the ECHP national data collection unit, also carries out studies of incomes and living conditions based on administrative and survey data. In 2000 there was a major interview survey of living conditions, following on similar surveys in 1976 and 1986.

The National Action Plan on Social Inclusion was drawn up in consultation with local authorities, social partners, and non-governmental organizations. It opens with the statement that 'the most important factors of the Danish strategy to combat poverty and social exclusion are found in social policy, but labour market, health, education, and urban and housing policies also play a pre-eminent role. Furthermore, fiscal policy contributes to the redistribution of income and thereby to the fight against poverty' (Government of Denmark 2001: 6). The activation approach of Danish social policy aims to raise labour supply, improve self-support, prevent marginalization, and ensure reasonable financial support without damaging incentives.

An appendix to the NAPincl makes a number of comments on indicators. The government notes, under the heading of financial poverty, its preference for using administrative register data rather than the ECHP. In the case of employment, it stresses the need to use the same data as the National Action Plans on Employment. Reference is made to the definition of a 'marginal group' and a 'social group' which over the last three years have spent more than 80% of their time unemployed, in activation, on training/educational leave, or (in the case of the social group) as recipients of cash assistance, sickness benefit, or rehabilitees (Government of Denmark 2001: 54). It proposes use of the 80%-over-three-years criterion when measuring long-term unemployment.

3.3. GERMANY

In Germany, the federal government has assigned a high priority to poverty reduction and in spring 2001 published a report on *Living Conditions in Germany*, described as the *First Poverty and Wealth Report of the Federal Government* (Bundesministerium für Arbeit und Sozialordnung 2001). (See also Becker and Hauser 2001, and for earlier studies of poverty in Germany, Becker and Hauser 1996.) The analytical part of the Report described the social situation in Germany. Poverty was investigated from a variety of perspectives, including relative income poverty, inability to participate in customary family activities, social crisis points in large cities, and homelessness. The Report set out guidelines for the future development of policy instruments. Central to the government's approach is the support of families, with increases in child benefit, family-oriented tax changes, and the encouragement of part-time work. There has been an intensive process of discussion—as a form of open coordination—involving politicians, academics, churches, welfare organizations, claimant groups and trade unions. Further work is in train on the measurement of poverty and social exclusion, including the measurement of non-monetary dimensions.

The National Action Plan on Social Inclusion for Germany describes the overall approach being adopted, noting that, 'because of the country's federal structure and constitutionally guaranteed right of local authorities to autonomy, the various strategies for combating poverty and social exclusion tend to differ regionally and locally' (Government of the Federal Republic of Germany 2001: 5). It emphasizes the role of the social partners and of health and welfare organizations. In some policy areas there are specific targets, such as reducing the number of unemployed severely disabled people by around 25% by 2002, but there is no general discussion of indicators.

3.4. GREECE

In Greece, the government takes the view that, given the current transitional state of the society and its administrative systems, it would not be sensible to define an official poverty line, because of the risk of missing people who need help and misdirecting resources to those who do not. (For academic studies of poverty in Greece, see Tsakloglou 1990; Tsakloglou and Panopoulou 1998.) Indicators related to unemployment, inflation, and state spending, and the monitoring of specific programmes, are given some prominence. A Poverty and Exclusion Network is being established to record, assess, coordinate, and target policy interventions, and data on incomes and living conditions are available from administrative sources, the household budget survey, and the ECHP.

The National Action Plan on Social Inclusion for Greece begins by highlighting key social developments in the recent past, including the move from a largely rural economy, increased participation of women in the labour market, and the reversal from being a country of labour export to being a migration destination. It expects that the next few years will see problems at both ends of the labour market: 'advances in the information society mean that some jobs [such as in the financial sector], which were previously considered impervious, might be placed at risk . . . On the other hand, social groups who used to draw their income on the informal sector . . . are likely to encounter increasing problems' (Government of Greece 2001: 10). The Appendix to the NAPincl, prepared by the Coordinating Committee, presents twelve 'stylized facts' about poverty and low income in Greece. It draws on evidence from the Household Expenditure Survey for 1999.

3.5. SPAIN

At present Spain has no official targets in the area of poverty and social inclusion, but a number of indicators have been prepared by different public bodies to monitor progress in these areas. (Studies of poverty and inequality in Spain are discussed in Ruiz-Castillo 1987.) The Family Budget Surveys for 1973–4, 1980–1, and 1990–1 allowed an analysis of the extent of poverty, and the Continuous Budget Survey in operation since 1985 allows indicators to be produced on a continuous basis. (These estimates have applied thresholds derived as proportions of average household expenditure.)

The official publication *Panoramica Social* [Social Outlook] includes a variety of indicators on social inequalities. Indicators currently in use from a policy monitoring perspective refer for the most part to social spending and programme activity levels, educational qualifications, housing facilities, and unemployment at both individual and household level. There is also considerable emphasis on regional and local aspects, given that much of the administration of social protection and the setting of minimum benefit levels are devolved. A panel of experts on poverty and social exclusion, convened by the Ministry for Social Action, Youth, and the Family in late 1999, made recommendations in the area of mea-surement of poverty and social exclusion. It highlighted *inter alia* the need to develop an indicator or a small set of indicators that would be pub-lished periodically to inform the public about key developments.

The National Action Plan on Social Inclusion for Spain describes as 'unprecedented in Spain' the production of a document that brings together for the country as a whole the different areas of action for social inclusion. The Plan presents social exclusion as structural, dynamic, multi-factorial, and multidimensional. Included is a matrix showing different social groups by domains of exclusion, with an 'X' indicating risk of exclusion (for example women from training) and 'XX' a serious risk of exclusion (for example ethnic minorities from housing). There is a list of indicators to be used in following the evolution of the NAPincl, and an Annex containing a report on social exclusion in Spain with a variety of social indicators. These include:

- *Financial*: poverty thresholds of 40, 50, and 60% of median income; child poverty; poverty rates by age and gender; 'extreme' poverty (less than 15% of mean disposable income)
- *Education*: adult illiteracy rate by age; percentage of adult popula-tion not having completed primary school; school non-attendance;

percentage of 15-year-olds with educational 'delay' (i.e. at an educational level below that appropriate to their age)

- *Employment*: poverty rate by employment status; underemployment (classified by age, education, and literacy level); long-term youth unemployment
- *Health*: percentage with disabilities
- *Housing*: percentage lacking specified amenities; number of homeless
- *Social participation*: ethnic minorities facing social exclusion; percentage with access to Internet and percentage using Internet

3.6. FRANCE

In France, the national statistical office (INSEE) regularly produces figures on poverty, defined as the share of the population having less than half of the median income per consumption unit (Conseil d'Analyse Economique 2001); INSEE also carries out a regular survey of living conditions. France has a long tradition of a multidimensioned approach to deprivation and precariousness. The Annual Report of the Observatoire National de la Pauvreté et l'Exclusion Sociale (2000) contains a wide variety of indicators. In addition to financial poverty, these indicators include difficulty in making ends meet, arrears of payments, and housing conditions. The numbers of beneficiaries of the RMI (*revenu minimum d'insertion*) or API (*allocation de parent isolé*) are also regarded as key social indicators. The studies include statistics on the *associations de solidarité*, on public opinion regarding poverty and exclusion, and on the coverage of these subjects in the media.

In 1998 a three-year programme to prevent and combat exclusion was adopted, which provided for action on four main fronts:

1. Guaranteeing access to fundamental rights
2. Preventing exclusion
3. Coping with social emergencies
4. Working together more effectively against exclusion

As well as defining policy measures to be implemented, the programme sets out indicators to be monitored, as follows:

- *Access to employment*: number of people helped to find work; number of young people admitted to schemes for joining the labour market; volume of schemes for entering the labour market mobilized

- *Access to housing*: number of social housing units built and number rehabilitated; resources deployed for schemes providing housing and keeping people housed; resources deployed on improving housing conditions
- *Access to health*: existence of health coverage for everyone; resources deployed to help the most deprived obtain health care
- *Access to culture, sport and leisure activities*: number of persons affected by new schemes
- *Prevention of indebtedness*: number of over-indebtedness files processed
- *Response to social emergencies*: the existence of round-the-clock call centres; number of new places in shelters

These indicators refer for the most part to activities under the programme rather than to outcomes. A new multi-year programme to combat exclusion covering the period 2001–3 is in the course of preparation.

The National Action Plan on Social Inclusion describes the general situation in France, emphasizing the role of social transfers and particularly child benefit, and refers to the measures put in place in the 1998 programme (see above). The NAPincl proposes a large number of indicators, distinguishing carefully between indicators of outcomes and administrative indicators of measures put into effect (Government of France 2001: Annex, p. 2). Among the indicators are:

- *Financial*: poverty threshold 50% (60% for international comparisons) of median income; decile ratio; poverty measured by living conditions (deprivation); poverty rate of single-parent families; percentage of children living in households below the poverty line
- *Education*: percentage of school-leavers without qualifications; young people with reading difficulties; relation between education of parents and children; rate of repeating school years ('*redoublement*')
- *Employment*: percentage of employees in stable (more than six months) employment; percentage of part-time workers who would like to work longer; youth unemployment rate; percentage of individuals living below the poverty line who are active in the labour market (referred to as 'working poor', although includes unemployed); percentage of children living in inactive households
- *Health*: life expectancy at 40; population whose daily activities are seriously restricted by state of health; percentage having had to go without medical care for financial reasons in past 12 months
- *Housing*: percentage lacking specified amenities; percentage living in overcrowded households; number who have had difficulties in the last

12 months in paying for water, electricity, and gas; percentage in rent arrears; number of homeless

- *Social participation*: percentage living more than ten minutes' walk from public transport; percentage not participating in cultural activity; percentage not going away on holiday; percentage not using computer for financial reasons or on account of unemployment; number of cases of debt registered at the national bank; rate of inscription on the electoral register

There is considerable similarity to the list discussed here, but there are also a number of indicators that warrant further discussion, and that we do not cover here. The NAPincl discusses in detail the potential data sources, noting in each case their periodicity—an important issue.

3.7. IRELAND

Ireland's National Anti-Poverty Strategy (1997) was developed following on the 1995 UN Social Summit in Copenhagen and was launched in 1997, to provide a framework for the efforts of various government departments and agencies and non-governmental actors. (For earlier studies of poverty in Ireland, see Callan *et al.* 1989, 1996; Nolan and Callan 1994.) Based on a stated understanding of the key causes of poverty and social exclusion and an explicit definition of poverty, the Strategy set out both a global poverty reduction target and five sub-targets. Ireland thus became the first EU member state to adopt a national poverty reduction target.

The Irish global poverty target relates both to the numbers below relative income poverty lines and to those experiencing 'basic deprivation', as measured by a set of non-monetary deprivation indicators, including having to go without a substantial meal all day, not being able to afford adequate heating, having to buy second-hand rather than new clothes, not being able to afford an overcoat. The basic rationale for adopting this dual approach, referred to as 'consistent poverty', was that households' current living standards are influenced not only by current income but also by resources and experiences (particularly in the labour market) over a long period. Combining low income with suitable direct indicators of deprivation—items generally regarded as necessities, which individuals or families must do without because they 'cannot afford' them ('enforced lack')—may then identify more reliably those experiencing exclusion because of a lack of resources than because of low income on its own. While alternative approaches to measuring poverty are discussed in detail in Chapters 5 and 6, it is worth noting here the way this Irish target and measure have performed over time, because of the light this sheds on central issues in designing social indicators.

Since 1994 Ireland has experienced remarkable levels of economic growth and dramatic declines in unemployment. Relative income poverty rates have not declined over this period, principally because social transfers per recipient, although rising significantly in real terms, have lagged behind the exceptionally large increases in average incomes. This has meant that, while the numbers relying on social transfers have fallen as unemployment has declined, more of those remaining reliant on them are below relative income lines. In these specific circumstances, such measures taken on their own fail to register change, despite what would be widely seen as genuine improvements in the circumstances of the poor, which violates our general principles for indicators set out in Chapter 2. The circumstances may be unusual, but could well arise with new EU member states if accession leads to rapidly rising incomes. On the other hand, in Ireland it is interesting that the poverty measure combining both relative income lines and deprivation indicators showed marked declines in poverty from 1994 as the extent of deprivation captured by these indicators fell. Indeed, this progress was such that in 1999 the original poverty reduction target was revised to be more ambitious. Success in terms of the official Irish target so far thus reflects declining levels of deprivation as measured by an unchanged set of indicators. Ireland's economic growth has been concentrated in such a short period that the use of an unchanged set of indicators can probably be justified, but the crucial issue remains of how best to capture and reflect changing expectations and views about what constitute necessities over a longer period.

We return to these poverty measurement issues in Chapter 5, but the Irish experience with an overall poverty reduction target serves to illustrate a number of the points made in our earlier general discussion. The Irish experience suggests that it is possible to obtain broad national consensus on a definition of poverty very similar to the one set out by the European Council of Ministers (see Chapter 1). However, embodying that consensus in a single indicator and target is likely to be very much more problematic. From an analytical point of view, and in order to inform both policy-makers and the public as fully as possible, it makes sense to look at a range of information rather than to focus attention on a single indicator. From a political perspective, however, a national commitment to attaining clearly articulated objectives is a crucial element in a strategy aimed at promoting social inclusion. A balance has to be struck so that the chosen indicators and targets meet the need for 'headline numbers', but still encapsulate key elements of the complexity of the underlying reality.

The Irish example brings out how complex that reality can be (see Nolan *et al.* 2000). When average incomes are growing exceptionally rapidly, then those on low incomes share in that growth and see their real living standards rise significantly; but when they lag somewhat behind the general movement, purely relative indicators of poverty miss an important part of the story. Indeed, a strong argument can be made that, over time, real income increases will not be sufficient to allow everyone to participate fully in society as general standards and expectations rise. The key challenge is to ensure that both these long-term consequences and the immediate impact of rising real incomes are reflected in the indicators chosen—to which we return in Chapter 5.

The sub-targets in the Irish anti-poverty strategy—in the areas of educational disadvantage, unemployment, adequacy of social transfers, disadvantaged urban areas, and rural poverty—also serve to illustrate the value of the general principles set out in Chapter 2. For example, the target in the area of educational disadvantage involves *inter alia* eliminating illiteracy and innumeracy problems at primary level, but there is no mechanism as yet for assessing whether that is being achieved. The targets on urban and rural disadvantage are so unspecific that it would be difficult to say whether they had been met. The target on adequacy of social transfers looks only one year ahead and leaves open the crucial issue of what is to happen to support rates in the medium term.

The Irish NAPincl 2001–3 (Government of Ireland 2001) summarizes the main features of the anti-poverty policy, setting the two-year EU NAPincl within the context of the ten-year Irish National Anti-Poverty Strategy, due to conclude in mid-2007. It brings out how, 'given the multi-dimensional nature of poverty, it cannot be the sole concern of a particular Government Department . . . poverty alleviation has to be a central priority for all policy-makers' (p. 11). It emphasizes 'the particular importance of building a shared understanding of the challenges to be faced and of achieving a broad consensus in the strategies to be adopted' (p. 3).

The section of the NAPincl dealing with indicators begins with a set of considerations that are similar in a number of respects to those we have given in Chapter 2. In particular, it states that 'targets should generally refer to desired outcomes and objectives, rather than policy interventions designed to attain those objectives' (2001: 35). The list of suggested indicators includes, in addition to the Commission's proposed indicators, the following.

- *Financial*: measure of 'consistent' poverty (see above); decile share ratio (see Chapter 6)
- *Education*: numbers lacking basic qualifications; early school leaving; training qualifications received
- *Employment*: youth unemployment; youth inactivity; percentage of employees below poverty line ('working poor'); children in jobless households; number of jobless households without basic qualification; differences in access to training for different social groups; levels of security of tenure in employment
- *Health*: concentrations of premature mortality; cancer deaths; health care access levels for different social groups; variation in life expectancy across social groups; low birth weight babies; variations in infant mortality; variation in cardiovascular disease; mental health levels
- *Housing*: homelessness; availability of affordable housing; housing standards
- *Social participation*: literacy and numeracy levels; access to services; public transport (in rural areas); levels of participation in community organizations; levels of integration of public services; crime levels

3.8. **ITALY**

In Italy an official Commission of Inquiry on Social Exclusion (CIES) has operated for some years and has recently been established on a permanent basis. This Commission, in collaboration with ISTAT, the official statistical agency, publishes annual statistics on poverty in Italy. These are based on expenditure data from the official household budget survey, and include both poverty rates and poverty gaps. In addition to regularly updating the expenditure-based poverty estimates (the time series of which were reconstructed backward to 1980), the Commission, in collaboration with ISTAT, has developed an 'absolute' poverty line, based on 'the monetary value of a basket of goods and services that are indispensable for a household of a given size to reach a "socially acceptable" level of living in the country' (ISTAT 2000). Statistics are now regularly published in addition to the standard figures on 'relative' poverty. The CIES Commission has also investigated deprivations in health, unemployment, education, and housing (results on the two latter aspects were published in Commissione di indagine sulla povertà e sull'emarginazione 1997*a,b*) and the gender dimension of poverty (Commissione di indagine sull'esclusione sociale 2000*b*). As well as looking at the variation in poverty rates across household types, particular attention is paid to territorial differences in poverty rates. An important feature of current Italian thinking is the devolution of policies to the regional level.

A National Plan to promote social integration has recently been formulated in which alleviating poverty is one of the stated priorities, along with supporting families, strengthening children's rights, and supporting the elderly and the severely handicapped, among others. The statistical information available for that purpose has been reviewed. A broad range of indicators has been presented to support analysis on social exclusion. Special attention is paid to indicators of labour market performance and integration, and to the evolution of state social spending; but importance is also attached to an approach that integrates the objective indicators with 'subjective' indicators based on the perception of poverty and non-monetary indicators.

The National Action Plan on Social Inclusion for Italy sets the scene by referring to the work of the earlier Commission on Poverty and Social Exclusion, and describes the main measures that have been adopted. The section on indicators emphasizes the need to take an approach that is multidimensional and dynamic. The indicators presented are primarily performance indicators that enable the appraisal of both the strengths and weaknesses of the national situation. In the near future, equal importance will be given to providing both outcome indicators and input indicators (e.g. the realized actions to favour families with children, elderly persons, etc.).

The section on indicators focuses its attention on the principal actors of the family scene in the different ages and phases of life. In fact, an interesting attempt is made to present the indicators following an approach for 'social subjects' (women, children, disabled persons, elderly persons, etc.). This aims at locating specific critical situations of social exclusion related to gender and generation. An example is isolated elderly persons, i.e. the elderly living alone without living siblings and/or children. Another example is disabled persons living in houses not modified to their needs. Among other indicators, statistics on access to new technologies are presented, in the belief that, although these statistics cannot yet considered as indicators of social exclusion, their evolution should be granted special attention in the future, since they will play a role in preventing social exclusion.

The NAPincl takes the European Commission's proposed indicators as a starting point, but seeks to develop them and extend the coverage. Among the suggested additional indicators are the following.

- *Financial*: absolute poverty measure; measure of the transitorily poor; rate of child poverty; rate of poverty among the elderly; percentage having difficulty in paying for necessities (food, clothing, health, housing, etc.); percentage of households that consider themselves as 'poor' or 'very poor'
- *Education*: percentage of schoolchildren failing to complete year; percentage without qualifications or who attended only primary school
- *Employment*: employment rate; youth unemployment; percentage of children in jobless households; percentage of women unemployed; percentage of women who interrupted their job after the birth of a child; percentage of women not in employment with children; percentage of households with two or more unemployed persons
- *Health*: infant mortality; percentage of disabled persons; percentage of disabled persons living alone; percentage of disabled persons with problems of mobility who do not live on the ground floor and without lift; disabled persons living only with disabled persons; percentage of seriously disabled persons; percentage of households with two or more disabled persons; percentage of households with serious disabled persons
- *Housing*: percentage lacking basic amenities (drinking water, hot water, electricity, toilet, telephone, refrigerator, washing machine); subjective perception of difficulty of access to some selected services (medical, food stores, schools, police stations, etc.)
- *Social participation*: percentage of elderly persons living alone without living siblings and/or children; percentage of persons using personal computers and frequency of use; percentage of persons using the Internet and frequency of use; percentage of households owning a personal computer.

3.9. LUXEMBOURG

In Luxembourg, the social protection system's guaranteed minimum income together with labour market activation are central elements in the strategy to combat poverty and social exclusion. The National Agency for Social Action publishes an annual report showing the numbers in receipt of the guaranteed minimum income. In response to the 1995 UN Social Summit in Copenhagen, a National Monitoring Centre for Social Development was established. The Centre has been studying the possibility of defining a social development indicator or set of indicators.

The Ministry responsible for drawing up the Luxembourg National Action Plan on Social Inclusion—the Ministry of the Family, Social Solidarity and Youth—invited the collaboration of other ministries, of the social partners, and of non-governmental organizations. The Plan sets out the measures envisaged to promote access to employment, resources, rights, goods and services, to prevent the risk of exclusion, and to aid the most vulnerable. The analysis contains statistics on the numbers in receipt of benefits and indicators of financial poverty (applying thresholds of 50, 60, and 70% of the median income).

3.10. NETHERLANDS

The Netherlands has since 1997 produced an annual Poverty Monitor (*Armoedemonitor*) assembled by the official Central Statistics Office (CBS) and the Social and Cultural Planning Office (SCP) (2001). (For earlier research on poverty in the Netherlands, see Dirven and Berghman 1992; Muffels *et al.* 1990.) It contains analyses of the trends in poverty and of the effect of policy measures, drawing on a particularly wide range of sources, including the Income Panel Survey (IPO) of tax statistics; the Socioeconomic Panel Survey (SEP), which follows a panel of individuals over time and forms the Netherlands component of the ECHP; the regular budget survey; and administrative data on benefit receipt and duration. Each year from 1996 to 2000 a conference on poverty and social exclusion was organized, gathering together organizations and parties involved. There have also been officially sponsored studies on social exclusion and participation in society as well as studies conducted on behalf of Eurostat. There are no official targets with respect to the numbers of persons in poverty or the numbers socially excluded, nor are there statistics that have been given the status of designated progress indicators in that context.

Policy priorities at present include increasing the number of people in employment, and providing of subsistence-level income via the statutory social minimum. Thus, considerable attention is paid to labour market indicators, such as the rates of unemployment, long-term unemployment,

unemployment rate differential of ethnic minorities, and labour force participation. An explicit target has been set with respect to women's labour force participation: that 65% should be participating by 2010. A good deal of attention is also paid to indicators of work incentives and the poverty trap. As far as benefits are concerned, indicators include the purchasing power of the social minimum benefit, the number of persons receiving disability benefit, the amount of social security benefits as a percentage of GDP, and the ratio of the number of persons receiving social security benefits to the number in employment. More broadly, there is a range of other indicators and targets of social policy relating to, say, education, health, the disabled, childcare, indebtedness, and ethnic minorities. The targets for education include halving the number of early school-leavers by 2010 and reducing the number of illiterate adults by 10% by 2003. Targets in the health area include decreasing the number of unhealthy years of life of people with a low socioeconomic status by 25% by 2020.

The Dutch National Action Plan on Social Inclusion states that 'the development of indicators and targets is in full swing in the Netherlands. [The indicators] set out in this first NAP can play a leading role in this national process' (Government of the Netherlands 2001: 39). Combating poverty and social exclusion in the Netherlands is a joint effort, embracing the national government, municipal and provincial authorities, and non-governmental organizations. All of these, and the social partners, were involved in the preparation of the Dutch NAPincl. The discussion of indicators appears both in a review of the current social situation in the Netherlands, where a variety of statistics are presented, and in the setting of targets for policy measures (referred to above). There is an Annex dealing with research that lists a number of valuable sources, including the Municipal Poverty Monitor, the Emancipation Monitor, and the Integration Monitor covering ethnic minorities. A key role is played in the Dutch analysis by the subsistence minimum income (*Algemene Bijstand*), which is related to the statutory minimum wage: 100% of the net minimum wage for couples, 70% for single persons living alone. The NAPincl shows the trend in the real value of the subsistence minimum, which it takes as an indicator of performance, and is particularly concerned with long-term receipt of the subsistence minimum (for four or more years). It proposes a financial poverty index, which is the ratio of the number of recipients (indexed at 100 in the base year) to the real value of the minimum (again indexed to 100 in the base year).

3.11. **AUSTRIA**

In Austria, there are official targets in the case of unemployment. The Ministry of Social Affairs publishes an annual social report, containing information on poverty and social exclusion, which is presented to and debated in the Parliament. The poverty measures included are based both on 'in danger of poverty' (having incomes below a relative income poverty line of 60% of median equivalized household income) and on 'poverty', i.e. falling below relative income thresholds and experiencing deprivation as measured by a set of non-monetary indicators. (For references to studies of poverty in Austria, see Förster *et al.* 2001.) This is similar to the Irish approach. The indicators used in Austria are: (i) lack of bath, shower or inside toilet; (ii) problems with the payment of rent, fuel bills, or debts; (iii) problems with heating; (iv) difficulties in affording new clothing; and (v) difficulties in affording to ask friends in for dinner. The ECHP is the main data source used in compiling these statistics.

The National Action Plan on Social Inclusion in Austria noted that there was little time for extensive dialogue. The report observes that 'poverty is no longer a mass phenomenon' and that the objectives of the social security system are much wider than helping persons at risk of poverty (Government of Republic of Austria 2001: 2). At the same time, combating poverty remains a key objective of social policy in Austria. The NAPincl lists a variety of measures and plans to promote access to employment, improve employability, promote access to resources, rights, goods, and services, and prevent exclusion. A task force for the development of social indicators has been established.

3.12. **PORTUGAL**

In Portugal, there is now an official poverty target to reduce the national poverty rate to the (1996) European average by the year 2005, i.e. from 23% in 1995 to 17% in 2005, and to reduce the absolute poverty rate by 50% again by 2005. (For earlier research on poverty in Portugal, see da Costa 1994.) The aim is to eradicate child poverty by 2005. Indicators for monitoring progress are based on administrative data regularly produced by various ministries including the Ministry of Labour and Solidarity (including information from the Minimum Income Guarantee introduced in 1996), and survey data on employment, family budgets, and living conditions by the National Statistical Institute (INE). Efforts are currently being made to bring about better coordination in the monitoring and evaluation of social exclusion. Portugal gives particular emphasis to regional and local perspectives.

The National Action Plan on Social Inclusion for Portugal reiterates the objectives described above and sets out a process for the development of the plan in consultation with the social partners. It states objectives for encouraging participation in the labour market, preventing the risk of exclusion, and protecting the most vulnerable. An Annexe contains many proposed indicators, in addition to those of the Commission. Indicators of outcomes include the following.

- *Financial*: child poverty rate; poverty rates by regions
- *Education*: early school-leaving; training qualifications received
- *Employment*: unemployment by age and education level; percentage low-paid workers; ratio of earnings of unskilled to average; percentage of employees who have received training
- *Health*: life expectancy; infant mortality
- *Housing*: housing lacking amenities
- *Social participation*: persons having basic competence in ICT.

3.13. FINLAND

At present Finland does not have any single official quantifiable target in the area of poverty and social inclusion. However, the dimensions of poverty and social exclusion are under close and frequent surveillance by public authorities. Statistics Finland publishes yearly statistics of income distribution and thereby calculates the number of persons and households whose income are below the poverty line. These calculations are based on register data. Also, the Ministry of Social Affairs employs a list of social indicators in its annual publication, *Trends in Social Protection in Finland*. The National Research and Development Centre for Welfare and Health has devoted many resources to investigating different approaches to poverty and social exclusion, including approaches based on a consumption basket and a consensus method. Furthermore, there are research units at universities that regularly evaluate the development and depth of poverty and exclusion: see Jäntti and Ritakallio (2000).

The National Action Plan on Social Inclusion was drawn up by a working party made up of, among others, government officials, researchers, representatives of the social partners and non-governmental organizations, including the European Anti-Poverty Network (EAPN). It held hearings for Third Sector organizations and other interest groups.

The Plan takes as its starting point 'current basic thinking in the field of social policy [which] has proved effective by international standards. . . . Most of the measures aimed at combating poverty and social exclusion have been incorporated as structural elements of the social policy systems' (Government of Finland 2001: 20,22). The main risk factors identified are economic/financial exclusion (including over-indebtedness), health problems, exclusion from the labour market, exclusion from the housing market, low education, and other types of exclusion such as alcoholism, criminality, and drugs.

The Action Plan presents a series of indicators, designed to illustrate resource deficiencies within different dimensions of social exclusion and the size of the groups affected. In addition to the indicators proposed by the Commission, these include the following.

- *Financial*: poverty threshold 50 and 60% of median income; persons in receipt of welfare benefits; persons subject to debt recovery
- *Employment*: persons employed as result of employment promotion measures; rate of non-participation; young people who have left school and are not engaged in work
- *Health*: percentage with poor self-assessed health; percentage of elderly with mobility problems; differentials by education in age-adjusted mortality
- *Housing*: percentage with inadequately equipped housing; overcrowding; waiting list for State Housing Board rental accommodation; homelessness
- *Other*: children subject to child protection; incidence of criminality, alcohol and drug-related problems

This list bears a considerable resemblance to the indicators discussed in Chapters 5–8 below, but contains some dimensions that we do not discuss, such as criminal offences and alcohol problems.

3.14. SWEDEN

In Sweden the approach adopted to combating poverty and social exclusion focuses on a general welfare system based on equality and universal participation. Historically, it has been founded on an economic policy of full employment, but this system had to cope with a large increase in unemployment in the first half of the 1990s. According to the May 2001 National Action Plan on Social Inclusion, 'the Swedish welfare systems rode out the crisis of the 1990s . . . they prevented the economic crisis turning into a welfare crisis too' (Government of Sweden 2001: 2). At the same time, the National Action Plan notes that 'the system has not fully succeeded in guaranteeing the welfare of young people, immigrants and single parent providers . . . [there are] groups with significant social problems such as substance misuse and homelessness' (2001: 2).

A range of indicators is used to monitor living conditions across various dimensions, based on the Swedish tradition of welfare research going back to the 1960s (the Low-Income Commission appointed in 1965 and the Level of Living Surveys dating from 1968), and the impact of policies aimed at combating poverty and social exclusion. There is no official measure of poverty in Sweden, but two indicators are commonly used. (For studies of poverty in Sweden, see Halleröd 1995; Gustafsson 2000.) The first indicator employs a poverty line expressed as a proportion (50% or, sometimes, 60%) of median income. As is noted in the National Action Plan, 'there is broad support in Sweden for using a measure in which the definition of poverty is related to overall income levels' (Government of Sweden 2001: 3). The second measure is based on an administrative standard: the proportion below the social welfare allowance norm.

The National Action Plan describes the theoretical basis on which Statistics Sweden carries out its Standard of Living Surveys: they 'apply a multidimensional welfare concept with . . . ten components: employment, income, material standard, housing, leisure, social networks, political participation, health, safety and security' (Government of Sweden 2001: 27). They note that, when using indicators to evaluate policy, 'a compromise must be made in view, on the one hand, of the fact that it is virtually impossible to summarize welfare in a limited number of general indicators and, on the other, of the need to use indicators as a tool for monitoring performance' (Government of Sweden 2001: 26). The NAPincl goes on to list four essential requirements: indicators must be 'well-defined', 'relevant to welfare', 'easy to communicate' and 'easy to follow up'. These seem close to the principles proposed here. There is no detailed discussion of individual indicators.

Focusing on specific policy areas, achievement of objectives relating to, say, children, the elderly, or those with disabilities is monitored by reference to programme participation, periodic standard-of-living surveys and household income surveys, employment statistics, and local authorities. One important objective announced in spring 2001 is to halve the number of people who are dependent on welfare between 1999 and 2004. The indicator of progress towards this objective is the number of welfare recipients calculated as full-year equivalents.

3.15. **UNITED KINGDOM**

In 1997 the new UK government indicated the priority it attached to the issue of social exclusion by setting up a new Social Exclusion Unit, which forms part of the office of the Prime Minister (the Cabinet Office). In 1999 the government set out a long-term strategy aimed at tackling poverty and social exclusion, under the heading *Opportunity for All* (UK Department of Social Security 1999). Key elements highlighted in the approach included tackling the causes of poverty and social exclusion as well as the symptoms, creating a fairer society, and investing in individuals and communities to equip them to take control of their lives.

In the present context, the distinctive feature of this strategy is that an extensive list of indicators of success was presented, covering the various areas delineated in the strategy—children and young people, those of working age, older people, and communities. Some of these indicators focus on incomes, some on wider aspects of welfare such as education, housing, health and local environment, and some on the factors that affect people during their lives and increase the risk that they experience deprivation at a later point. The first progress report a year later (UK Department of Social Security 2000*a*) assessed performance against more than 30 indicators, and further indicators are being developed. (See also the reports of the New Policy Institute: Howarth *et al.* 1998, 1999; Seymour 2000.)

The indicators of success focusing on incomes cover three distinct elements:

1. The proportion living in households with relatively low incomes, measured against relative income lines set at 50, 60, and 70% of median income and 40, 50, and 60% of mean income;
2. The proportion living in households with low incomes, measured against lines derived as relative thresholds in 1996/7 and fixed at that value in real terms subsequently;
3. The proportion living in households with persistently low incomes, measured against relative income thresholds but including only those below the thresholds in at least three years out of four based on panel survey data.

The indicators of success focusing on wider aspects of current welfare or well-being fall into four main groups:

1. *Employment*: for example the proportion of working-age people in employment; the employment rate for disadvantaged groups

2. *Health*: for example low birth weight; drug and tobacco use; life expectancy
3. *Housing*: for example numbers in poor housing; numbers sleeping rough
4. *Fear of crime*

Indicators concerned with the risk of poverty and social exclusion later in life fall into two categories:

1. *In childhood*: for example educational attainment at 7, 11, and 19 years of age; truancy; teenage pregnancy
2. *During working age*: for example employment during working age; whether contributing to a private pension.

The indicators focusing on communities relate to the difference between employment rates in the most deprived districts and the national average, burglary rates, and housing quality. Further indicators are currently being developed focusing on gaps in educational attainment and in health. Many indicators are not UK-wide. In particular, the UK NAP details a range of different indicators that only apply to either England or Scotland.

For the most part, the stated objective in terms of these indicators has been simply to see them move in the right direction—to see a reduction in numbers on relatively, absolutely, or persistently low incomes, for example, or an increase in the proportion in work. Specific targets have been set for certain objectives as part of separate institutional processes, notably one whereby each government department sets out its aims in terms of service provision and outcomes. In addition, a high-profile commitment to eradicating child poverty in 20 years and halving it in ten was made in 1999 (Blair 1999). This was not accompanied by a specification of how child poverty was to be measured. It was subsequently stated that progress would be monitored using a subset of 'headline indicators', namely the proportion of children living in low-income households where 'low income' is defined in relative, absolute, and persistent terms; the proportion of children living in households where nobody is in work; the proportion living in poor housing; and two indicators to be developed reflecting gaps in educational attainment and in infant and early childhood mortality. Intermediate targets for the period to 2004 have also been set out:

1. to reduce the number of children living in households with an income of less than 60% of the median by at least a quarter;

2. to reduce the number of children in households where no one works—taking account of the economic cycle;
3. to reduce the number of households living in social housing that falls below the set standard of decency by a third (England only).

The UK experience to date with social indicators represents an interesting contrast to the Irish case. Whereas the latter brings out the dangers of concentration on a single global poverty reduction target, at the other extreme the UK use of a wide range of indicators brings out the complications of that broad-brush approach. Just focusing on child poverty, for example, it is not clear how the headline indicators can be used to measure whether child poverty has been halved, or eradicated, at a particular date. One approach would be to combine them into one summary measure, but, apart from the many problems faced in doing so, the result would not be transparent—one of the key principles we outlined earlier. In practice, it is the headline indicators relating to low income that seem likely to receive most attention, and it is interesting to note that the intermediate target to 2004 in those terms refers to the number in households below 60% of the median. Recent UK government statements have also used relative measures to describe the extent of poverty. A range of views has been canvassed (see CASE 2001) in the course of considering the best way to monitor progress towards meeting the target of eradicating child poverty.

Finally, the criteria set out in choosing suitable indicators in the UK are themselves of interest. These were that the indicators had to be relevant to the overall strategy for tackling poverty and social exclusion, capturing key aspects of current poverty or factors increasing the risk of deprivation in later life; related to outcomes rather than processes; based on data that are publicly available and statistically robust; and unambiguous in interpretation.

The National Action Plan on Social Inclusion reflects the strategy described above. It gives particular importance to a life-cycle approach, structuring interventions around different stages in the life course, and to narrowing the gap between the most deprived communities and the rest of the United Kingdom. A wide variety of indicators is detailed. A selection of these is summarized below, reordered according to the headings employed here.

- *Financial*: low income indicators 50, 60, and 70% of median income, 40, 50, and 60% of mean income; percentage of children living in households with low incomes; percentage of older people living in households with low incomes

- *Education*: percentage of university students from under-represented and disadvantaged groups (Scotland); performance in literacy and numeracy tests of primary schoolchildren; reduction in school truancies and exclusions
- *Employment*: percentage of children in jobless households; percentage of working-age population in employment (cyclically adjusted); employment rates of disadvantaged groups; unemployment rates of most deprived local authority districts
- *Health*: percentage of low birth weight babies (Scotland); reduction in gap in infant mortality between manual groups and whole population (England); gap between quintile of health authorities with lowest life expectancy at birth and population as a whole (England)
- *Housing*: percentage living in housing that does not meet decency standards (England); percentage of households with children living in temporary accommodation (Scotland); number of rough sleepers
- *Social participation*: percentage of elderly able to live independently; percentage of homes in disadvantaged areas with access to the Internet (Scotland)

3.16. CONCLUSION

There is considerable variation across the member states in the way social indicators are employed to monitor progress and evaluate the success of policies aimed at promoting social inclusion. There are however signs of convergence in thinking and in policy. The UN 1995 Social Summit in Copenhagen undoubtedly acted as a catalyst in putting the eradication of poverty high on the agenda. Increasingly, there is a shared view that poverty has to be seen in broad terms, encompassing not only financial poverty but also wider dimensions of deprivation. The National Action Plans on Social Inclusion have given further impetus to this process. The preparation of NAPincl is now an obligation placed on member states every second year, but it is one that runs with the grain of national thinking. At the same time, there remain significant—and interesting—differences in the NAPincl. Their length varies from around 40 pages to over 100. Some countries have entered into a detailed analysis of different indicators; others have limited themselves to broad principles. Some member states have carried out computations of the indicators provided, an exercise that has been both time-consuming and highly instructive, since certain problems become evident only when one reaches the implementation stage. In some member states, non-governmental organizations have played a role in the construction of the NAPincl; in others there is no reference to such bodies. But the common elements dominate. If we look at the lists of additional indicators proposed by member states, they reflect specific national concerns, but there are recurring themes. Overall, there is remarkable similarity in approach. The European Social Agenda can definitely be said to be building on common concerns and ambitions.

4

Portfolio of Indicators as a Whole

Against this background of national policies to combat social exclusion, we now examine the use of social indicators to monitor progress in the European Union towards greater social inclusion. We first consider the portfolio of indicators as a whole, and examine the relation with the principles set out in Chapter 2.

4.1. STRUCTURE OF THE PORTFOLIO OF INDICATORS

Consideration of the principles set out in Chapter 2 leads us to support a three-tier structure of indicators.

Recommendation 5. There should be three levels of indicators for use in the EU monitoring process.

Level 1 would consist of a restricted number of lead indicators (around ten) for the main fields that we believe should be covered, including material deprivation, lack of education, lack of productive role, poor health, and poor housing.

Level 2 would support these lead indicators, providing greater detail, and describing other dimensions of the problem. There would be no limit on the number of Level 2 indicators, but we should avoid unnecessary proliferation, since each additional indicator involves agreement being reached and increases the statistical and other resources required.

Level 3 would consist of indicators that member states themselves decide to include in their National Action Plans on Social Inclusion, to highlight specificities in particular areas, and to help interpret the Level 1 and 2 indicators. No doubt these national indicators will provide a source of ideas and experience about new indicators which may be adopted by the EU as a whole at Level 1 or 2, in time replacing those initially proposed.

Both Level 1 and Level 2 indicators would be commonly agreed and defined. Member states would use them in their NAPincl and they would be used in the Joint Report on Social Inclusion. While member states will be encouraged to complement the EU indicators in this way with their own choice of indicators at Level 3, it is important that the portfolio of EU indicators should command general support as a balanced representation of Europe's social concerns. The focus of the present book is on the common EU indicators, i.e. Level 1 and Level 2.

The three-tier structure has a number of advantages. Definitely the most important one is that it allows the principle of balance across different dimensions to be satisfied without restricting the scope for the development of individual fields. Certain areas are more developed, methodologically and empirically, than others. Financial poverty, for example, may be measured in a number of ways (poverty count, poverty gap, etc.). (This is reflected in the number of pages we devote to this subject.) The three-tier structure allows there to be several indicators of poverty at Level 2 without their coming to have disproportionate weight in the overall assessment at Level 1. By appropriate choice of the lead indicators, it will be possible to satisfy the requirement that the significance of the components be 'proportionate', i.e. that the individual fields have degrees of importance that, while not necessarily exactly equal, are not grossly different. Member states may differ in the relative weight that they attach to the different fields, but there is likely to be broad agreement that each of them is relevant to the construction of a *Social Europe*.

It is clear that no set of indicators can be exhaustive, and there are costs in terms of lost transparency from having too extensive a range of indicators. A selection has therefore to be made. We should say, first, that this is a subject where further research would be valuable. It may be that there exist empirical findings on the degree to which different information is assimilated and understood by members of the public, which could be applied to the present issue. If not, then we recommend that such research be undertaken. On *a priori* grounds, we would expect that a list of some ten lead indicators would be relatively easily understood by members of the public. A European scorecard that involves several dimensions should not be too taxing for those citizens who watch ice skating, particularly since in this case there is a single set of marks. Whether five or 15 would be better in this respect than ten is a matter of judgement, but we believe that a number of lead indicators of this order would be more transparent than a larger number, and that a single indicator would be regarded by many citizens as painting too limited a picture. For national governments, there will undoubtedly be advantages in the fact that rankings will differ across the fields; so that we may expect greater willingness on their part to diffuse the results of the Commission's evaluation.

4.2. PRESENTATION OF INDICATORS

The common indicators should be presented in the form of a level of performance, not as a ranking. This recommendation is made for several reasons. The aim of policy is to improve performance and, ideally, bring all countries to a high level. If such a high level is obtained more or less uniformly, then the rankings will have little meaning. Equally, all member states may be performing equally badly, and a ranking would give no indication of the need for action. In a situation where countries are improving their performance, but with no changes in ranking, then no change would be recorded. Finally, where indicators are measured with error, rankings do not allow one to show this as clearly as poverty rates plus or minus two percentage points.

In considering the performance measures to be adopted, one has to consider the relation between different fields, not least on account of the appeal of adding up the aggregate indicators to arrive at a total score for each member state. Such a synthetic score would attract the attention not only of newspaper headline writers, but also of policy-makers and the general public. An aggregate performance measure can, as argued by Micklewright (2001), serve the twin functions of (i) summarizing the overall picture and (ii) communication. The Human Development Index produced by UNDP is often cited as an example. The simple addition of separate indices for gross domestic product (GDP), life expectancy, and educational attainment has been much criticized, but it has served to broaden the focus from looking only at GDP. (Alternatives to simple addition are considered, in the context of poverty indices, by Anand and Sen 1997.)

Such an aggregation has to be done with care, giving appropriate weight to each of the components. If the portfolio contains, for instance, the total poverty rate (say 15%) and the rate of homelessness (say 0.5%), then simply adding these would give a highly misleading impression. In the context of the EU, there are evident difficulties in reaching agreement on such weights, given that each member state has its own national specificity. Moreover, how should we aggregate? Here it is important to distinguish two different forms of aggregation. The first combines aggregate indicators; the second combines different elements of deprivation at the individual level (which are then summed over individuals to form an aggregate index for the country). In a theoretical sense, this is simply an issue of the order of summation. Do we sum first across people and then across fields, or do we sum across fields for an individual and then across individuals? But there are substantive differences, both in the way in which the summation is done and in the way in which the information is presented. For the purposes of the present exercise, we feel that the first form of aggregation should be avoided. The whole thrust of the European social agenda is to emphasize the multidimensionality of social disadvantage. Politically, the process will not encourage member states to learn from each other if attention is focused on a single rank order. Our view is that the three-level design proposed here, with Level 1 limited to a handful of key indicators, is a good balance between multi-dimensionality and communication.

The second form of aggregation—at the individual level—is however one that we believe to be important. The cumulation of deprivation for a person or a household is a serious source of concern. At several points we refer to indices that combine elements, such as consistent poverty defined as being both materially deprived in particular dimensions and below an income threshold. Twenty per cent of the population may be below on each dimension taken separately, but the overlap may only be 10%; i.e., only 10% of the population may be both deprived and income-poor—there may be another 10% who are income-poor but not deprived, and a further 10% who are deprived but not income-poor.

Such composite indices of individual disadvantage raise two important issues. The first is the form of aggregation. The consistent poverty index is the *intersection* of those deprived on both dimensions. There are attractions in examining, for instance, the number of households that are at risk of financial poverty *and* have poor housing *and* have poor health. We may also be concerned with the *union* of all those who are deprived on any dimension. In the consistent poverty example, this would give a figure of 30% of the population. There are other possibilities. The aggregation of different dimensions at an individual level is discussed by Bourguignon and Chakravarty (1997) and by Brandolini and D'Alessio (1998), who provide an exploratory application to Italian data.

The second issue is the availability of data and the statistical reliability of such composite measures. The first prerequisite is micro data linkable at the micro level across dimensions, as we have emphasized. The second issue concerns sample sizes. Studies of multiple deprivation have revealed the problems of the small numbers that can arise (see Atkinson and Sutherland 1989), and this needs further investigation. This may mean that we have to consider a subset of the fields. We do not at this juncture recommend a composite index covering all dimensions, but believe that systematic attention should be paid to the possibility of developing indicators that capture the cumulation of disadvantage at the individual level. We would like to see member states testing such composite indicators, as an example of what we see to be an important function of Level 3 indicators. Through peer review, the exchange of best practices may allow future agreement on a Level 1 and/or 2 indicator of this type.

In the presentation of the indicators, it is important to convey as clearly as possible the uncertainty that surrounds the numerical magnitudes. In Section 2.3 we have described how the statistical sources are subject to a variety of errors. More generally, the variables employed as indicators may be only imperfect measures of our underlying concerns. As has been emphasized in the literature on national league tables for schools and hospitals (see e.g. Goldstein and Spiegelhalter 1996), the uncertainty needs to be made explicit. The user will ask whether a reduction of one percentage point in the rate of illiteracy is larger than the margin of error. This is not, however, an easy question to answer. Intervals can be supplied that take account of sampling variability, such as standard errors for the proportion of the population living below an income cut-off. But other forms of error are less easily formalized. Ultimately, a judgement has to be made as to the reliability of specific indicators for the purpose in question. These judgements will no doubt become more secure as we gain greater experience of the use of indicators in the EU.

4.3. DISAGGREGATION OF INDICATORS

It is envisaged that the indicators would be disaggregated by a number of key variables, subject to the data constraints. We have already made clear the importance of disaggregation by gender. In determining the degree of other disaggregations, it will be necessary to carry out a detailed consideration for each of the Level 1 and Level 2 indicators of the dimensions along which disaggregation should take place. We do not attempt here to provide such a discussion, but refer to some general issues and then consider the specific dimension of region.

There are at least three senses in which indices can be disaggregated. The first—and perhaps the most natural—interpretation is to consider *values of the indicator for specified sub-groups* of the population; for instance, we are interested in the rate of long-term unemployment by age groups. For this purpose, the sub-groups need not be exhaustive. We may look at the poverty rate among children (i.e. the proportion of children living in households below the poverty line) and the poverty rate among the older persons, without considering the intermediate age range. Secondly, we may consider the *variation of the indicator across sub-groups* of the population. This may involve looking at the ratio of the poverty rates of children and older persons; it may mean looking at the standard deviation of regional unemployment rates. The third disaggregation involves the *decomposition* of the identified population by exclusive sub-groups; for instance, we may be interested in the composition by age of the long-term unemployed.

In considering what disaggregations are possible, the first issues are statistical. The statistical reliability of the results depends on the sample sizes, and they can easily become too small if the population is divided into several groups, generating standard errors so large that no distinctions can be drawn between the sub-groups covered. Sampling errors may also limit the conclusions that can be drawn about changes over time. Against this, where the values of the indicator are sufficiently different, the differences may still be significant. This may apply, for example, to the poverty rates for one-parent families, where the proportion of the population is relatively small but the differences in poverty rates is large. A further statistical problem is that the data sources in some member states may not contain the variable required for the disaggregation, or the coverage may be different (for example, including or excluding non-nationals). Indeed, in some member states there may be legal or constitutional prohibitions on collecting certain information—for example on ethnicity—in statistical inquiries. Or the information may be deemed too sensitive to be collected without adversely affecting response rates.

A second issue concerns the definition of sub-groups, and their comparability across member states. For example, we may want to classify people according to their activity status: employed, self-employed, unemployed, retired, and otherwise inactive. These activity states have to be defined consistently across member states. As far as household composition is concerned, we may distinguish between classifications based on household composition and those that seek to take account of the relations between different household members. For example, a household may consist of two adults and a child. This may be sufficient to classify the household in terms of its potential economic activity, but is consistent with several different familial relationships: the two adults may be married or a cohabiting couple; they may be mother and grandmother, or mother and adult child; etc. It may be difficult to secure comparability in the definitions across countries. For a number of policy purposes, we may wish to have indicators for those with disabilities, but, as discussed in Chapter 8, there are serious measurement problems related to cross-national differences in definitions.

A distinction may therefore have to be drawn between indicators where the within-country differences *can* be compared across countries, and cases where we do not recommend across-country comparisons.

Regional breakdowns

Region is a characteristic that needs to be singled out. As noted in Chapter 2, a number of member states have decentralized major elements of policy to regional, provincial, or local governments. Regional break-downs do however raise specific questions.

The Commission has indicated the weight it attaches to the regional dimension in specifying a certain indicator concerned with regional disparities, based on the variation in regional unemployment rates. We would depart from the Commission's proposal in two important respects.

In one sense, we would go further, giving regional information for *all* indicators of social inclusion where it is meaningful and where data permit the disaggregation to be made in a reliable way. We would locate the regional analysis within each of the indicator fields, and not rely on a single Level 1 'regional indicator'. This means, for example, that, subject to availability, low educational attainment would be reported not just nationally but also by communities in Belgium, regions in France, *Länder* in Germany, and so on. We believe that this would give greater importance to the regional dimension, which is of considerable significance to member states. The example of educational attainment illustrates this point, since there is concern that disparities in education and training mean that certain parts of the country may be less able to benefit from the development of an information-based economy.

We would however pull back from comparing the degree of regional disparities across member states, an exercise that we feel has real problems where there are differing numbers and sizes of regions. Comparisons of indicators calculated for households have a clear meaning across countries, but indicators for different types of aggregative unit are less easily compared. Member states differ in their definitions of local government units. Regions differ in number and in size. Who will decide on the appropriate level of region? A measure based on units that distinguish

London boroughs may reflect greater dispersion than one that is based on French *départements*, and the latter may in turn have greater dispersion than one based on UK regions. A direct comparison of the dispersion of unemployment rates between regions, for example, would depend sensitively on the number of regions. It would tend to be less in a country with three regions than in a country with 30 regions.

The same would apply if we took employment rather than unemployment rates. If the regional disaggregation is seen as a means for interpreting the national position, then it will be possible to take account—in that specific context—of the differences in size and number of regions. It could be included as a Level 3 indicator. Where the focus is on comparison with the national aggregate, rather than across member states, this difference in structure can more easily be taken into account. Moreover, consideration of the national aggregate directs attention to our central concern, which is with the level of the indicator. A member state that had a 10% unemployment rate across all regions might score well on consistency, but this can hardly be a performance to be commended. For this reason, the regional differences have to be interpreted in the light of the overall national picture. We would be interested to know that, behind an overall unemployment rate of, say, 5% were regions with rates as low as 1% and some as high as 10%.

5

Financial Poverty

In this and the next three chapters we examine individual indicators. We begin with a single field: risk of poverty. We devote a whole chapter to this one indicator, for two reasons. First, poverty is intrinsically important, and, as described in Chapter 1, estimates of the extent of poverty in Europe have played a major role in the evolution of European social policy. Secondly, the design of poverty indicators serves to illustrate many of the issues that arise with indicators in general. The problems that we discuss in this chapter, and the resolutions that have been offered in the rich literature on which we draw, should be borne in mind when considering the other fields of indicators in later chapters.

5.1. THE CONCEPT OF POVERTY

In the European Council of Ministers decision of 1975, the poor are defined as 'individuals or families whose resources are so small as to exclude them from the minimal acceptable way of life of the member state in which they live'. This and similar definitions (see e.g. Townsend 1979; Room 1995; Atkinson 1998) imply that poverty cannot be defined unequivocally, as it is essentially a relative, graduated, and multi-dimensional notion. Its latent ambiguity must be taken into account and transcended when establishing a poverty standard. It is on account of the potential ambiguity that some prefer to use alternative expressions, such as 'low income', rather then 'poverty'.

Poverty is a *relative* notion, because it is defined in relation to the general level of prosperity in a country or population group at a given point in time. As such, poverty is a relative concept in two senses. First, what is regarded as a minimal acceptable way of life depends largely on the prevailing life-style in the community concerned and thus on its level of social and economic development. It is senseless to search for an absolute standard whereby the content of poverty can be determined accurately for all countries and for any moment in time. On the other hand, the relative nature of poverty should not be overemphasized or exaggerated to the extent that confusion arises between the notions of poverty and income inequality, as this would undermine the credibility of the poverty standard. It would, for example, make no sense to use the term 'poor' to apply to those below the bottom quintile, since there would by definition always be 20% of the population in poverty. (The bottom quintile group could, on the other hand, enter a measure of income inequality—see Chapter 6.)

The second sense in which poverty may be relative concerns the uprating of the poverty standard over time. The initial poverty standard may be determined relative to current living standards, but in examining changes over time, whether at the individual level or at the aggregate level, we may wish either to uprate the scale by the overall increase in living standards (average income) or to maintain it constant in purchasing power (consumer prices). Poverty in 2000 may be compared with poverty in 1995 either by using 60% of the median in both years, calculated specifically for each year, or by using 60% of the median in 1995, adjusted by the consumer price index for the increase in prices between 1995 and 2000. If, for example, median equivalized incomes are increasing by 2% per year, then in five years the median is some 10% higher. Put the other way round, simply adjusting in terms of consumer prices causes the poverty standard to fall to $60/1.1\% = 54\%$ of the current (2000) median.

Poverty is a *graduated* notion because it concerns many different circumstances. A distinction needs to be made between subsistence insecurity (i.e. households living in difficult financial circumstances, but who have not (yet) been excluded from a minimal acceptable way of life), those whose insufficiency of resources is far-reaching, and the inframarginal (i.e. individuals who are entirely outside the social system, such as the homeless).

Poverty is *multidimensional* because it does not consist merely of an insufficiency of resources, but also encompasses cumulative deprivation in relation to income, housing, education, and health care. In other words, it concerns non-participation in various important areas of life. The various elements of the quality of life have been developed in the Scandinavian studies of living conditions (e.g. Erikson and Åberg 1987). In his capability approach, Sen (1985, 1999) has shown how different dimensions affect the capability to achieve various combinations of functionings, and hence provides a link with individual freedom. This offers the possibility of a fuller theoretical grounding, but here we adopt a more pragmatic approach to identifying the essential dimensions. One key element, for example, is that of access to public services. An individual below the poverty line in a country with access to extensive social provisions (education, health care, sociocultural services) may be better off than an individual just above the poverty line in a country lacking such provisions. This needs to be taken into consideration in order to ensure the credibility of the poverty standard put forward, and to recognize the contribution of social transfers in kind. As we have seen in Chapter 3, the multidimensionality of poverty has been stressed in the National Action Plans on Social Inclusion.

Finally, we should underline the *temporal dimension* of poverty. Being poor for a period of months is less problematic than being poor for many years. In other words, a distinction needs to be made between short-term poverty resulting from, for example, sudden loss of income, which is essentially a cyclical phenomenon, and long-term or structural poverty resulting from a substantial erosion of the socioeconomic position of a household, which manifests itself in a permanent lack of resources. The different phases of life are important in this respect. Longitudinal research, involving panel studies of persons and households over consecutive years, has offered an insight into the nature, the causes, and the duration of poverty.

Insufficiency of resources

Our discussion here begins with one dimension of poverty—insufficiency of resources—measured at a point in time. Even with this narrowing of scope, the threshold applied, and the corresponding number of poor, depends on whether one defines poverty in terms of standards of living or in terms of minimum rights. Moreover, in making the transition from an academic analysis to a policy concept, one must realize that the method of measurement will never be perfect. There are likely to be errors of measurement and errors that arise from the misspecification of the variable studied.

To make the discussion more concrete, we have set out the following logical tree:

Measured resources

Errors of measurement/recording/processing

True current resources

Transitory variations

Permanent or normal resources

Relation between resources and standard of living

Standard of living

We have to work with measured resources, but how we interpret this observed variable depends on whether we are concerned with people who score low on true current resources, on permanent resources, or in terms of standard of living. There are three relevant elements here. The first is that of measurement and related error; the second is that the current measure may differ from the more normal situation on account of transitory variation; the third is that the variable being measured may not be that in which we are interested (i.e. we are measuring income but are interested in standard of living). The impact of measurement error and transitory variation is discussed below (and we return to the subject when considering poverty dynamics). There will be both Type I and Type II errors; i.e., the count of those in poverty will miss some people who are indeed in poverty ('false negatives') and will incorrectly identify as poor some people who are not ('false positives').

At this point, we focus on the difference between resources and standard of living, a distinction that is often overlooked. It is commonly taken for granted that poverty is concerned with *standard of living*, or the achieved levels of living. In this case we are concerned with the final line in the logical tree. If income is taken as an indicator, then it is as an indirect measure of standard of living (Ringen 1988). Historically this was the case, in studies such as that by Seebohm Rowntree (1901) in the UK. But the shift to a participation approach to measuring poverty has also been accompanied by interest in a second conception of poverty, which is concerned with the *right to a minimum level of resources*, the disposal of which is a matter for individual decision. In this case we are interested in the second or third—not the fourth—line of the logical tree; and the fact that people with the same level of resources may have different standards of living is irrelevant.

The implications of the difference between standard of living and minimum rights conceptions of poverty may be illustrated by a historical example. The United States used to have different poverty lines for men and for women. On a standard of living approach, this could be justified on the grounds that women had smaller nutritional requirements. On a rights approach, such differentiation would be hard to justify. A second example is provided by the notion of 'core poverty' introduced by Bradshaw (1972) and developed in Bradshaw and Finch (2001a). This method, which embraces both different indicator variables and different poverty lines (discussed in Section 5.2), seeks to refine the definition of poverty by considering the subset of those below the financial cut-off who are also classified as poor by other criteria. Those in the overlap are the 'core poor'. A similar approach is adopted by Lollivier and Verger (1997), who examine the overlap between poverty in terms of living standards, monetary poverty, and subjective poverty in France. The Irish definition of 'consistent poverty' is equally an example of such an approach. The attractiveness of this method depends on the view taken of poverty. If our concern is with standards of living, then it does indeed seem natural to consider, for instance, the subset of those with low incomes who also have low scores on consumption measures. If, however, our concern is with a rights concept of poverty, then the financial indicators may be sufficient: people below a specified income level are at risk of being unable to participate in the society in which they live.

Income versus expenditure

The logical tree is helpful in considering the choice between collecting information about a household's total income or about its total expenditure. Eurostat in recent years has come to use income as the indicator of financial poverty, principally because it is now available in a harmonized way across the EU from the ECHP. Earlier studies (see e.g. Hagenaars *et al.* 1994; McGregor and Borooah 1992; Zaidi and de Vos 2001) have used information on both total income and total expenditure, or have used only expenditure. The National Action Plan on Social Inclusion for Greece presents estimates for both income and expenditure.

There are two main arguments that people can make in favour of using total expenditure. The first is that we should be concerned with standards of living, and that these are measured better by expenditure. This argument clearly depends on the premiss that standard of living is our concern, and it would be rejected by those adopting a minimum rights approach. The second argument accepts that income should be our concern, but suggests that expenditure may be a better proxy for 'normal' income than measured income. A family may be able to sustain its consumption through a temporary period of low income by running down its savings. On the other hand, a counter-argument is that the variable measured (expenditure) is not the same as consumption. The amount spent in a month may differ from consumption in that households run down stocks, purchase consumer durables, etc. Recorded expenditure may be misleading.

We recognize the arguments in favour of using expenditure, and we return to the limitations of current income when considering the persistence of poverty; but there are counter-arguments and, overall, we do not feel that there are strong enough grounds to reverse the move to an income basis. Moreover, income measures are directly available on a regular (annual) basis from the ECHP, and considerable research has been done on their validation.

Recommendation 6. The risk of financial poverty should be measured in terms of household income.

We should note that if this recommendation is not followed, and household expenditure is employed, then this would involve use of the harmonized household budget surveys, and, as noted earlier, this means that the access conditions would need to be relaxed. There could be only limited confidence in a central EU poverty indicator based on the use of surveys not open to external validation. The adoption of an expenditure basis would create pressure for household budget surveys to be conducted annually by all member states and for the Eurostat harmonization exercise to be carried out annually. We should stress that the switch to use of expenditure would have to be made by all member states. Consistency across member states in the approach adopted (income versus expenditure) is clearly of major importance, and we would not wish to see variation in practice across countries

5.2. OVERVIEW OF EXISTING METHODS OF SETTING THE FINANCIAL POVERTY LINE

In the literature, a number of methods have been developed for deriving poverty lines and identifying the poor. In general terms, these methods may be divided into the following types: the *statutory* method, the *relative* method (used in the Commission's indicators 2 and 3), the *food ratio* method, the *subjective* method, and the *budget* method. As noted in Chapter 2, the term 'subjective' may be applied in three different ways. Here we are concerned with setting the poverty threshold to be applied to household income (or expenditure), and not with the evaluation of individual household circumstances. We are therefore referring to the first of the usages of the term 'subjective' listed in Chapter 2: household responses as to where the poverty line should be drawn. Non-monetary indicators of poverty are treated in the next chapter, and subjective assessments of financial strain are considered in Section 8.5 on financial precariousness.

In the *statutory*, official or political method, the poverty line corresponds to the minimum income that is applied in social or fiscal legislation (e.g. subsistence income in Belgium, or the social welfare allowance norm in Sweden). The main advantage of this method is that it provides a poverty line that represents a political translation of an established view on poverty. As subsistence income is the income that is guaranteed to every Belgian, it would at first sight appear to be a good candidate for a (politically validated) poverty standard in Belgium. However, the statutory method begs the question of whether the legal threshold corresponds to a genuine social need. The level at which subsistence income is set is the result of incremental policy decision-making, where governments balance conflicting objectives and are faced with budget constraints, and the subsistence income is not guaranteed to keep people out of poverty. Moreover, in terms of being able to assess social security and poverty policy, it is not logical that a standard should be applied that is derived from the very policy pursued. A proper assessment of social policy performance thus requires an independent threshold. Analysis of the extent to which people fall below statutory subsistence standards in a given country is of course essential in assessing effectiveness in meeting the social security system's own objectives, but that is a separate issue. (On this, see the NAPincl for the Netherlands.)

In the *relative* income method, the poverty line is set at a percentage of a macroeconomic variable such as per capita national income, mean or median net household income, or equivalized net household income (i.e. taking into account household size and/or composition by means of equivalence scales). This method is usually applied in comparative international research, but is also one of the bases for the poverty objectives set in Ireland and the UK (as described in Chapter 3). The most commonly applied threshold was initially 50% of mean equivalized income. In 1998 Eurostat put forward a standard of 60% of median equivalized income, calculated over persons rather than, as in the past, over households, and using the modified OECD equivalence scale (see below); and this is the basis for the Commission's Indicators 2 and 3. The main advantage of the relative method is that it provides a poverty line that facilitates cross-national comparison. The main drawback is that this method leaves open a range of choice about the percentage to be applied. Subject to the limitations imposed by considerations of data quality, the threshold could be 40, 50, 60, or 70% of average or median equivalized income. The precise threshold selected will be far from neutral in its impact on cross-national comparisons. The number of individuals that are identified as being poor will tend to be high or low depending on the percentage that is chosen to different degrees in different member states.

Food ratio poverty lines are based on the assumption that households that spend the same proportion of their incomes on certain basic needs (food, clothing, heating) are equally well off. This method is used by Statistics Canada to calculate Low Income Cut-Offs (LICOs) (Wolfson and Evans 1989). The procedure first determines the average share of household income that is spent on the defined basic needs. It then identifies the income levels at which households (of different types) spend on average 20% points more on such basic necessities than the average household. These income levels for different household types are referred to as LICOs. The method has a number of technical drawbacks (see Wolfson and Evans 1989). One fundamental problem within the context of poverty measurement is the degree of arbitrariness involved in the choice of goods to be included in the basic needs category and in the determination of the low income cut-off point, i.e. the relevant excess proportion (20%) of total income spent on necessities.

In the USA, the recent recommendations formulated by the Panel on Poverty and Family Assistance charged with reassessing the measure of the official poverty line may be regarded as a variant of the food ratio method (Citro and Michael 1995). The existing poverty line had been established in 1964 using a hybrid budget method (see below), and since then had been adjusted over time only on the basis of the Consumer Price Index. The Panel recommended that the median annual expenditure on necessities of life (food, clothing, and shelter) be calculated for a reference household (two adults and two children). The poverty line for this type of household is calculated by taking a percentage of this expenditure and adding slightly to this amount to cover for other expenditure. For other types of household, the relevant poverty line can then be calculated by applying specific equivalence scales to the line for the reference household. As real expenditure on food, clothing, and shelter tends to rise over time, but more slowly than total real expenditure, the evolution of this poverty line can be expected to be at a rate somewhere between that of a purchasing-power-linked poverty line and that of a relative (prosperity-linked) poverty line. The method appears to be effective in the USA. However, one would need to ascertain whether it is adequate in a comparative EU context. If the food ratio method proves to be workable in the EU too, this standard is likely to constitute an attractive policy objective, as the income thresholds would increase relatively predictably as the general level of prosperity rises, though the two would not develop identically. In other words, this approach is a compromise between purchasing-power-linked and prosperity-linked thresholds.

In the *subjective* income method, a poverty line is constructed, as described in Chapter 2, on the basis of views expressed by the population itself (Van Praag *et al.* 1982; Muffels *et al.* 1990; Deleeck *et al.* 1992). A question of the following kind is put to a sample of the population: 'What is the lowest net monthly income, all included, that your household needs in order to make ends meet?' The answer to this question (i.e. the 'required lowest income') appears to increase as the actual income of the households increases. In order to eliminate excessively high estimates from wealthy households, the procedure adopted in the studies cited above is to take account only of answers from respondents who are balancing on a 'budgetary tightrope', i.e. who are on the verge of subsistence insecurity. Other studies have made use of the responses from all households.

Compared with the statutory and the relative methods, the subjective method yields socially more realistic income thresholds, as these thresholds are based on judgements by the population. One could argue that subjective thresholds are rooted in households' day-to-day experience with managing their budgets. The main drawback of this approach is that different respondents will regard different standards of living as minimal. Moreover, it is not always clear which circumstances and budget items are taken into consideration when answering the question about 'required income'. In practice, subjective income thresholds tend to be rather higher than absolute or relative ones. Furthermore, they can differ quite substantially from year to year. There are indications that small changes to the phrasing of the question about 'required income' can affect the income threshold obtained quite significantly (Van den Bosch 2001).

The *budget* method is the oldest and, to some extent, the most obvious method of determining income thresholds. This approach is based on a list or 'basket' of goods and services that are deemed to be essential. The main advantage of budget standards is that they are extremely tangible: their content is entirely clear, and so is the living standard that they allow. The main drawback of this approach is that it is hard to determine which ingredients should be included in the market basket, and that any selection, even where made by experts, is a matter of judgement. The minimum budgets thus obtained are almost inevitably influenced by the actual standard of living and the prevailing life-style in a particular country and at a given point in time. The budget method has been applied in the USA (from 1964) and Germany to determine official poverty lines. In the USA the basket contained food items only: in order to determine the poverty line, the cost price of this basket was multiplied by a coefficient of three. In Germany the required minimum is equated to the total cost of a more generalized goods basket. Often, budget standards are based on data regarding actual household expenditure. If this is the case, they approximate to the results obtained through the food ratio approach, or the variant proposed by Citro and Michael (1995). A recent study (Bradshaw 2000) has explored the use of the Eurostat harmonized budget surveys for constructing budget standards, and exploring the food ratio method.

5.3. EVALUATION OF DIFFERENT METHODS

In Chapter 2 we set out a set of principles that should be applied to individual social indicators used by the European Union. The five methods discussed above may be assessed as follows in relation to these criteria.

Identifying the essence

The *statutory* threshold is politically validated, and might therefore appear to be acceptable to the general public. As a policy objective, however, this standard is ambiguous, as it is at the same time both a goal and a tool of social policy. In some cases, the statutory minimum is the standard applied when judging adequacy. The NAPincl for the Netherlands, for example, gives central place to the subsistence minimum, which is related to the minimum wage. We should however distinguish between a measure of the number of households depending on the minimum benefit, and a measure of the number of households in financial poverty. The minimum income may be above the poverty line, so that the recipients are not poor. On the other hand, governments may—explicitly or implicitly—set the statutory entitlement level below their target level, since actual policy outlays are constrained by budgetary and other factors. As emphasized by Veit-Wilson in his study of minimum incomes, a government minimum income standard, or what it regards as a defensible standard of adequacy, may depart from the actual social assistance rates (Viet-Wilson 1998: 3). The amount provided under social assistance may, for example, be constrained by considerations of work incentives. The aim of policy may be to fill part, but not all, of the gap. And, where the social assistance minimum is set at the target level, it cannot be assumed that all those entitled do in fact receive the minimum guaranteed level of income or indeed any assistance. People may not claim the assistance to which they are entitled; there may be errors in administration that deny them the benefit. As stressed by the European Anti-Poverty Network, there are potential beneficiaries who 'are not claiming or are excluded from access to resources, rights, goods, and services' (EAPN 2001: 3).

As the *subjective* approach to determining thresholds is based on public perception of poverty, general acceptance should in principle be high, and it has an apparent justification. As the *food ratio* method (particularly the US variant proposed by Citro and Michael) is based on expenditure on basic needs, this approach too may well appeal to the general public. There can be debate about the choice of basic needs to include, but the standard has an evident anchor. The same applies to the *budget* standard.

In contrast, the *relative* poverty approach provides no direct guidance to the choice of any particular percentage, within a range limited at the bottom by considerations of statistical reliability. For this reason, the public acceptability of this approach may be considered to be rather low, although the fact that relative standards such as 50 and 60% of the median or mean have been used for some twenty years in the European Union means that they have gained increasing recognition. The thresholds put forward in the more affluent EU countries may be accepted more easily if they approximate to the statutory minimum. In the poorer member states, however, the amounts may well be considered inadequate.

Robustness and statistical reliability

The criteria to be applied using the *statutory* threshold are likely to be complex, involving for example income and assets tests. This means that the measures may be difficult to implement statistically, requiring detailed data, and their reliability may be open to question. The *relative* criteria involve less complex calculations, and Eurostat already has experience of their calculation, but this experience has also demonstrated the need for care in definition and measurement even at a national level. As noted earlier, the validity of these measures needs to be assessed on a continuing basis, in the light of other existing data. Experience with *subjective* indicators for poverty thresholds has found that they tend to fluctuate inexplicably over time within a given country, as well as varying inexplicably across countries (see Van den Bosch 2001). The robustness of the *food ratio* method still requires further testing in the EU context; and the same applies to the *budget* method.

Responsiveness to effective policy interventions

As already mentioned, the fact that the *statutory* threshold is determined by policy choices means that it can be used only with care as an indicator of policy performance. The other methods appear to rank equally on this criterion. It is true that a policy may make people below the poverty line better off but fail to raise them above the line; in this case, no improvement may be recorded in the poverty rate. This is however a property of the headcount measure of poverty, not of the standard applied. We return to this when considering the poverty gap and other alternatives to a headcount of those in poverty.

Comparability

The *statutory* threshold is hard to apply at EU level. First, statutory subsistence income schemes do not exist in all member states. Where the schemes do exist, they differ considerably in their method of operation. In some countries, for example, entitlement to the minimum benefit depends on both an income test and on an assets test. When applying the statutory threshold, do we want to apply the asset test in the latter cases? In some countries certain forms of income are disregarded, so that a household may qualify as being below the statutory threshold but have a total income comfortably above. Do we wish to take account of such disregards? Statutory threshold incomes fulfil different roles within the countries' respective social security or tax systems, and therefore cannot be compared. Attempts to apply statutory thresholds empirically across EU countries (notably in Bradshaw *et al.* 2001, using the ECHP) highlight the complexities involved in formulating what that safety-net minimum actually is on a country-by-country basis across the wide variety of household circumstances that actually occur in practice, as opposed to a small number of hypothetical or model families. The data on social protection routinely collected at the European level by MISSOC have serious limitations in this context, preventing the safety-net level actually provided in each country's overall package of income support to different types of household from being identified.[1]

---

[1] Bradshaw *et al.* (2001) point out, for example, that one cannot tell from the MISSOC tables whether income tax is paid on social assistance, or whether child benefits should be added to social assistance, or whether the family would be expected to pay any health charges out of their income, and/or whether there are any charges or benefits in respect of education to take into account. Also, MISSOC does not provide enough information on the

In contrast, the *relative* income threshold can more easily be applied across countries, both within and outside the European Union, which is one of the reasons why Eurostat opted for this method. This being said, it is important to keep in mind that achieving an agreement on a definition of income (gross/net income, income from self-employment, status of housing costs), of an equivalence scale, of an appropriate threshold, etc. are no easy things. Although major steps have been made in those areas, significant progress is still required.

The *subjective* approach to poverty thresholds has been applied to compare countries, but such comparisons will evidently reflect both differences in social conditions and differences in public perceptions. The latter may lead to problems in extending this approach to the European Union as a whole. The *food ratio* method too may not easily extend to international comparisons, since the resulting differences in poverty rates may reflect differences in spending preferences rather than differences in deprivation. The *budget* method, as noted above, shares some of the same features as the food ratio method, being based in part on actual spending behaviour. The attraction of these methods in terms of public acceptability (see below) means that their application EU-wide warrants further investigation, but we have to recognize that the application of a common method to all member states would not mean that the resulting poverty line bore the same relationship to average living standards. A EU-wide budget approach, for instance, could be implemented by requiring that the ingredients be chosen according to commonly agreed criteria. (Bradshaw and Finch 2001*b* applied a standard derived for food expenditure in the UK to other countries, simply to illustrate the potential of the approach.) The resulting total income would vary across countries as a proportion of the median or mean, depending on differences in the relative prices of the items selected. Moreover, changes in poverty numbers over time would happen on account of relative price changes as well as changes in the distribution of income. These are not necessarily arguments against such an approach; they do however complicate the interpretation of the findings.

Timeliness

There do not appear to be major differences between the methods on this account as far as the regular application of thresholds is required, but there

---

scales of social assistance to calculate entitlement for the range of household types actually found in the population.

are differences when it comes to the uprating of standards. The *relative* measure is self-updating, but the *budget* method must, in the medium term, be adapted to rising levels of prosperity and changing patterns of consumption. The *food ratio* method raises rather different issues, but also involves regular reconsideration. The relative method has therefore a certain advantage, but we should not lose sight of the fact that all poverty measures depend on the availability of household income survey data, and that these data are typically available with considerable delay.

Burden of data requirements and procedures

As already noted, the data required to implement the *statutory* threshold are likely to be more detailed, necessitating information on components of income but also on assets. The *relative* method requires information about the population as a whole, in order to determine the threshold. The *subjective* method typically requires only a modest addition to the survey questionnaire. The *food ratio* method as well as—in most cases—the *budget* approach require information on food and other expenditures, and hence presume the existence of (and access to) household budget data; the budget approach requires input from experts in nutrition and other branches of consumption.

5.4. EXAMINATION OF PROPOSED FINANCIAL POVERTY INDICATORS

The European Commission has proposed as a structural indicator the proportion of people below the poverty line before and after social transfers (defined as 60% of national median equivalized income). We consider first the relative nature of these indicators. We then analyse some of the detailed features: the level of the threshold when measuring financial poverty, the equivalence scale used to adjust for differences in household composition, and pre- and post-transfer poverty.

Relative measure

In the previous section we evaluated different approaches to the measurement of poverty against the six principles set out in Chapter 2. This showed that each had certain advantages and disadvantages. However, because of the large EU experience gained through years of research, the relative measure has the unique advantage of being practicable and immediately applicable on a comparable basis. The relative approach has also been widely applied in member states, so that 60% of the median is now quite widely recognized. Moreover, it is, we believe, possible to 'demystify' the choice of percentage, and thus the level of the poverty line, by explaining what it means in terms of purchasing power in each individual member state (see below). This leads us to conclude that the Commission's choice of a relative measure has considerable merits in the first stage of European social indicators, although we believe that other approaches should be investigated with a view to their use in the medium term.

Recommendation 7. In the first stage of European indicators, the risk of financial poverty indicator at Level 1 should focus on relative poverty, the threshold being expressed in relation to the general level of incomes in the member state; in the medium term, other approaches should also be investigated.

The relative approach is taken here to involve a poverty line that is set relative to the current income. As discussed in Chapter 2, it would be possible to choose a percentage of the median at a base date and then update the poverty standard only in line with consumer prices. Given sufficient economic growth, poverty measured with such poverty lines should decrease fairly rapidly. In contrast, with a relative measure, economic growth, whereby (percentage-wise) everyone benefits equally, will not reduce relative poverty. In fact, measured by a relative standard, poverty will remain more or less stable, even if there is a constant and unequivocal improvement in prosperity, as long as the distribution of income stays more or less the same. This holds for each member state separately, but also for any comparison between member states with different growth rates. Conversely, in the case of economic decline, whereby (percentage-wise) everyone is affected equally, relative poverty will not increase. The latter seems particularly problematic for a poverty standard that is expected to have policy relevance.

In fact, relative poverty may tend to increase rather than decrease in periods of economic growth. A substantial improvement of the incomes and labour market positions of households and individuals above the poverty line can translate into a significant rise in poverty, as the poverty standard is increased without a corresponding rise in the incomes of those at the bottom (for example benefit recipients). Benefits may provide only a fixed purchasing power, so that they will lag behind wages; in that case, only in the long-term, through various direct and indirect linking mechanisms, will benefit recipients share the general increase of prosperity. The possibility that poverty may not decline, or rise, in periods of prosperity is illustrated by the experience of Ireland since the mid-1990s, as described in Chapter 3. Conversely, in a period of economic crisis, during which average income rises very little, if at all, relative poverty may be reduced. This is illustrated by the experience of Belgian Flanders from 1976 to 1985, when poverty fell, but the drop in relative poverty occurred exclusively among the elderly population, while poverty among the working population was unchanged. Achieving an improvement of the incomes of people below the poverty line who are of working age may require radical changes in terms of income distribution. Minimum benefits for those out of work can hardly rise above the lowest earned incomes. And if the lowest wages increase, so may higher wages. Creating more labour market opportunities for the low-skilled may, in the first instance, benefit more privileged workers, who do not necessarily come from poor households.

For the reasons given above, we recommend including at Level 2 a measure of poverty based on a poverty line fixed in real terms at 60% of the median at a specified date for a limited period—see Recommendation 8 below. The price-only adjustment approach raises the question as to the length of time for which the constant real standard would be applied. The number of years for which the standard can reasonably be carried forward depends on the growth of real income and on the changes that have taken place in the distribution of income. Where there has been substantial change, then the price-adjusted line may cease to be seen as acceptable in the light of prevailing life-styles. A period of about five years seems likely to be acceptable, but any longer period would risk the fixed poverty standard losing contact with overall living standards. The poverty threshold would then lose its interpretation in terms of social participation.

Counting households or people?

As noted in Chapter 2, there is a choice as to whether to count households or individuals. Are a couple and two children in poverty counted once or four times? It used to be common practice, when measuring poverty at the European level, to consider the proportion of *households* below the poverty line (and then the number of people living in those households). However, the Eurostat Task Force report (1998) on *Statistics on Poverty and Social Exclusion* recommended that the proportion of *persons* be counted. The Commission in its proposed social inclusion structural indicators refers to the 'share of the population', or individuals. If a couple and two children are in poverty, then on this basis we count four people. Since individuals are at the heart of our concern, we find this approach persuasive. It means that the total population remains the same independently of differences in household composition. If Alice marries Bob, she does not disappear from the statistics. Following our overall recommendation that statistics should in general be presented in terms of counting individuals or their circumstances, we recommend that the calculation be based on persons.

Poverty level

The Eurostat Task Force (1998) on *Statistics on Poverty and Social Exclusion* recommended not just the change from households to persons, but also the use of a poverty line fixed as a percentage of the median in place of the previous use of a percentage of the mean. The use of the median rather than the mean has been justified on the grounds that (i) it is less sensitive to extreme observations (see Cowell and Victoria-Feser 1996), (ii) it is not affected by top-coding and bottom-coding, and (iii) it is, under certain assumptions about the underlying distribution, less sensitive to sampling fluctuations. We should however note that the median shares with the mean the properties of being affected (though to a much lesser extent) by the deletion of observations, such as those for (very) low income, and could be affected by the inclusion or non-inclusion of the non-household population. Moreover, the ratio of the median to the mean varies across member states, so that a change of reference value is not completely neutral across countries.

What should the percentage be? Should we take 60% of the median, as in recent Eurostat publications (Eurostat 2000*b*)? Should we take 50% of the median, as is the practice used by the United Nations and OECD (Oxley *et al.* 1997) and in certain member states (France, for example)? Table 5.1 summarizes the low-income thresholds used in the NAPincl. The 50% level is employed by 11 of the 15 member states, and the 60% level receives more qualified backing. The 40 and 70% levels also have their supporters. It is an intrinsic disadvantage of the relative method (as defined above) that it offers no direct answer to that question, except of course those linked to the robustness of income data. There is a gradation, not a sharp cut-off, in the risk of poverty associated

Table 5.1. *Low-income thresholds in national action plans*

Country	Median (%)				Other
	40	50	60	70	
Belgium	X	X	X	X	50% mean and continuous graph
Denmark		X			
Germany					
Greece	X	X	X	X	Income and expenditure
Spain	X	X	X		
France		X	(X) exclusively for international comparisons		
Ireland					Consistent poverty
Italy		X			Absolute measure
Luxembourg		X	X	X	
Netherlands					Alternative financial poverty index
Austria			X		
Portugal		X			
Finland		X	X		
Sweden		X	(X) sometimes		
United Kingdom		X	X	X	40, 50, and 60% mean

with different income levels. A person living in a household whose (equivalized) income is below 50% of the median is at greater risk than a person living in a household whose income lies in the range 50–59% of the median.

The reasons why 50 and 60% of the median have been widely used are in part to be found by reference to the results of applying the other approaches discussed in Sections 5.2 and 5.3, such as the levels of statutory subsistence minima. This is one ground for our recommending further investigation of these other approaches at the EU level. Here we refer to more pragmatic considerations: measurement error and accepted practice.

Purely random measurement error means that a poverty measure based on observed income is likely to include more people whose income has been under-recorded than people whose income has been over-recorded and vice versa. If the error is uncorrelated with the true value (as might be the case with random coding errors), then this adds noise to the distribution, spreading out the lower tail. Measurement error may then indicate taking a lower cut-off. Some people believe therefore that, in order to arrive at a credible and politically acceptable poverty standard, a narrow approach is most appropriate, applying a lower threshold and seeking to minimize 'false positives' (people wrongly classified as poor when they are in fact above the poverty line). Others believe that one should aim for the best estimate, recognizing that there will be errors in both directions.

Measurement error may not however be unrelated to the true value. Certain classes of income, such as that from self-employment or investment income, are particularly prone to measurement error, and these are not distributed in the same way as other income. Some independent workers with high true incomes may have zero or negative recorded incomes. Equally, this may arise because transitory fluctuations are more significant for this group. The problem becomes even more severe when we consider the difference between income and expenditure or material deprivation. Studies based on the ECHP (e.g. Layte *et al.* 2000*b*) have shown that deprivation, measured by enforced lack, exhibits considerable mismatch with financial poverty. The results suggest that deprivation does not fall monotonically as income rises. The same is true if expenditure is taken as a measure of consumption capability (UK Department of Social Security 1996*a*: 28). The proportion of the actually poor may be a declining function of observed income over an initial range; for example, some people with zero or negative incomes (making losses) may enjoy a comfortable standard of living. If this is the case, then restricting the poverty cut-off to a lower value may have the consequence of reducing the absolute number of false positives but increasing their proportion in the population. By the same token, the composition of the population identified as poor will change with the poverty line (see, in the case of Ireland, Nolan and Whelan 1996*a*: ch. 3). With a low cut-off, the poverty figures may give undue emphasis to special groups in the population. This is especially likely to be important if we are concerned with standards of living (rather than minimum resources), since, with a cut-off of, say, 40% of the median, those identified as poor may include sizeable numbers of people who are in fact well above the poverty line.

Accepted practice points to use of the threshold of 60% of the median, in that it provides a degree of continuity with the earlier use of 50% of the mean, and it has already been widely used, especially since the 2000 Lisbon Summit, where EU poverty estimates—calculated on this basis and using ECHP data—were presented to heads of state and governments. One might run the risk of being accused of manipulating poverty figures if these were suddenly to be reduced drastically (solely because of a change in the definition). On the other hand, if a change is to be made, the formal adoption of the social indicators by the European Union would be an appropriate occasion. As we have seen, the threshold most commonly used in the NAPincl by member states was 50% of the median. Moreover, 50% would bring the EU into line with the UN and OECD. It can also be argued that it would be politically easier to defend a line that is criticized mainly for being too low than one that is criticized mainly for being too high.

There are therefore justifications that can be given for both 50 and 60% of the median, and we recommend that both be included at Level 1 and be reported on as a situation of *risk of poverty* rather than one of poverty as such.

These considerations lead us to welcome the current Eurostat practice of providing an assessment of the robustness of the conclusions to the precise choice of poverty level, with estimates based on 50, 60, and 70% of the median and of 40, 50, and 60% of the mean. This is particularly important in view of the massing of incomes around certain income levels in member states where there are flat-rate benefits. Such robustness calculations, which provide information on the dispersion of poverty estimates around the reference thresholds, are a good example of indicators that should appear in the second level, providing material to help interpret the lead indicators. At the same time, we recognize that a threshold of 40% of the median is close to the bottom tail of the distribution in a number of countries, and that the ratio of noise to signal may be sufficiently high for statistical offices not to regard such a statistic as reliable. The recommendation is therefore made subject to considerations of statistical reliability.

To summarize, we recommend the following.

Recommendation 8. There should be two Level 1 indicators for (risk of) financial poverty, one calculated on the basis of a threshold set at 50% of the national median equivalized income, and the other at 60% of the median; there should be Level 2 indicators, set at 40% (where statistically reliable) and 70% of the median; Level 2 financial poverty information should also include the value of the 60% 'poverty line'

**(in purchasing power standards—PPS) for a one-person household
and for a household consisting of two adults and two children. There
should be a Level 2 indicator based on a poverty line fixed in real
terms (i.e. uprated only for inflation) at 60% of the median at a specified date for a limited period (say, about five years).**

The Belgian NAPincl suggests that a diagram could illustrate the
sensitivity of the poverty count to the poverty cut-off, where the hor-
izontal axis shows the level of equivalized income in euro, ranging from
40 to 70% of the median, and the vertical axis shows the percentage
below that ceiling. Individual member states could truncate the lower
part of the diagram depending on the reliability of the data in different
countries.

Household unit, equivalence scales, and weighting

The most widely used unit of analysis in measuring poverty is the
household. There are some reasons to be concerned that the household
unit assumes full income-sharing, which in reality does not take place.
An unequal distribution of income between men and women living
together may be concealed by the household unit of analysis. (On the
within-household distribution, see Jenkins 1991 and Sutherland 1997.)
Inequality between different generations may be hidden. Adults and
children may not have the same living standards; the elderly may not
share fully in the resources of the household. We believe that inequality
within the household is an important issue, which warrants fuller investigation, in particular because of its importance to measuring poverty
among women. For the present, however, the limitations of the available
data mean that we do not propose any departure from what has become
widely established, and therefore we recommend that a household unit
be adopted. This does not mean counting the number of households:
as just emphasized, we should count the number of people living in
households.

Differences in household size and composition mean that an equivalence scale has to be applied to adjust total household income. The
Schmidt household containing a couple and two children cannot be
treated as having the same needs as a single person. On the other hand,
a per capita income calculation, dividing the family's total income by
four, seems to go too far in the direction of adjusting for household size.
The most frequently used equivalence scale up until the 1990s was

that devised by the OECD (1982), which consists of the following weights: 1.00 for the first adult, 0.7 for every additional adult, and 0.5 for every child. This would lead us to divide the Schmidt's family's income by 2.7 to arrive at its 'equivalized income'. In research based on the Luxembourg Income Study, an equivalence scale that is often used is equal to the square root of the number of household members, which would give the rather lower figure of two equivalent adults in our example. Today one predominantly uses, as with the Eurostat estimates, the so-called OECD-modified scale, which was proposed by Hagenaars *et al.* (1994), and which encompasses the following weights: 1.00 for the first adult, 0.5 for every additional person aged 14 or over, and 0.3 for every child under 14. The value in our example of the Schmidts is then 2.1, and in practice, the latter scale often approximates to the square-root equivalence scale.

The choice of equivalence scale will increase or decrease the number of poor, especially among large households, and will affect the composition of the poor population (including the number of poor children). The results of Becker and Hauser (2001) show that in Germany in 1998 the poverty rate (with a threshold of 60% of median income) for a married couple and two children was similar to that for single persons when using the original OECD scale, but under half the rate for single persons when using the modified OECD scale. For the purposes of comparing total poverty rates across member states, the OECD-modified equivalence scale seems a reasonable compromise, but the sensitivity of the findings regarding the composition of the poor population means that the choice of equivalence scale needs to be regularly assessed. It should be stressed that, in this case, disaggregation by household types (for instance looking at families with two children) on its own is not sufficient. The use of a scale giving a low weight to children may mean that families with children record a low poverty rate. What is required instead is a series of estimates with different equivalence scales.

The introduction of differences in household composition means that we have to consider once again the weighting to be attached to each observation. The natural starting point is to count the number of individuals in poverty. We have earlier argued against treating a household as a single unit, and in favour of it being weighted by the number of people. This is the procedure we recommend. It should however be noted that this means that total income does not 'add up'. It would add up if our couple and two children counted as 2.1 equivalent persons (not as four persons), i.e. if total income were divided by 2.1 to get the individual equivalized income and then multiplied by 2.1 when we add across the individuals in the household: the 2.1 terms would cancel. This is of particular significance when in the next chapter we come to the measurement of the poverty gap. If we weight households according to the number of people they contain, then it can happen that giving a specified amount of money to two people can raise them above the poverty line if they are a couple but not if they live singly, even though the households are in both cases below the poverty line by the same amount of equivalized income.[2] But this simply means that the impact of a transfer depends on the circumstances of the recipient. We do not see this as a sufficient reason to depart from our core principle of counting people as individuals. Moreover, a weighting equal to the number of equivalent adults is far from transparent. It would be hard to explain to the four people in the Schmidt family that they counted for 2.1 of the x million in poverty; or that Alice and Bob, in getting married, reduce their weight in the poverty calculation from 2 to 1.5. These considerations lead us to recommend use of a weight equal to the number of the people in the household, although we recognize that, in terms of income, this leaves an adding-up problem, and that the sensitivity to use of the alternative set of weights should be examined.

The choice of weighting affects both the poverty count and the determination of the median. We envisage here that the median is obtained by considering the distribution of adult equivalized income among individuals. This will typically differ from the median of the distribution among households or among households weighted by the number of equivalent adults. The sensitivity in the case of the mean is investigated by Callan *et al.* (1996: 70), who show that there can be differences of the order of 5%.

Recommendation 9. The poverty risk measure should be based on household income adjusted for differences in household size and composition by the OECD-modified equivalence scale, each household being given a weight equal to the number of household members, with the sensitivity of the results being assessed on a regular basis.

---

[2] Suppose that the poverty line is 100 for a single person and 150 for a couple. The two people living singly have each an income of 90. Giving them each 9 will not raise them out of poverty. To have the same equivalized poverty gap, the couple has an income of 135. Giving them 9 each will raise them above the threshold of 150. The same applies in income distribution terms if we consider a transfer of income between two households with different composition but the same equivalized income: the impact will be neutral only if the weighting is equal to the number of equivalized persons—see Ebert (1997).

One way in which sensitivity may be gauged is by considering poverty rates for different types of household. As is clear from the NAPincl, there is considerable concern about the extent of child poverty (see also Cornia and Danziger 1998; UNICEF 2000; Vleminckx and Smeeding 2000), and this is one of the disaggregations that we recommend. Poverty rates among the elderly should also be examined. If we are interested in disaggregating the poverty figures, considering sub-groups of the population, then we may wish to extend the dimensionality of the equivalence scales, taking account of characteristics apart from the household size and composition. Poverty among the elderly may require us to consider scales that vary with degrees of disability: the need for personal care is an important example. Research on expenditure by families with disabled children (e.g. Baldwin 1985) has shown how estimates can be made of the additional costs.

The Commission's indicators apply the same equivalence scale to all member states, and this seems a natural starting point. If however we were to follow a different approach to the definition of the poverty line, such as the adoption of a Europe-wide budget approach, then this could well lead to different equivalence scales in different member states (see Muffels *et al.* 1992). Suppose for example that we consider the relative cost for a child compared with the scale of 1 for a single person. On a budgetary approach, we are concerned with the extra costs of a child, i.e. the budget needed for a single parent plus one child, compared with that for a single person. In the case of food this would not double, but it would increase more than for shelter. This means that, in a country where shelter is less expensive relative to food, the proportionate additional cost for the child will be larger, and hence the equivalence scale will be larger. (In all cases, we are considering the position relative to a single person.) Alternatively, if we were to adopt a subjective approach to the definition of poverty, then the population of one member state might attach a higher weight to the needs of children, relative to single people, than another. Our willingness to accept different equivalence scales for different member states is therefore part of a wider question of our willingness to consider alternatives to the Commission's relative approach to poverty measurement.

Definition of resources

Ideally, resource measurement used to determine whether or not a family is poor should be as complete as possible, including both cash and in-kind income components. Using only monetary income is likely to produce misleading results, especially in the context of cross-country comparisons. Examples may include poor farmers in the South living in owner-occupied dwellings and consuming a considerable proportion of their own production as well as poor urban households in the North receiving substantial amounts of assistance in-kind in the form of welfare programmes.

Our recommended measure for poverty analyses is *disposable or net income*. The definition, and other methodological issues, have recently been reviewed by the Canberra Group (Expert Group on Household Income Statistics 2001; see also Smeeding and Weinberg 2001). Following the Canberra Group classification, disposable income includes total income (cash employee income and cash value of fringe benefits, cash and imputed in-kind income from self-employment, rentals, property income, and current cash transfers received) less current transfers paid (social contributions, taxes, regular inter-household cash transfers, and regular cash transfers to charity). In most income surveys, however (including the ECHP and the new EU-SILC), some of these elements are not included for practical reasons, mainly because considerable work is needed in order to assess the best means of measuring and valuing them in each country. This is usually the case for non-monetary employee benefits other than company cars and imputed income from self-employment (goods from own gardens and farms). The EU-SILC task force, however, proposes to develop the concepts and measurement in order to include those resource components in a later stage; we would like to support this.

Another important issue for welfare comparisons between both households and countries is the *income generated from owner-occupied housing and housing beneath market rents*.[3] As for other income in-kind, accurate measurement of imputed rent is a main problem. In theory, imputed rent is the difference between the cost of renting one's housing (in a

---

[3] The calculations carried out in Britain (see e.g. UK Department of Social Security 2000*b*) are made on two bases: before and after housing costs. In the former case, the figures relate to the distribution of equivalized net income, which includes housing benefit but makes no deduction for housing costs. In the latter case, what is measured is net resources, defined as net income minus housing costs (rent, water charges, mortgage interest, structural insurance premiums, ground rent, and service charges). The second of these calculations—that of net resources after housing costs—may appear rather strange to observers from outside the UK. It can however be justified on the grounds that housing expenditure is a relatively exogenous element of a household's outgoings, and one that varies across households in a way that reflects accidents of geographical location and tenure rather than the quality of the accommodation occupied.

competitive market) and the cost actually incurred in owning the home (or renting it at below a market price) (Expert Group on Household Income Statistics 2001). Inclusion of this element of income can make a significant difference. The NAPincl for Greece presents estimates for 1999 that show that the proportion with income below 60% of the median was reduced from 20.0 to 17.3% by the inclusion of imputed income from housing. The problems in measuring imputed rent are twofold. First, a lot of detailed information is needed both on the house, to estimate its rental value, and on the costs of owning the home. Secondly, matching of similar houses is needed to estimate the rental value of the owner-occupied houses. This may be problematic in countries with a high percentage of owner occupancy. Here again, the EU-SILC task force proposes to develop the concepts and measurements in order to include this resource component in a later stage; and we would like to support this as well.

The *assets* of a household are part of its command over goods and services. This theoretically valid point is important only if the income-poor actually do possess assets. Empirical studies (e.g. Ruggles and Williams 1989; Ruggles 1990; Wolff 1990; Rendall and Speare 1993; Van den Bosch 1998) indicate that few among the income-poor have financial assets of any substance, though many—especially among the elderly—own the house in which they live. However, it is doubtful whether the owned home can be considered fully fungible in current economic and social conditions, so that it cannot be used to finance current consumption. Therefore there may not be a case for allowing anything over and above the imputed rent attributed to home ownership. On the other hand, the situation differs geographically and across member states. The role of assets may need to be revisited.

Should *social benefits in kind* (i.e. free or subsidized services to individual households, such as education or health care) be included in the income concept? As the level and distribution of individual services does affect comparisons across households and across countries where the extent of state provision differs, social transfers in kind should in principle be included in the definition of income. However, there remain important conceptual and practical obstacles. First, it is not clear how to think of the income equivalent of services provided. Most in-kind benefits are not fungible, in the sense that they cannot be applied to different consumption needs. Recipients may place a lower value on the benefits than the cost of providing it. And it is difficult to see why poor households should be reclassified to a 'rich' category because they require extensive medical care. Health care is provided only to those in need, covering costs so that the amount received has to be netted against the extra costs, which could well leave the household's overall welfare unchanged. (In other words, the household has extra needs in terms of health care costs, and these are cancelled out by the provision of that health care.) The same argument applies to education. Second, from a practical point of view, it remains unclear how the value of in-kind benefits can be estimated (on the basis of entitlement, of actual take-up, or of what the household would be prepared to spend to receive the service). In any case, to value in-kind benefits in each country, a large amount of data is needed (for instance the frequency and type of delivered health care services). A consensus on definitions and methods has not yet been reached. We therefore share the conclusions of the Canberra Group, that more research is needed in this field.

Questions regarding income should be as detailed as possible. Traditionally in income surveys, household heads are asked about the total disposable household income after having been reminded of all income components. Additionally, each household member is asked about the various personal income components. Thus, the total disposable income of the household can be calculated by adding up all separate incomes of the household members, complemented with any income that cannot be allocated to a particular individual within the household (e.g. housing allowance). Comparison of these two methods reveals that questions about overall household income often result in an underestimation of the household income. It would appear that household heads fail to take into account all income components, or underestimate certain components. Moreover, the degree of underestimation increases as household size increases. This may indicate that the head is insufficiently aware of the incomes of, for example, working children within the household, or that more calculation errors are made because of the greater complexity involved when more incomes come into play.

It has to be decided how to measure accurately *net and gross income*. The Canberra Group proposal distinguishes income components at the gross level only, and records total tax and total net income. The rationale is that several income components may be considered jointly for tax purposes, so that net income at component level has no clear meaning (if any). However, depending on the country (and hence the tax system applicable), many survey respondents may be able to report a net figure with greater accuracy. Therefore the EU-SILC task force suggests that countries could collect in their surveys net income components, in which case a country would develop a model to derive the gross from this net figure. In this, one should draw on the expertise built by teams that have constructed micro simulation models—especially the EUROMOD model, which is an EU-integrated one (see Section 9.2). In the ECHP questionnaire, most income components are reported net of tax and other deductions. The only exceptions are income from self-employment and rental/property income, while income from capital may be specified as net or gross depending on the respondent. With the exception of France, all gross amounts in the constructed variables have been converted to net values on the basis of an estimated net–gross ratio calculated at household level. Although we share the caution by Immervoll and O'Donoghue (2001) against using simplified methods, this pragmatic solution seems to be appropriate in an early stage.

Current or previous year income?

A choice also needs to be made with regard to the *observation period*. Should we use monthly or annual income? Does it suffice for an individual's income to be below the poverty line in a particular month, or is the income obtained over a longer period a more appropriate indicator? Theoretically, a longer reference period will result in less income inequality; a short observation period (e.g. monthly income) might register coincidental fluctuations that would have been evened out over a longer period. Consider the following example. If a respondent happens to be asked about his monthly income during a short spell of unemployment, the income registered in the survey will be 'unrealistically' low in comparison with his annual income. Conversely, a short observation period may register incomes that are 'exceptionally high' in comparison with the respondent's annual income. Thus, if the objective is to measure income inequality, and if one accepts that the majority of the population is able to spread out its income in order to compensate for a temporary drop in income, then a longer observation period may be called for. Therefore, the Canberra Group recommends that the accounting period to be used for income distribution analyses should be the year. This has the further advantage that comparisons can readily be made with total income figures in national accounts.

The choice between monthly and annual income in poverty research will depend on the assumptions made regarding the effect of short-term income fluctuations on the economic well being of individuals and households. Some households will be able to maintain their consumption level during short spells of lower income by using their savings, or borrowing, or postponing some expenditure. However, this is likely to be more problematic for households at the lower end of the income scale. The extent to which this is the case is likely to vary across member states. In some countries the institutional and family structure may facilitate income smoothing. In other countries it is harder for low-income groups to spread their income out evenly over a year with a view to retaining a minimum level of spending, and it may be more appropriate to observe monthly incomes. Moreover, the yearly income will not be a very useful measure for governments of member states where benefits are weekly or monthly based. Measuring income on a yearly basis in these cases makes it difficult to assess to what extent monthly benefits are targeted at low-income households.

The empirical implementation of the income measure raises a number of issues, some of which plead in favour of an annual income approach, others of which favour a monthly approach. An annual-income approach can be implemented where countries have access to register data. It is however unrealistic to suppose that register data will be available for all member states in the short- or even the medium-term. We have therefore to take account of the position of those countries reliant on survey data. Respondents are often unaware of their overall annual income. As the most important income components (salaries, social transfers) are usually received on a monthly basis, these are the amounts that respondents are most familiar with. On the other hand, other types of income (such as interest, holiday pay, and scholarships) are received less frequently—for instance annually—so that for these components respondents may be asked to indicate a yearly amount. This can subsequently be calculated back to a monthly sum. For the self-employed it may be necessary to take the monthly equivalent of earnings calculated over a longer period. These amounts can be incorporated in the monthly income in so far as households may be assumed to take this income into account in their monthly spending.

Alternatively, one could conduct a survey that runs through all sources of income for every month during a whole year. This would, however, increase the interview burden considerably. Moreover, such an approach may yield unreliable data. The ECHP gauges the annual income in the calendar year prior to the year in which the survey is conducted ($N-1$) rather than in the last 12 months. The main reason for this is to make it possible for respondents to use, at the moment of the interview, their annual pay slip or their tax declaration. (With the exception of the UK, the tax year is 1 January–31 December in all the member states.) Cantillon *et al.* (2001) have carried out an in-depth analysis of the quality of the Belgian ECHP income data, exploiting the fact that in data relating to 1993 a direct comparison can be made of the two approaches: income for the previous month versus income for the whole previous calendar year. This study brings out the difficulties in measuring past annual income accurately.

The most important consideration in choosing the reference period is, we believe, that we want to be in a position to analyse income in conjunction with the socioeconomic and demographic information pertaining to the same date. When the reference period is taken as the preceding calendar year, then the income refers to a different date from other measures (household composition, labour market situation, and social exclusion indicators). A person may have become unemployed a couple of months before the time of interview and be recorded as unemployed, but the survey records their earnings from a year before when they were still working. This is a particular problem for households where fieldwork takes place later in year *N*. In view of these problems, we recommend that consideration be given to the alternative concept of 'current modified income', i.e. annualized current regular income components (wages, regular social benefits, pensions, multiplied by 12 if paid monthly) and, for irregular components or those best collected on an annual basis, figures for the most recent and appropriate period (e.g. self-employment income, capital income, annual bonuses).

'Current modified income' has advantages but also limitations. When we come to the measurement of poverty persistence, the current measure may be more subject to transitory variations than previous year income. An example is provided by the periodic uprating of social transfers. A family may have an income that, averaged over the year, retains the same relation to the median; but if the family is interviewed one year before a benefit uprating and next year after the uprating, then this may induce spurious mobility. We also recognize that a move to a current modified definition would involve major changes in national statistical data collection systems.

Against these disadvantages are to be set significant benefits. There would be greater consistency between the income variable and other indicators. It would avoid a situation where, as at present, the poverty status is assessed by dividing the income of the previous calendar year by an equivalence scale based on current household composition. It would allow the indicator of jobless households (Section 7.3) to be related to current poverty. It would allow indicators to be constructed of the number of working poor based on current income, rather than an approximation based on current status and past income (see Section 7.4). From the standpoint of social inclusion indicators, these merits in our view outweigh the drawbacks.

Recommendation 10. In order to be able to link income with house-hold and individual variables, either income should be measured as 'current modified income', or countries should collect information about household and individual characteristics for the period to which the income data relate.

Pre- and post-benefit poverty headcount

The Commission has proposed indicators of poverty before and after the impact of social benefits. (For a detailed examination, see Marlier and Cohen-Solal 2000.) Transfers here do not include pensions, so poverty 'before transfers' refers to income including pensions, whether paid privately or by the state (as the available data do not allow the split to be made between public and private pensions). Poverty after transfers (i.e. based on total income) is a natural outcome measure, but the status of the measure of poverty before transfers needs to be clearly understood. In our view, it is a measure of the efficiency of state transfers. This is of considerable interest when assessing the effectiveness and coverage of policy, particularly if related to the total amount spent on such transfers; but it should be seen in these terms, not as an outcome indicator for social inclusion. Countries may choose different methods of combating social exclusion. A country that encourages labour market participation by one-parent families, for instance, will have a lower rate of poverty pre-transfers than a country that relies on social transfers for this group; but no particular significance can be attached to this difference from the standpoint of achieving social inclusion. A country may convert transfers into tax credits, reducing poverty measured before transfers (since the households now pay less income tax), but leaving poverty post-transfer unchanged. There seems no reason to record such a bookkeeping change as a policy improvement.

While we understand the usefulness of the pre-benefit indicator to the Commission, we do not recommend its inclusion in the portfolio of measures considered here. This is for two reasons. The first is that the assessment of the effectiveness of policy depends on formulating a counter-factual: one has to identify the level of poverty *in the absence of the transfers in question*. Such a counter-factual situation almost certainly does not coincide with the level of poverty measured by subtracting transfers from disposable income. If benefits did not exist, then people would change their decisions. For example, unemployed young people would live with their parents. The measurement of such a counter-factual is far from easy. The second reason is that, taking the broad approach that we adopt here, there seems no reason to examine the policy effectiveness of transfers but not of other policy interventions; nor is there any reason to confine our attention to the poverty indicator. If we were to extend our coverage to pre-benefit poverty indicators as measures of policy efficiency, then readers might well ask why we have not considered the effectiveness of labour market policy in reducing long-term unemployment.

6

Depth of Poverty and Income Inequality

The indicators of financial poverty described in the previous chapter provide a measure of the extent to which people face the risk of serious deprivation in terms of their standard of living or the extent to which they fall below a specified minimum level of resources. To measure the seriousness of the risk people face, or the depth of their poverty, we have to associate further indicators. In this chapter we consider the persistence of poverty (Section 6.1), measures of the poverty gap (Section 6.2), and the extent to which those with low financial resources are suffering enforced deprivation (Section 6.3). Are people below the poverty line year after year? How far do their incomes fall below the poverty line? Can we combine financial and non-monetary indicators of deprivation? In the final section we turn to the broader issue of the overall distribution of income.

6.1. PERSISTENCE OF FINANCIAL POVERTY

The longer people remain in poverty, the greater their risk of being permanently excluded. If survey returns show the Leblond family as having incomes below 60% of the median for three years running, then we can be more confident that they are genuinely facing financial pressure, and that this is not due to measurement error or to temporary deviations in income. Moreover, this financial pressure, sustained over three years, is more likely to have led to problems of social exclusion. We welcome therefore the proposal by the Commission of a dynamic indicator of poverty (the share of the population below the poverty line for three consecutive years). In particular, where the income poverty level has been set at the higher level of 60% of the median, this provides a valuable way of focusing attention on those most likely to be at risk of social exclusion. At the same time, we should note that the dynamic approach raises a number of issues, which mean that its implementation is less than straightforward. (These issues are discussed by OECD 2001a: 43.) In terms of the principles set out earlier, the issues affect the burden of data collection, the reliability of the results, and the interpretation/acceptability of the indicator. The problems are both immediate, in that they affect the implementation of indicators in the EU in the next couple of years, and continuing, in that they apply to dynamic indicators in general.

Collection of data on poverty dynamics requires either (i) panel data, or (ii) that respondents to a cross-sectional survey provide accurate recall data (which in the case of income is highly problematic), or (iii) administrative data which can be linked over time. The third of these has been used, for example, in studies of the receipt of social assistance in Denmark and Germany (Leisering and Leibfried 1999). Though feasible in some member states, the application of register data has stringent requirements. Not only must we be able to link individuals over time, but we must be able to link together data for those living in the same household. For this purpose, there would have to be considerable advances in the availability of, and access to, administrative data.

Where administrative data are not available, survey information is crucial. It is for this reason that the European Community Household Panel has been so important, offering possibilities of measuring change over time for the same persons and households. We understand that the new EU-SILC will incorporate a panel element, although member states will be able to use different sources for the panel and cross-sectional information. The data on poverty dynamics may be obtained from either a 'pure' panel or a rotational panel design for the main survey, or by use of other sources such as register data. The cross-sectional and the panel elements can be separate, while requiring full linkages at an individual level within (and not obligatory between) each dataset. In our view, it is important that the sample size of the panel element be sufficient to allow proper longitudinal analysis, particularly if there is significant attrition (loss of sample members over time)—see below.

Recommendation 11. High importance should be attached to the measurement of the persistent (risk of) financial poverty and to the collection of appropriate data.

There will however be a hiatus between the two sources, ECHP and EU-SILC. In most member states the final round of the ECHP is being conducted in 2001, with results expected in mid-2003. The EU-SILC will be in full operation, after a pilot, as from the year 2003. If one is seeking to measure persistence over a minimum of three years (see below), then the results for 2005 (with the first EU-SILC three-year panel data) are due in mid-2007. There will therefore be a period in the mid-2000s where the most recent panel data on income will remain those relating to 1998–2000. It may be argued that the extent of persistent poverty does not change greatly over time, so that out-of-date data may be adequate. However, a number of current policy initiatives are designed to reduce persistent poverty, and we would like to be able to monitor their success. For this reason, we recommend that a systematic review be made of alternative sources, to be used as a stop-gap, including the possibility that administrative data may be supplied on a temporary basis.

Turning to the more general issues, we would like to emphasize that panel data have to be used with care. Panel data have been enthusiastically embraced by social scientists, but research has also demonstrated their limitations. A number of these limitations apply to the measurement of the persistence of poverty. Even if the panel were to be complete, the existence of *measurement error* can cause mobility (in or out of poverty) to be mis-measured. The importance of the error depends on its correlation over time. A permanent error in the measurement of income, for example, which caused income to be understated by a constant amount would not affect measured mobility (but would affect the population identified). However, measurement error is not always going to take this form. For instance, where one source of income is not reported in the survey questionnaire, the amount of missing income is likely to vary over time.

Where the panel suffers from *attrition*, then there is a further source of unreliability. Where those least likely to escape poverty are also those most likely to drop out of the panel, we may expect the poverty escape rate to be overstated. Conversely, the bias is in the opposite direction if those who have enjoyed a positive change in their circumstances are less likely to be interviewed at subsequent stages, for example because they have moved to a more prosperous region and are lost in the tracing process.

There are equally problems of *interpretation*. The person in the street may regard mobility as a natural part of human life. Children become older and women re-enter the paid labour force, both events which change the economic circumstances of the family, but in a way that forms part of the natural life-course. To record such developments as mobility may seem rather different from those changes associated with the ending of unemployment or the acquiring of new skills. There may also be a difference between permanent and transitory status. A family may be correctly recorded as being above the poverty line, but this may only be a temporary escape, while they enjoy a short-run windfall or piece of good luck. The 'carousel' effect means that, for some of the most disadvantaged, they may disappear from poverty for a period but will return before long. An example is where children are taken into care by public authorities during a period of family crisis. In such a situation, the needs of the household measured by the equivalence scale are reduced, and the family may be recorded as rising above the poverty line; but there is no permanent change, and when the crisis is over they will fall once again below the poverty line.

These considerations are important when we come to the length of time over which mobility is measured. From the standpoint of policy, we are interested in relatively long periods, but the limitations outlined above point to a shorter rather than a longer period. Attrition becomes increasingly serious with the length of the panel; changes in household formation are more likely to enter the picture. Weighing these factors, and taking account of the hiatus in data availability to which we have already referred, we feel that a period of three or four years may be a reasonable choice.

Closely related is the question of whether we require for the definition of persistent poverty that households be below the poverty line in all years studied. Measurement error and transitory variations mean that we may want to ignore one year's departure, where this is not the current state. In terms of data for three years, we would start with those currently poor (denoted by P) and require that they have been non-poor (denoted by N) in only one of the previous two years, i.e. taking the sequences PPP, PNP, and NPP. If, as recommended here, we take data for four years, then we are allowing the sequences PPPP, NPPP, PNPP, and PPNP.

The study by the OECD (2001*a*) suggests an alternative approach to the dynamic measurement of poverty, which is to take a multi-year average of income. Following the permanent income approach pioneered by Friedman (1957), the OECD defines as 'permanent-income-poor' families whose average equivalized income over three years falls short of the average poverty threshold income. According to the OECD figures derived from the ECHP for 1993–5 reference years, the average annual poverty rate (using 50% of the median) was 11.7%, and 3.8% were below in all three years, but 7.9% were permanent-income-poor. These findings support the proposal in the previous paragraph that the persistent poverty measure should not require families to be poor in all observed years: the proportion with an *average* income over three years below the poverty line (the 'permanent-income-poor') is significantly higher than the proportion below the line in all three years.

In the same way, Berthoud (2001a) defines families as 'chronically poor' if average income over six years is below the average poverty threshold. This brings us back to the question of the choice of reference period, with the horizon now being extended from one year to three years or six years. The same concerns as noted earlier arise about the incapacity of low-income households to smooth out fluctuations in income. If we accept that smoothing is indeed a problem, then use of a multi-period average of income has to be justified on the grounds that we are distinguishing between degrees of severity. We are not dismissing current poverty, measured by the Level 1 indicator, but are supplementing it by an indicator of persistent (i.e. repeated) poverty and of chronic (i.e. long-run average) poverty.

These considerations lead us to make the following recommendation.

Recommendation 12. Level 2 indicators of persistent poverty risk should include (a) the percentage of persons living in households currently below 60% of the median who have been below this threshold in (at least) two of the previous three years (the persistently poor); (b) the percentage of persons living in households whose income averaged over the last three years is below the average for these three years of the 60% of median threshold (the chronic poor).

The first of these measures requires data for four years, the second for three years. Under the first element of this indicator, the persistently poor are a proper subset of those currently below 60% of the median. This has a particular value when it comes to relating persistent poverty to the current characteristics of the individual and his or her household. The second element, on the other hand, captures a broader notion of persistence, including some who are not currently below the income threshold. The two elements therefore serve as useful complements and provide a more rounded picture of persistence.

6.2. POVERTY GAPS

The poverty headcount has the advantage of being easily explained, and lends itself to headline figures: '*X* million poor in Europe'. However, it has serious shortcomings. It gives no indication of the depth of poverty.

All of the X million could, in theory, be only 1 euro short of the poverty line. As this—hypothetical—example illustrates, the headcount can be very sensitive to precisely where the line is drawn. By the same token, it can be affected by small changes in policy. A modest increase in flat-rate pensions, for example, can lift a significant proportion of the elderly above the poverty line. More importantly, the headcount may be quite unresponsive to policy improvements. A government may raise the incomes of all those in poverty without necessarily raising anyone above the threshold (as with a transfer equal to half the gap between the total poverty line for the household, allowing for its composition, and the household's total income). The lack of policy responsiveness means that the headcount scores badly on our third principle.

The obvious next step is to consider the *poverty gap*, as has already been extensively used in poverty measurement, for example by Eurostat. The total poverty gap, G, measures the total shortfall of households/persons from the poverty line, and can be related for instance either to the total population of a country or to only that part of its population below the poverty line. If we divide G by the poverty headcount, H, we obtain the mean poverty gap, which is a measure of the *intensity* of poverty. For comparability across countries, the gap may be expressed as a % of the poverty line. As is shown by Förster *et al.* (2001: figure 2.1), high-poverty countries are not necessarily those with a high intensity of poverty.

The poverty gap is a natural measure, but it is not without problems. First, it requires careful definition to take account of the adjustment made to incomes by the chosen equivalence scale. As discussed in the case of the headcount, there is a choice as to how observations are weighted. If every household consisted of a single person, then we would simply take everyone with income less than the poverty line, z, and add up the shortfall. This would be both the poverty gap in terms of welfare and the amount of income required to bring everyone up to the poverty line. But if households differ in composition we need to adjust by an equivalence scale, treating a couple, say, as equivalent to 1.5 single persons. Suppose there is a couple below the poverty line. Both have equivalized income equal to two-thirds (1/1.5) of the household income, y. With a weight equal to the number of people in the household, the gap in equivalized terms is twice (for two persons) $\left(z - \frac{2}{3}y\right)$. On the other hand, the cost in money of bringing the household up to the poverty line is $\left(\frac{3}{2}z - y\right)$, which is smaller. This alternative calculation in effect gives a weight to the household equal to the number of equivalent adults, which can also be expressed as subtracting total household income from a specific poverty line computed from the standard (one-person household) poverty line for each household, taking into account their size and composition.

There are therefore two different interpretations of the poverty gap. One—the sum of the income shortfall—is often described as the 'cost' of abolishing poverty. This is however a misleading description. It assumes perfect targeting, in that there is no spillover to anyone above the poverty line, and it assumes that there are no changes in before-transfer incomes. Even if the former could be attained, there are likely to be behavioural responses that change before-transfer incomes (as where people decide to reduce their working hours, or to retire earlier). For this reason, we prefer to see the poverty gap treated as a measure of the welfare of the individuals living in households below the poverty line, and this leads us to adopt an equivalized income measure. As in our discussion of weighting in the previous chapter, we are not persuaded that the advantages in terms of adding up are sufficient to overthrow the arguments in favour of each person receiving a weight of 1, irrespective of household composition. The poverty gap is measured, then, as the mean over all people below the poverty line of the difference between their adult equivalized income and the poverty line (for a single person).

The second issue concerns reliability of the calculation of the poverty gap. Unlike the headcount, it is sensitive to the precise value of incomes below the poverty line, so that the poverty gap places greater demands on the reliability of the data. Of particular concern here are observations of very low, zero, or negative incomes. This may, as discussed earlier, result from errors—whether of the interviewees, the interviewers, the coder, or the imputation process (if any) applied for missing income—causing reported income to depart from true income. Or it may reflect differences between current income and standard of living. One standard procedure is to apply a bottom-coding procedure (Atkinson *et al.* 1995: 37). A value of, say, 10% of the median equivalized income could replace any values below that amount. (The bottom-coding procedure would be applied where there is a response to the relevant question(s); in the case of item non-response, the observation would be excluded from the analysis.) Such a procedure would leave the median unaffected, and would therefore have no impact on the poverty line or on the headcount. On the other hand, the choice of 10% of the median is a matter of judgement. If we are adopting a minimum resources approach to the definition of poverty, with income as the variable of concern, then the precise choice may not be too critical. The impact on the mean poverty gap is also reduced if we take the higher 60% cut-off. If, however, we are adopting a standard-of-living approach, then people in the bottom percentile could well have expenditure above the poverty level. In this case bottom coding would not be adequate—although we should note that the headcount too is overstated.

An alternative procedure to bottom-coding, proposed to us by Professor John Hills of the LSE, is that we take the *median poverty gap*, i.e. the extent by which, in equivalized income, the median poor person, ranked by equivalized income, falls below the poverty line. Such a measure is still sensitive to errors of measurement that define the poverty population (headcount), but, with a 60% of median poverty cut-off, the median poor person is unlikely to be in the very bottom group with extremely low or negative income, where income may be a particularly bad indicator of standard of living. This is an attractive measure of the intensity of poverty suffered by the 'typical' poor person. It is also easily explained and therefore scores high on transparency. On the other hand, there are circumstances in which it may be more sensitive to fluctuation than the mean poverty gap (bottom-coded), and we suggest that experience be gained with its use before a choice be made between the median and mean poverty gaps.

The poverty gap is only one way in which to allow for the depth of poverty, and it can be criticized as being insensitive to the distribution of the poverty gap. One alternative is the *Sen measure*. This, like a number of other measures, weights the poverty gaps, rather than simply adding them. A gap of 250 euros is treated as more important than two gaps of 125 euros. The Sen (Sen 1976; Sen and Foster 1997) measure applies a weight based on the household's rank in the distribution. A household right at the bottom of the poverty population gets a weight of 1.0, a household ranked 15% from the bottom gets a weight of 0.85, etc. This procedure is similar to that involved in the construction of the Gini coefficient but is limited to the population below the poverty line (see Section 6.4). While the significance of rank order weights may be quite persuasive in the case of measuring inequality, as with the Gini coefficient (Sen 1974), it is less evident that we wish to weight poverty gaps in this way. Why should the severity of poverty depend on how many other people are poorer? For these reasons, we do not here pursue this further.

We make the following recommendation.

Recommendation 13. As measures of the intensity of poverty, Level 2 indicators should include the mean equivalized poverty gap (with bottom-coding) and the median equivalized poverty gap for a poverty line set at 60% of the median.

As noted, after experience has been gained with the median poverty gap, it may be decided that the mean gap can be dropped, allowing the number of Level 2 indicators to be reduced. But it should be emphasized that the poverty gap indicators should be used in conjunction with the total poverty headcount. The significance of a large poverty gap depends on how many people are affected.

6.3. DEPRIVATION INDICATORS

Income, while a central determinant of household living standards, has limitations in the measurement of poverty and social exclusion. Deprivation indicators can provide a valuable complementary source of information about the extent of the poverty risk (Callan *et al.* 1993; Nolan and Whelan 1996*a,b*). This applies both in seeking to identify those experiencing poverty and exclusion at a point in time, and in seeking to assess changes over time.

Indicators of deprivation are generally based on asking survey respondents whether they have a specific item or participate in a certain activity. We have cited in Chapter 3 the examples used in the Irish national poverty target, such as going without a substantial meal all day, having inadequate heating, or not having an overcoat. It is important to distinguish between situations of deprivation—not *having* an overcoat—and *not being able to afford* an overcoat. Such enforced lack in effect combines non-monetary and monetary components. For this reason, we do not refer to measures of enforced deprivation as purely 'non-monetary' indicators. The Eurostat (2000*b*) report on *Income, Poverty and Social Exclusion* contains information on both bases. It shows for example that in 1996 more than a quarter of the EU population was experiencing a housing problem such as lack of bath, shortage of space, or damp, and that 5% had cumulative housing problems. It shows that 1 in 8 lived in a household that could not afford new clothes owing to insufficient income.

It is important to distinguish different uses of deprivation indicators.

1. One approach, pioneered by Townsend (1979) in the UK, is to construct an index of deprivation from a set of non-monetary indicators and derive an income poverty line on the basis of the relationship between scores on this index and household income. This could be used as a guide to the appropriate percentage of median income to be used in a relative poverty measure (for example whether 50 or 60% is the more appropriate), or to derive a different method of

uprating: for example, it might rise more or less rapidly than median income.

2. A second approach is to identify the poor directly on the basis of deprivation scores, or to rely primarily on the enforced deprivation scores in measuring poverty (as for example Mack and Lansley 1985 did using British data, and the major follow-up, the Poverty and Social Exclusion Survey of Britain, carried out in 1998 and 1999— Gordon *et al.* 2000).

3. The third possibility is to use both income and enforced deprivation scores in identifying the poor, and this is the approach applied in framing the Irish official poverty target and is one of the measures in official use in Austria, as described in Chapter 3 above (see Layte *et al.* 2000*a*).

The rationale for using deprivation indicators in a cross-sectional context is that current living standards and deprivation levels depend on having a command over resources and experiences (particularly in the labour market) over a long period, not just on the flow of income into the household this week, month, or even year. This, along with the difficulties in accurately measuring income in household surveys, means that some of those observed on low income are not in fact experiencing what would generally be seen as high levels of deprivation and exclusion. Non-monetary indicators of deprivation, on the other hand, provide direct measures of exclusion, but taken alone do not necessarily allow one to relate such exclusion to inadequate resources. This provides the essential rationale for combining both low income and non-monetary indicators of deprivation to identify those experiencing exclusion because of a lack of resources at a specific point in time.

As well as helping to identify the poor at a point in time, deprivation indicators have considerable value in assessing changes in poverty over time. The dilemma faced in using income alone is that a purely relative approach can miss an important part of underlying trends. Accepting that poverty is relative, changes in real living conditions are still relevant and need to be captured in the measurement process. While one can use both purely relative income lines and ones held fixed in real terms, this may still fail adequately to capture and convey changes in living conditions. Deprivation indicators can do so in a direct way, which can be easily understood and conveyed to a broader audience. In addition, in assessing trends in poverty one can then incorporate changing standards and expectations in the society in question into what constitutes 'necessities' and what represents exclusion.

Application of deprivation indicators in a EU context

In applying deprivation indicators to the monitoring of social inclusion in the EU, even more complex issues have to be faced than in the context of an individual country. The best approach will depend on precisely what it is that one is most anxious to capture. To illustrate this, it is worth comparing some of the options based on the types of indicator available in the ECHP.[1]

The first and simplest option is to take a subset of key indicators, look at deprivation levels in terms of these indicators across each of the member states, and see how those levels change over time. For example, as noted above, the Eurostat (2000*b*) report presents results from the ECHP showing the percentage in each country reporting that they could not afford selected items in 1996. Three items were presented to represent 'basic needs': a meal with meat, chicken, or fish every second day; new rather than second-hand clothes; and a week's holiday away from home every year. Three further items were presented separately to represent consumer durables: a telephone, a car, and a colour TV. (Items relating to other dimensions including housing and health were also presented.) Unsurprisingly, there are very substantial differences across the member states in the percentages reporting that they have to do without these items. For example, only 15% of the Danish sample, compared with about 66% of those in Greece or Portugal, reported having to do without at least one of the 'basic needs' items.

This brings out the first key feature of this option. Because, effectively, a common standard is being applied across countries, rather than a relative standard that takes the average level of living in the country in question into account, there will be much wider gaps between countries at a point in time than with, for example, relative income poverty rates. (The same of course would be true if a common income line were to be applied.) The second key feature relates to trends over time. If the same set of indicators is used from one year to the next, then progress is being measured against a fixed standard rather than against one that reflects the evolution of average levels of living over time. This also has the great advantage that the indicators it produces are easily understood.

A second option would be to take a common set of indicators across all the member states, but apply them in a way that takes average levels of

---

[1] Layte *et al.* (2000*b,c*) and Whelan *et al.* (2001) explore the factors determining deprivation levels across households and countries, and analyse the relationships between low
income, deprivation, and self-assessed economic strain, using ECHP data.

living in the country in question into account. For example, a summary deprivation index could be constructed in which each item is weighted by the percentage *not* deprived of the item in the country in question. So it would be a more serious deprivation to be unable to afford a week's holiday in Denmark (where only 14% report such deprivation) than in Portugal (where a majority report this). The key indicator would be a deprivation score, and mean deprivation scores could be compared across countries. The gap between countries would then be narrower than if one simply constructed a summary index weighting each item equally. With the three basic items employed in the Eurostat study, for example, the mean score for Portugal on such a summary index with country-specific weights would be about three times that in Denmark—much closer to the gap between those countries in relative income poverty rates. So this would produce in effect a relative deprivation indicator at a point in time. In looking at trends over time, the weights for each item in each country would adjust automatically as the extent of deprivation in the country changed. Whether time-varying weights would suffice to capture changing living patterns and expectations over any prolonged period is doubtful, but over, say, a five-year period there would be advantages in focusing on an unchanged set of indicators.

The third option is to seek to use indicators specific to the country in question, but designed to capture the same underlying condition of exclusion owing to lack of resources. For example, one could select only items possessed by a substantial majority in the country in question, or regarded as a necessity by such a majority. This would mean that certain items would count as deprivation in Denmark but not in Portugal, where most people actually lacked them, while items serving as useful indicators in Portugal might be essentially irrelevant in Denmark because so few Danes are doing without them. Over time, certain items might then be dropped and others added for specific countries as the extent of possession changes. While this would certainly have some attractions in terms of coherence with the definition of poverty as exclusion resulting from a lack of resources, it would pose significant problems both analytically and in terms of ease of understanding.

These indicators might also be *combined with income* to produce measures or indicators of 'consistent' poverty. One option would be simply to look at the numbers *both* falling below relative income thresholds *and* reporting the enforced lack of a common set of items, held fixed over time. So people would be identified as 'consistently poor' if, for example, they were below 60% of median income in their own country and reported being unable to afford one of the 'basic needs' or consumer durables items. Across countries, this would in effect represent a combination of a common (European) deprivation standard and a (country-specific) relative income standard. Correspondingly, over time it would represent the combination of a fixed deprivation standard and a relative income standard. This would highlight those who are experiencing deprivation in terms of a generally accepted set of basic needs across the member states, and whose resources are constrained compared with the average in their own country. It would however imply that someone unable to afford new clothes and below 60% of median income in Denmark is 'poor', whereas someone in Portugal reporting such deprivation and on a lower income in purchasing power terms is not 'poor' because that income, while low, is still above 60% of median income in Portugal.

An alternative is to combine relative income thresholds with a set of items using country-specific and time-varying weights. So people would be identified as 'consistently poor' if, for example, they were below 60% of median income in their own country and scored above a threshold on a summary deprivation index, with that index constructed from a weighted set of 'basic needs' or basic plus consumer durables items. The key question is then how such a deprivation threshold would be derived in each country. (This is of course exactly analogous to the problem of where to draw an income threshold to distinguish the 'income-poor'.)

If one could instead identify a country-specific set of items representing what was generally regarded as deprivation *in that country*, and reflecting the underlying condition of exclusion one is trying to capture, this would be in line with the logic of the 'consistent poverty' measurement approach as developed in Ireland. If in addition the set of items were adjusted over time, that would again be in line with the underlying logic of the approach. However, obtaining consensus on a methodology to identify the appropriate set of items for each country, and to adapt the set over time, remains a significant challenge. Conveying what such a measure means—including the rationale for the selection of items—to a broad audience would also be challenging but essential if it was to be employed as a key EU social indicator.

Our overall conclusion from this discussion of the use of non-monetary indicators of deprivation is that they can certainly serve in country-specific efforts, using indicators appropriate to that specific setting and together with income, to identify those experiencing exclusion because of a lack of resources. This is particularly valuable because income, on its own, will not capture comprehensively the command over resources and living standards of different households, and may mislead as to the extent and nature of such exclusion. For this reason, we hope that member states will where possible include these measures at Level 3. In a comparative context, they can also bring out differences in the average standard of living across countries, or in the living standards of those falling below relative income lines, in a more concrete, comprehensive, and easily conveyed fashion than income alone. At present, however, there is no simple generally accepted approach to using such indicators— either on their own or together with income—to measure the same underlying concept of relative poverty in different countries in the same way. We believe that a major effort should be made to overcome these problems.

Recommendation 14. Non-monetary indicators of deprivation should where possible be included by member states at Level 3, and a significant investment should be made in developing these indicators in a comparative context for use in the EU monitoring process.

6.4. DISTRIBUTION OF INCOME

Measures of income inequality are concerned not just with the bottom part of the distribution but also with the whole range of incomes. This can be represented in different ways. Traditionally, individual observations were arranged into a frequency histogram or density function, indicating the proportion of the population falling in selected income bands: e.g. 50–59% of the mean. Other representations of the distribution of income in a given sample include the 'cumulative distribution curve' and the Lorenz curve. The former simply cumulates people below a given income level, showing the proportion of the population with incomes below, say, 50% of the mean. Looked at from the vertical axis and from bottom to top, this curve corresponds to the famous parade of Pen (1971), where all individuals in the population march in the order of their size, itself proportional to their income. The slope of the cumulative distribution at a given point gives the frequency at that point, so that we can work back to the frequency distribution. The Lorenz curve cumulates the population in increasing order of income, as depicted in Figure 6.1. It shows the share of total income received by the bottom $x\%$ of the population. Suppose that we rank the population according to the equivalized income of the household in which they live and divide them into fifths (quintile groups). The shares may be denoted by S_1, S_2,

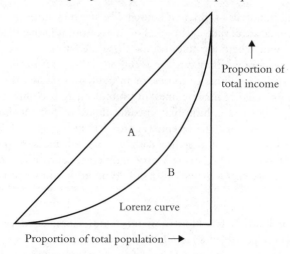

Figure 6.1. *The Lorenz curve*

S_3, S_4, and S_5 (which is equal to $1 - S_1 - S_2 - S_3 - S_4$). For example, for the EU 'average' (over 13 member states covered) in 1996, these were 8, 13, 17, 23, and 39% (Eurostat 2000b: table 2.1). The Lorenz curve is obtained by cumulating. The first point is 8%, the second is $(8\% + 13\%) = 21\%$, the third point is 38%, and so on. So the bottom fifth of the EU population had 8% of total income, and the bottom two–fifths had 21%.

The Lorenz curve can be used to make rankings of countries. Where the Lorenz curve for country M lies everywhere above that for country N, this means that the lowest x% always receive a larger share in country M. In other words, the distribution in country N is more unequal than that in country M. The problems with such an approach for our purposes are (i) that we are not concerned with the ranking of countries, but rather with deriving a measure of performance relative to the standard of equality, and (ii) that the Lorenz curves yield only a partial ranking: where the Lorenz curves cross, we cannot reach a definite conclusion. For this reason, we have to resort to one or a few scalar 'inequality measures' which summarize the departure of the distribution from equality and satisfy various basic properties.

The Commission has proposed use of the ratio of the share of the top quintile group to that of the bottom quintile group, which in the case of the EU data for 1994 would yield a value of 39/8, which is close to 5. People are ranked according to the equivalized income of the household in which they live. This identifies the top and bottom fifth of individuals. We then calculate the ratio of the shares of the two groups, adding the equivalized incomes for each person. (This will not add up overall to total income, on account of the equivalization; the numbers would add up only if we gave each person their equivalized weight, rather than a weight of 1.) This measure is referred to below as the quintile *share* ratio. The italicized word is important, since this indicator is different from the ratio of the quintile points, which is the income of the person at the bottom of the top 20% as a ratio of the income of the person at the top of the bottom quintile. A similar calculation to that taken by the Commission, and preferred by some, is the decile *share* ratio, i.e. the ratio of the income share of the top 10% to that of the bottom 10%. This would concentrate more on the extremes, but places greater demands on the reliability of the data, the shares of the decile groups being more subject to influence by outliers. On the other hand, the ratio of the decile points (the decile ratio) appears a robust indicator and is widely employed.

The quintile share ratio measure differs from that most commonly used, which is the Gini coefficient. The reasons for the popularity of the Gini coefficient are not entirely clear, but may be due to its graphical interpretation as the area between the Lorenz curve and the diagonal, denoted in Figure 6.1 by A, relative to the whole triangle, denoted by $(A + B)$ in the figure. In the case where the data are in the form of quintiles, then $(1 - \text{Gini coefficient})$ may also be calculated as the average of $9 \times S_1$, $7 \times S_2$, $5 \times S_3$, $3 \times S_4$ and S_5, i.e. as a weighted average of the shares, the weights declining with rank. This brings out one of the arguments in favour of the Gini coefficient, which is that it responds to changes in all shares. In contrast, the quintile share ratio is responsive only to changes in the top and bottom shares. For example, if the quintile shares for the EU in 1994 had been 8, 15, 17, 21, and 39%, rather than 8, 13, 17, 23, and 39%, then the quintile share ratio would have shown no change, despite the fact that the bottom 40% had a larger share. The Gini coefficient would fall by 1.6 percentage points. (It is reduced by $2 \times (7 - 3)/5$.)

The Gini coefficient tends to be more sensitive to changes that take place around the middle rather than in the tails of the distribution, since the weight attached to a small transfer of income depends on the difference in the cumulative frequencies (Atkinson 1970: 256). Since, from the standpoint of social inclusion, we are concerned more with the bottom of the distribution, this may be seen as pointing to the use of an index that gives explicit weight to a redistribution towards the bottom. The equally distributed equivalent (in a different sense from equivalence scales) measure (Atkinson 1970) has such a property, calibrating aversion to inequality by a parameter that can be chosen by the investigator. In the limiting case of variation of this parameter, as aversion to inequality becomes infinite, we are concerned only with the share of the bottom group (a 'Rawlsian' measure). Countries would be compared simply on the basis of the share in total income of the bottom $x\%$ of the population, where x could for example be 10 or 20%. The choice of x would be governed by both theoretical and practical considerations. It could not be too low, since we would then encounter the problems of statistical reliability discussed in Section 6.2 on the poverty gap. It could not be too high, as this would vitiate the objective of concentrating on the bottom group.

An inequality measure based on the share of the bottom 20% (defined earlier as S_1) can be contrasted with the Commission's proposal of the ratio of S_5 to S_1. The former is concerned solely with the position of the bottom group, whereas the latter is concerned with the position of the bottom group *relative to the top group*. It is the inter-group relative nature of this indicator that distinguishes it from a poverty measure. From the standpoint of inclusion, there is a distinct concern with the gap between the bottom and the top of the distribution. The case for so doing may be illustrated by a much earlier writer concerned with social cohesion. Plato argued that 'if a state is to avoid . . . civil disintegration . . . extreme poverty and wealth must not be allowed to rise in any section of the citizenbody, because both lead to disasters. This is why the legislator must announce now the acceptable limits of wealth and poverty' (quoted by Cowell 1977: 26). Plato proposed that the maximum limits should be set at 4 to 1. It may be noted that Czechoslovakia, one of the least unequal Eastern European countries under Communism, attained a value for the ratio of S_5 to S_1 as low as 2.7 in 1985 (Atkinson and Micklewright 1992: table 5.1). (This may of course still have breached the Platonic maximum for the range of all incomes.) A different argument in favour of the quintile share ratio is that it is more easily explained to the general public than the Gini coefficient, or other relatively complex statistical measures. This seems to us a strong reason, although the decile share ratio would be equally easy to explain.

If we are concerned with the relation between top and bottom, should we use the quintile share ratio or the quintile ratio? That is, should we use S_5/S_1 or the ratio of the income of the person at the bottom of the top 20% to that of the person at the top of the bottom quintile? (The same question would arise if we took the decile ratio.) The quintile share ratio will normally be higher than the quintile ratio, since there will be inequality within the top and bottom quintile groups. The quintile ratio has a weakness that does not arise with the quintile share ratio. It is possible for the distribution to become less unequal but for the quintile ratio to indicate a worsening. Suppose that social transfers become more targeted, and this involves reducing payments to the person at the top of the bottom quintile and increasing them to people with significantly lower incomes. This shifts the Lorenz curve upwards, but the quintile ratio rises. On the other hand, use of the quintile points, not the shares, has statistical advantages. The quintile ratio (and even the decile ratio) is less sensitive to the precise value of incomes at the very top and very bottom. The share of the top income group may be highly sensitive to a few outliers. The argument is parallel to the earlier comparison of the poverty headcount and the poverty gap. Those concerned about the data demands of moving to measures of poverty intensity may prefer to stay with the quintile ratio, rather than the quintile income share, even though—like the poverty headcount—it does not always respond to policy changes in the expected way.

There is an *'embarras de richesse'*. We make the following recommendation.

Recommendation 15. Income inequality should be measured at Level 1 by the ratio of the top and bottom quintile shares measured in terms of equivalized income, with the decile ratio and Gini coefficient (both also measured in terms of equivalized income) being included as complementary measures at Level 2.

7

Education, Employment, and Unemployment

In this chapter we examine the fields of education, unemployment, and employment. We start in each case from the indicators proposed by the Commission, but we go beyond these, covering for example access to education, employment activation, and the working poor. We draw on the indicators proposed by member states in their National Action Plans on Social Inclusion, and those used in other sources.

The principal concern of this chapter is with labour market issues, but education has wider significance. The educational level of the retired, for example, is relevant to their capacity to participate in society and to take part in the democratic process. These aspects are considered in the next chapter, as is functional literacy and numeracy; but there is no sharp dividing line, and in our recommendations in this chapter we take account of the fact that education is concerned with more than employment and accelerating economic growth.

The indicators in this field proposed by the Commission are:

(4) proportion of jobless households;
(5) regional disparities (coefficient of variation of regional unemployment rates);
(6) low education (proportion of people aged 18–24 who are not in education or training and have only lower secondary education);
(7) the long-term unemployment rate.

All of these indicators differ from those of poverty and income distribution in being absolute, although in different senses. Unemployment rates and rates of joblessness are naturally anchored by a lower limit of zero, whereas the educational indicator adopts a particular absolute standard for low education. All indicators are based on objective criteria. They differ however in other respects, as we bring out below.

7.1. LOW EDUCATIONAL ATTAINMENT AND DIFFERENTIAL ACCESS TO EDUCATION

Indicators relating to education are widely used as general social indicators. The World Bank and the UN (including the UNDP's widely cited *Human Development* and *Human Poverty (2) Indices*), for example, give prominence to adult literacy and school enrolment rates. For industrialized countries, the OECD's list of social indicators put forward in the early 1980s included years of education and literacy among those who have left the education system, as well as the extent of participation in adult education. The publication *Society at a Glance: OECD Social Indicators* (OECD 2001*b*) includes indicators for the distribution of the population by level of educational attainment, the percentage that has attained at least upper secondary education, and the proportion that has attained tertiary education.

Education is an area reasonably well provided in terms of comparative statistics. The range of comparative data now available on education is illustrated by the annual *Education at a Glance* compendium (OECD 2000*a*). This presents data on, *inter alia*, education expenditure, numbers of students currently enrolled at different levels of the education system and participation rates, numbers of teachers and their salaries, labour force participation and earnings by educational attainment, and mathematics achievement levels of students. The main source for OECD and Eurostat are the so-called UOE annual statistics—with E(urostat) collecting the data for EU countries, O(ECD) collecting the data for OECD countries that are not members of the EU, and U(NESCO) collecting data for the other participating countries.

To facilitate comparisons across countries, these international organizations have developed a framework for comparing educational programmes called the International Standard Classification of Education, the first of which (ISCED-76) was adopted 25 years ago, and the revised one (ISCED-97) in 1999. ISCED provides a basis for comparisons across systems that differ in terms of institutional structures. It distinguishes six main *levels* of education to which the range of programmes in different countries are allocated. It also distinguishes, using a three-digit classification (broad, narrow, and detailed), the *fields* of education. Of particular relevance here is the distinction between ISCED 2 'education at the lower secondary level' and ISCED 3 'education at the upper secondary level'. We return later to the way in which these are interpreted in different countries with different structures of secondary education and different examination systems, problems that may arise *within* countries where there is a diversity of curricular pathways.

Information is also available from sample surveys. The Labour Force Survey is a key data source in this respect. Surveys such as the ECHP and household budget surveys seek information on the highest education level attained by respondents. These surveys provide data on the level of completed education of those no longer in education for a representative sample of the general population, and allow this information to be disaggregated (e.g. by age and gender). Secondly, they provide a basis on which educational attainment can be related to other features of the individual and his or her situation, such as employment and unemployment experience, earnings and household income, and a wide range of objective and subjective variables.

This wealth of data does not mean that the identification of suitable indicators to fit within a social inclusion framework is unproblematic. Many of the data relate to inputs, and much less is known about the success of the education system in imparting specific or general skills, and about skills and competencies within the general population. Some such comparative data on current school pupils have been gathered on a one-off basis. The OECD compendium, for example, presents comparative data on student performances in mathematics and science. These performance indicators, and measures of literacy, are discussed in Section 8.3; here we are concerned with the relation to educational attainment. In a study carried out as part of the Framework Programme IV, under the NEWSKILLS project, Steedman and McIntosh (2001) have examined the relation between the ISCED classification of educational attainment and performance on mathematics and literacy tests. They conclude that those who do not continue with education and training are likely to have only low levels of basic mathematical skills (p. 574). From evidence on adult literacy (see Section 7.3), they find that there is a strong positive correlation with the ISCED classification. Defining as 'low education' those with only lower secondary education or less (ISCED categories 0–2), the proportion of those in this category performing at a low level of literacy was between 46% (Sweden) and 73% (Ireland).

When we consider the outputs of education, we have to recognize that it serves many functions, not only that of fitting people for the world of work and enhancing their productivity, but also developing the capacity of individuals to lead a full life, and transmitting societal norms and values. The choice of appropriate indicators will thus reflect not only data availability and comparability, but also the perspective from which education is being assessed. In focusing on social inclusion, our main concern will be with the major role educational attainment plays in influencing the risk of subsequently experiencing poverty and social exclusion, and with the extent to which access to education is itself structured by socioeconomic status.

So what indicators in the area of education appear most suitable in the context of a focus on social inclusion? The Commission's proposed indicator of low education, derived from the Labour Force Survey, is the proportion of people aged 18–24 who are not in education or training and have only lower secondary education. The use of the ISCED category 2 or lower as a cut-off seems to us a good starting point. While there are problems of translation across countries (see below), the intention of the cut-off is easily explained and the indicator scores well on transparency. As we have seen, it has a degree of coherence with measures of mathematical skills and literacy. Where upper secondary education is required to enter third-level or advanced vocational programmes, then failure to cross the ISCED 2/3 divide is prime facie evidence of exclusion from the possibility of educational advancement along these lines.

From a social inclusion perspective, it is particularly important to capture the extent of low educational attainment, given its role in influencing subsequent life-chances and the risk of experiencing poverty and exclusion. Concentrating on low attainment among the age-group flowing out of the education system provides an indicator that is amenable to change over a relatively short period. We endorse the use of a flow indicator as proposed by the Commission: the proportion aged 18–24 who have only lower education and are not in education or training. We should however elaborate on the reasons for excluding those currently in education or training. This is presumably because they are assumed to be in the course of acquiring at least the equivalent of upper secondary qualifications. We want to exclude the person who left school at the age of 16 with only a lower qualification but at age 22 entered university on an access course; we want to include the person with only lower secondary schooling who is on temporary training scheme with no qualification at the end of the training or a qualification less than equivalent to upper secondary. In order to achieve this, we therefore propose the following modified version of the Commission's indicator.

Recommendation 16. There should be a Level 1 indicator measured as the proportion of those aged 18–24 who have only lower secondary

education and are not in education or training leading to a qualification at least equivalent to upper secondary.

The use of a flow measure of attainment may be compared with the educational attainment measure included by the OECD in its new set of indicators, which is the education level attained by the working-age population (defined for the purpose as those aged 25–64), distinguishing between below-upper-secondary, upper-secondary, and tertiary. The OECD attainment indicator in effect aims to capture the educational attainment of the whole working-age population, as a proxy for the stock of human capital. This measure will change only slowly, as older cohorts with relatively low levels of education exit and younger ones with higher levels enter.

We understand why the Commission chose to take a flow indicator. A focus on those leaving the education system allows the indicator to be related more directly to policy interventions and outcomes in terms of, for example, retention of students through to completion of upper secondary level. None the less, entirely ignoring the situation of those aged 25 and over will miss a key element in current exclusion. While the indicator suggested by the Commission could indeed serve as the leading indicator of low educational attainment, it would thus be useful to complement it with the proportions in older age groups who attained lower secondary level or less.

We therefore propose a Level 2 indicator of the educational attainment of the working age population. This indicator may be best derived from the regular Labour Force Survey conducted in each country, and converted to a common basis using ISCED. The age ranges do however require some consideration. In the EU Employment Strategy, the age range of 15–64 has been adopted. Here it would make no sense to begin with those aged 15, since they cannot be expected to have completed upper secondary education and in a number of member states compulsory schooling extends to those aged 15, 16, and 17. We therefore take the range 18–64. It should however be noted that, since education continues to provide benefits in terms of leisure activities and social participation, there is case for taking the entire adult population (all aged 18 and over).

Recommendation 17. There should be a Level 2 indicator measured as the proportion of those aged 18–64 who have only lower secondary education or less.

In considering the use of these indicators, we have to bear in mind the problems of making international comparisons of educational attainment. As is noted by the OECD, 'the diversity of education systems and differences in the structure of the governance of education pose a challenge for international educational comparisons' (OECD 1997: 8). Steedman (1999) provides a classification of different interpretations that may be given to the attainment of a specified education level, such as 'upper secondary'. All students completing a course of study may be awarded a certificate or diploma; students may be examined by an external body, and those who pass are classified as having attained the specified level; the external test may be a single grouped examination, which is either passed or failed, or students may pass or fail in individual elements, in which case a number of passes has to be specified. Where there is an external body, this may be public or private. Where it is public, then there may be different ministries involved, or there may be qualifications awarded at different levels of government. These different forms of assessment are relevant in that, in some countries, only certain qualifications may be taken into account, for example those awarded by public bodies.

The problem of defining comparable standards is not new. As Steedman (1999) notes, within most countries there is a long tradition of making judgements about the equivalence of qualifications (for example between vocational and academic baccalaureates). In the UK there is a particularly wide range of qualifications, and equivalences have been developed for use, for example, in determining eligibility for university entrance. Inter-country equivalences are however an order of magnitude more complex, and may make a considerable difference to the ranking of member states. An example is provided by the UK qualification General Certificate of Secondary Education (GCSE), an examination typically taken at around the age of 16. If one defines upper secondary education as commencing at age 14, then the GCSE taken after two years of study may be regarded as reaching Level 3, and hence a person with a specified performance in GCSE would not be classified as suffering 'low education'. On the other hand, GCSE does not qualify people to be admitted to university, so that it is not an entry qualification for the next ISCED category. According to the estimates of Steedman in 1996, this makes a great deal of difference: the proportion of the UK population in 1992 aged 25–64 classified as having lower secondary education or less is 32% on the former basis but 47% on the latter basis (Steedman 1999). The UK is unlike a number of other member states in having a sizeable proportion of those with good academic attainments leaving at 16. This was more common in the past, so that the stock figure is particularly affected. These important issues of classification need more attention than we can give them here, and should form part of the continuing refinement of the indicators employed by the EU.

Other indicators of educational disadvantage

The National Action Plans of member states refer to other indicators of educational disadvantage. Some concern non-attendance at school (Spain and the UK) or school exclusion (UK) or early school-leaving (Ireland and Portugal). Some concern under-performance, such as repeating years (France) or failure to complete a year (Italy and Spain). These relate to the school population. In the case of the adult population and their past school attainment, the NAPincl for Spain suggests taking the proportion who have not completed primary education, which is a more severe version of the indicator proposed above in Recommendation 17. As has been shown by Klasen (1999), there is considerable variation across countries in the proportion of the age group not enrolled in an educational institution at the minimum school-leaving age.

Finally, from a social inclusion standpoint, the concern is not only with the role played by educational attainment in influencing the risk of experiencing poverty and social exclusion, but also with the extent to which access to education is itself structured by socioeconomic status. This issue is raised, for example, in the Belgian and French NAPincl. The NAPincl for the UK refers to the under-representation among university students of those coming from disadvantaged groups. While substantial differences across socioeconomic groups in educational level are seen in all countries, it is extremely difficult to make valid comparisons across countries on a harmonized basis. Studies have sought to make comparisons across countries of social class differentials in both school dropout rates and participation in third-level education. There are serious problems both in measuring social class and in defining what school dropout or third-level education means in very different institutional structures. The structural inequalities these reveal are highly significant from the point of view of social inclusion, but we need harmonized data sources that allow them to be reliably compared and tracked over time.

The ECHP does seek to measure both parents' social class and education level attended for those currently in education, and so in principle would provide a basis for comparing, say, numbers still in school at age 17/18 across the classes. (Information on the student's parents is available, provided the student lives with them.) However, both social class and education measures need to be validated from a comparative perspective and perhaps further developed before they can be relied on, and the relatively small size of the samples also limits the use of this source for making comparisons, for example, of educational participation across classes. For older age groups, focusing on participation by those aged 18–21 or attainment in the immediate post-education cohort, the major gap in the data is that parents' social class is available only for those still living in the parental home. Parents' level of education can be measured reliably in such surveys and could usefully be added to the new EU-SILC from 2003, opening up new possibilities of tracking differential educational attainment that are important for the multidimensional approach to poverty and social exclusion. The reasons for differential access do however need to be probed, including the affordability of education. When considering this aspect, it is essential to distinguish the costs of compulsory education from those of other studies (in particular tertiary education).

Recommendation 18. A significant investment needs to be made in the investigation of indicators, on a comparative basis for use in the EU monitoring process, of differential access to education with a specific focus on parents' level of education and the costs of education.

7.2. EMPLOYMENT AND UNEMPLOYMENT

The National Action Plans on Social Inclusion attach considerable weight to employment. The Finnish Plan, for instance, refers to 'the importance of work as a source of social security and welfare' (Government of Finland 2001: 11). There are similar references in other NAPincls:

Employment and participation in the social community of the workplace is very important to the individual as well as society. This is a precondition for a cohesive society and solidarity between various social groups. (Government of Denmark 2001: 7)

One of the main causes of poverty and social exclusion is long-term unemployment. Work generates economic independence and makes it easier for people to become involved in society. (Government of the Federal Republic of Germany 2001: 6)

Access to employment becomes increasingly important for equal participation, especially due to the diminishing importance of family business. (Government of Greece 2001: 10)

L'emploi est un important facteur d'inclusion sociale. (Grand-Duché de Luxembourg 2001: 26)

A vigorous employment policy is the key to the fight against poverty. (Government of Sweden 2001: 11)

In what follows we take as given the objective of the European Union to raise employment rates, but we note here that there is a case for taking a wider measure of the *contribution* that people make to society. This extends beyond paid work to include caring and other unpaid socially valuable activities. Such an extension would have real meaning for many people, particularly women.

Employment and poverty reduction

Typically, the incidence of poverty is much higher among work-less households than among work-rich households. When poverty rates are disaggregated, the unemployed, and more widely those living in jobless households, are usually found to have higher poverty rates. A study for 16 OECD countries found the average poverty rate for households without earnings from work to be more than 35%, versus an average of around 13% for single-earner households and 3% for double-earner households (Förster 2000). International evidence points to a strong association within countries between individual unemployment and poverty (Hauser *et al.* 2000*a*).

On this evidence, one would expect poverty to drop as more jobs become available. Yet, the relationship between work and poverty is not as linear as it seems, as can be inferred from historical trends and from international comparative research. In many EU countries, growing unemployment in the 1970s and 1980s did not coincide with an increase in poverty (Atkinson *et al.* 1995; Cantillon *et al.* 1997; Förster 2000). Conversely, recent studies have shown that job growth does not necessarily result in a reduction of poverty. Moreover, although unemployment is generally regarded to be one of the principal causes of poverty, comparative international research has demonstrated that there is no linear relation between unemployment in a country (including long-term unemployment) and the poverty rate. Some countries combine low poverty rates with a high level of non-employment, while others register high poverty and high employment rates.

This observation highlights the importance of social protection. Unemployment does not necessarily lead to financial poverty. The fundamental purpose of benefit systems is to provide sufficient income to those who are jobless. As Hauser *et al.* (2000*a*) have shown, differences in poverty risks across countries are heavily affected by the systems of social transfers. Factors affecting the outcome of social benefits in terms of poverty alleviation can be divided into context variables (i.e. characteristics of the unemployed and their families, such as unemployment duration, the number of workers in the family) and institutional features of the unemployment compensation scheme, such as the degree of coverage, the level of benefits, and the combined effects of benefit and tax regulations. To assess the adequacy of social protection schemes in a comparable way, all these factors should be taken into account. As a result, poverty among the unemployed varies according to family status, duration of unemployment, and other circumstances. Poverty risks should therefore be disaggregated by different sub-groups, although sample sizes may limit the degree to which this is feasible. For example, the sample size of the ECHP in most countries is too small to make reliable estimates of the poverty risks faced by lone mothers in long-term unemployment.

Unemployment need not lead to financial poverty where social protection is well designed. Conversely, employment does not guarantee escape from poverty. There are at least two obstacles on the road from more work to less poverty. The first is that additional job vacancies will not necessarily be filled in by members of vulnerable work-poor families. Recent job creation has tended to benefit households with already at least one person in work, not households with no adult in work (Gregg and Wadsworth 1996; OECD 1998). The second obstacle is related to the extent to which 'activation policies' are combined with adequate wages (Marx and Verbist 1999) and adequate job quality. Working poverty is the subject of Section 6.4; we first consider employment quality and dimensions of social exclusion other than financial poverty.

Employment quality and social integration

Employment is important not only because of its potential contribution to reducing poverty. Labour market participation is an important means of social integration: in an individualized society, lack of work holds a danger of social exclusion and detachment from the prevailing life-style and culture in society. According to traditional sociological theory, the foundations of social cohesion consist in mutual interdependencies that are created through work (Durkheim 1893). As work implies cooperation with and for others, it is through work that one becomes aware of mutual dependency and becomes more closely involved in broader and more abstract social relations, whereby the foundations are laid for social cohesion and solidarity. More recently, Sen, in his capabilities approach to individual freedom, has stressed the costs of unemployment that go beyond income loss: 'psychological harm, loss of work motivation, skill and self-confidence, increase in ailments and morbidity (and even mortality rates), disruption of family relations and social life, hardening of social exclusion and accentuation of racial tensions and gender asymmetries' (Sen 1999: 94).

Socio-psychological research has shown repeatedly that both the objective and the subjective well-being of the employed is considerably higher than that of the unemployed. Unemployed persons have more health complaints, they feel more socially isolated, and in general they are less satisfied than the employed (Clark and Oswald 1994; Gallie and Russell 1998; Gallie 1999). Benefit dependency increases dependency on rules and control by often-anonymous bureaucracies (Schuyt 1995). The least well-off citizens also tend to possess the fewest bureaucratic skills, and they often suffer because of this (De Lathouwer and Bogaerts 2000). About a quarter of all the long-term unemployed in Flanders feel desperate or discouraged, and they experience unemployment as truly difficult (De Witte 1992). However, this also means that a large proportion of the unemployed have a much more positive perception of unemployment: almost 38% of the long-term unemployed in the EU15 are not (or no longer) work-oriented (Gallie and Alm 2000). Especially significant numbers of housewives, persons in early retirement, and the disabled tend to regard their non-employment as rather positive (Hoff and Jehoel-Gijsbers 1998; De Lathouwer and Bogaerts 2000; de Beer 2001).

The considerable degree of heterogeneity in how people experience unemployment and economic inactivity cannot be explained (entirely) by differences in income. It would appear that the value that one attributes to paid work *as such* is a more influential factor. Value research has shown that, in all European countries, paid work is still considered as the second most important domain of life—after the family, but more important than friends or leisure time. On the other hand, studies have shown there to be differences in legitimization for not working among certain groups (Hoff and Jehoel-Gijsbers 1998; de Beer 2001). Housewives, the disabled, and elderly unemployed persons feel fewer obligations to work, as a result of which the individuals concerned are affected to a lesser extent by the negative consequences of non-work.

It cannot be assumed that all work offers scope for personal development and social orientation. Semi- and non-skilled workers in particular are often deprived of job characteristics associated with personal development and enhanced opportunities for social participation (learning opportunities, job security, and job satisfaction) (Gallie 2001). Moreover, it is noticeable that individuals feel a stronger desire to develop themselves through work than used to be the case (De Witte 2000). Consequently, quality of work and working conditions are becoming increasingly important. Research into the status of low-skilled labour has shown that the high-skilled get much more satisfaction from work than the low-skilled. Lack of skills leads to a lower professional status, inferior quality of work involving less autonomy, variation, and contacts, lower earnings, and a greater physical burden. This has negative effects on personal well-being and attitudes towards work. Absenteeism, for example, is higher among the low-skilled than among the high-skilled (Pollet *et al.* 2000; De Witte 1999).

Although there are no indications of a general decline in quality of work, the work pace has gradually increased (de Beer 2001). This is the result of increasing competition, technological change, and more professional specialization, whereby 'redundant tasks' (often stress-reducing) are eliminated through rationalization. Besides the quality of labour, the altered context of 'double earnership' is also very important. Today, both partners must learn to cope with increased pressures of work, while the combination of family and work represents an additional burden. The cry for downshifting and the prevalence of stress, absenteeism, and burnout are illustrative of the often-problematic nature of working conditions.

The role of employment in directly addressing social exclusion therefore needs to be interpreted carefully. The extent to which employment offers a solution for social exclusion depends critically on the quality of jobs (Gallie 2001). While we believe that indicators of employment and unemployment are important, they have to be seen in a wider context. As we have noted at the outset, we do not want to underestimate the value of other activities that contribute to society.

Unemployment, non-employment, and underemployment

The longstanding concern about unemployment means that the basic concepts have been extensively discussed. We do not rehearse here the definitional issues, but simply adopt the ILO standard definition (see e.g. OECD 1987: 125): in order for an individual to be considered unemployed, he/she must be without work throughout the reference period, be taking active steps to find work within a specific time frame, and be readily available to start work.

Particular concern attaches to the long-term unemployed. *Long-term unemployment* usually refers to those who have been unemployed for at least one year, and its extent is expressed as a percentage of the total labour force (i.e. the economically active persons, which consist of both people at work and the unemployed). The definition has evolved over time: in 1968 the OECD regarded as 'long-term' unemployment lasting more than six months (OECD 1993: 86). At that time, overall unemployment rates in Europe were much lower, and Sinfield suggests that this may be an example of how, 'consciously, or unconsciously, we can act to redefine and so diminish the apparent scale of a problem as it becomes more intractable' (1981: 95; cited in OECD 1983: 53). The choice of cut-off will affect the relative position of different member states. The significance of the long-term unemployment rate also depends on the labour market institutions. For example, where the unemployed are offered training programmes or subsidized work after a given period, then the clock may be reset. The figures have to be interpreted with these differences in mind.

The overall and long-term unemployment rates in member states can be derived from the Eurostat harmonized Labour Force Surveys. It may also be possible to obtain data from the ECHP, in which individuals are followed over time. In *Employment in Europe* (European Commission 2000c), data are presented on the flows into and out of long-term unemployment. By linking the three ECHP waves for which data existed (reference years 1993, 1994, and 1995), it was possible to track the employment status of individuals over a period of 36 months using a *calendar of activities*, which registers the activity status of the respondent for each month of the year prior to the survey.[1] Data were available for all member states except Austria (only two years of data collection), Finland (only one year of data collection), Sweden (does not participate in the ECHP), and the Netherlands (calendar of activities not included in questionnaire). Dynamic measures of economic activity and unemployment developed by Marlier and Verma from the calendar of activities can be found in Marlier (1999). However, as the ECHP data cover a relatively

---

[1] In the 'calendar of activities', the activity status is provided by the respondent—it is *self-defined* and is therefore not constructed using the strict ILO criteria. For the current year, both the self-defined and the ILO status are available.

small number of people, the possibilities for constructing a comparable indicator on flows are limited. Use of calendar data would allow different measures of long-term unemployment to be developed, such as that described in the Danish NAPincl (Government of Denmark 2001: 54). The long-term unemployed could for example be defined as those who had been unemployed or on training or active labour market program-mes for more than 80% of the time in the previous three years. We recommend that labour market calendar measures be further explored, but in the meantime suggest the following.

Recommendation 19. The overall unemployment rate and the long-term unemployment rate, measured on an ILO basis, should be Level 1 indicators.

These indicators would be disaggregated by gender and by region. There is also considerable concern in the NAPincl with long-term unemployment among youth and among older workers, and it would be useful to have breakdowns for those aged under 25 and those aged 50 and over.

The merit of these unemployment indicators lies in their simplicity and wide use. However, they are either too broad or too restrictive for gaining full insight into the problematic aspects of unemployment and non-employment in terms of social inclusion. *Non-employment* is defined as the sum of the economically inactive and the unemployed, expressed as a fraction of the total of these groups plus those at work. In calculating the economically inactive, we have to decide on the definition of the poten-tially active population. As noted earlier, in the EU Employment Strategy the age range of 15–64 has been adopted. On the other hand, the NAPincl reveal a wide range of opinion in member states, as is illu-strated by the NAPincl for Finland, which takes the age range 25–54 (Government of Finland 2001: 49), whereas the NAPincl for the UK (Government of the United Kingdom 2001: 16) takes 16–64 for men and 16–59 for women. It seems to us that there are good reasons for setting the lower age limit at 18, not 16. As observed earlier, in a number of member states compulsory schooling extends to those aged 15, 16, and 17. At the top end, we can see merits in both 59 and 64. The first of these may be seen as a compromise between those who wish to allow early retirement from 55 and those who would regard 65 as the retirement age (and therefore would choose 64). Choice of the age of 59 has the further advantage that it avoids having to make any distinction between men and women in those countries where the retirement age is 60 for women.[2] On the other hand, 64 would be consistent with the Employment Strategy. We also propose that those aged 18–24 in full-time education (and inactive) be excluded, on the grounds that this is closer to the intention of those who regard the non-employment rate as a performance indicator.

The notion of 'non-employment' includes those who do not—or do no longer—wish to work (retirees, women, and students) and for whom non-work would therefore not appear to be problematic, at least from the perspective of social exclusion. Conversely, the standard definition of unemployment is very strict: only those satisfying the three conditions for being considered to be unemployed (jobless, job search, and readily available on the labour market) are taken into account. Discouraged workers (see below), involuntarily part-timers (see below), and some of those who would call themselves unemployed but who are on special schemes and therefore considered either to be employed or outside the workforce (e.g. early retirement) are not included. Nor do these definitions provide insight into the degree to which people move into and out of the labour force.

Therefore, non-employment and unemployment rates need to be qualified by means of additional indicators. Although 'unemployment' remains the most significant slack in the labour market, one must also take account of the population of *discouraged workers*, i.e. individuals who would like to work but are not seeking employment because they feel that no suitable job is available. They are classified as inactive according to the strict ILO definition, but from the perspective of 'social exclusion' there are good reasons for including an indicator of 'discouraged workers'. It is apparent from research (by the OECD 1987: chapter 6, among others) that a large proportion of discouraged workers tend to remain jobless for long periods of time. In many surveys, the reasons given for being discouraged are lack of skills, education, or qualification. A substantial proportion of discouraged workers appear to have experienced long-term unemployment. Moreover, data for the USA and Australia indicate that discouraged workers who do enter the labour force actually fare worse than other non-participants. In the Eurostat Labour Force

---

[2] A possible compromise would be that each country uses its own official retirement age. Countries where there is no single retirement age would then have to choose a retirement age that best reflects their retirement pattern. As retirement ages vary between member states, it will limit the ability to make meaningful comparisons across Europe. In our view, this approach should therefore not be followed.

Survey, a person not seeking employment because he/she believes that no work is available or because he/she does not know where to find work is identified as a 'discouraged worker' (rather than as inactive). It should be noted, though, that this is a subjective criterion: it is highly dependent on how individuals perceive the questions and, indeed, on the order in which they are put to them.

Under the strict definition of unemployment, a person who works, but for fewer hours than he or she would choose to work, is considered to be employed. Therefore, indicators on *involuntarily part-time workers* (or *underemployed*) are generally added to the conventional definition of unemployment (OECD 1990: chapter 7). The European Anti-Poverty Network (2001) has proposed that the EU indicators should include the percentage of the workforce in non-voluntary part-time employment. In the Eurostat Labour Force Survey, involuntarily part-time work refers to three categories: full-time workers who worked less than their usual hours, part-time workers who worked less than their usual hours, and those working part-time because full-time employment could not be found. In the context of 'social exclusion', it should be noted that not all involuntary part-time jobs are precarious, and they may lead to voluntary part-time or full-time work. However, in many cases they may be a cul de sac. They do not tend to be stepping stones for the unemployed to return to full-time jobs (OECD 1995: 75). The importance of these considerations, especially for women, leads us to recommend including an indicator of the proportion in involuntary part-time work.

Several additional indices of unemployment and underemployment have been put forward to complement the unemployment rate. Almost all of these indicators include discouraged and involuntarily part-time workers: see e.g. the U6 and U7 measures published by the Bureau of Labour Statistics up until 1993, the OECD Jobs Study (OECD 1994*b*) and *Employment Outlook* (OECD 1994*a*, 1995). The index of labour slack adopted by Standing (1999) also takes account of those in employment but on lay-off or not working for economic reasons.

To conclude, we recommend as follows.

Recommendation 20. There should be Level 2 indicators for the proportion of discouraged workers, the proportion non-employed, and the proportion in involuntary part-time work, expressed as a percentage of the total population aged 18–59 (or 64), excluding those aged 18–24 in full-time education (defined as those that are both in education and inactive).

7.3. **JOBLESS HOUSEHOLDS**

Labour market trends are conventionally measured at the individual level. But what matters most from the viewpoint of poverty, economic welfare, and various other aspects of well-being is not so much the labour market status of individuals, but that of households. It has been demonstrated that individual-level employment trends can be very misleading as to what has happened at the household level (Gregg and Wadsworth 1996; OECD 1998). A rise in the employment rate of individuals may mask 'employment polarization' at the household level, i.e. a rise in both the share of households with no person in work and the share of households with two or more persons in work. We therefore propose joblessness at the household level as an indicator. This measure could, in its most rudimentary form, be defined as follows: the proportion of working-age households with no adult in work (employed or self-employed), where a working-age household is defined as a household with at least one person of working age. It may prove desirable, however, to define the class of eligible working-age adults more narrowly, e.g. to exclude full-time students under a certain age.

The Commission proposed in its September 2000 Communication a definition of an indicator of jobless households that would measure the proportion of working-age households with no person in employment, where working-age households were defined as households in which there is at least one person aged 25–55. The definition has however changed over time. The indicator presented to the Stockholm Summit in March 2001 showed the share of households in which no member is in employment as a proportion of households in which at least one person is active. This later implementation gives a different set of households to form the denominator. John, aged 56, living on his own, was excluded from the base in 2000 but included in 2001. His younger brother Peter, also living on his own but aged 53 and early retired, was included in the 2000 definition but not in the March 2001 implementation.

It seems to us that the definition must start from the class of eligible people, a household then qualifying if it contains at least one eligible person. Eligibility includes all persons in paid employment, defined to include employment and self-employment, and everyone else in the population who is not explicitly excluded by the following criteria designed to truncate the beginning and end of the working life, i.e. *excluding*

- children aged 17 and under;
- those aged 18–24 in education and not included in the active population, whether employed or unemployed, using the ILO main activity status concept;
- those aged 60 or over.

The age criterion embodied in the last of these is, as before, a compromise between those who would regard 65 as the retirement age and those who wish to allow early retirement from 55 on as not indicating 'joblessness'. The definition described above will include both John and Peter in the example given, and will continue to include John if he continues work after the age of 60. Compared with the Commission's 2000 version, the proposed definition includes those aged 18–24 who are not in full-time education, all those aged 56–59, and those employed aged 60 and over. It is therefore more extensive than the original definition and the March 2001 implementation. If precedence is given to the upper age adopted in the Employment Strategy, then that could be used instead.

The second departure proposed here is to base the indicator on people not on households. As argued earlier, our basic concern is with the situation of the citizens of the EU, and this leads us to prefer to count people living in jobless households. Here too there is a decision to be made. We could count the total number of people, or we could count the number of 'eligible' people as defined above. The choice depends on the purpose of the indicator: whether it is a generalized measure of contact of the population with the world of work, or a measure of the contact with work of those who might potentially be in the labour force. Here we take the wider concept as applying to the population as a whole, because we are potentially interested in the entire population. Within this group, we are likely to be concerned with sub-populations, such as the percentage of working-age people living in jobless households and the percentage of children living in such households, but our starting point is the whole population. To this end, we begin with the total, N, of all people living in households that contain at least one eligible person (as defined above). N includes everyone, not just those who are eligible—Elisabeth living with two children aged under 14 and a grandmother aged 80 counts as four. We then consider the total of all people, P, living in the subset of these households where there is no person in employment or self-employment or on a government training scheme. If Elisabeth is at home looking after the children and the grandmother, then this family is included, and adds 4 to the total P. The proportion of people living in jobless households is then given by P/N.

In view of the complexity of the definition of joblessness, it may be helpful to give some examples to show how changes in labour market status affect the proposed indicator:

- Elisabeth taking up employment reduces the numerator by 4, but does not change the denominator.
- Elisabeth marrying an employed man from a single household reduces the numerator (by 4) but leaves denominator unchanged (whereas it would have changed a household measure).
- The death of the grandmother reduces both P and N by 1.
- John retiring at age 58 leaves the denominator unaffected but increases the numerator.
- John retiring at age 60 reduces the denominator but does not change the numerator.

If we consider the total of people, P', living in the eligible households where there is at least one person in work or on a government training scheme, then P'/N is the complement of the joblessness indicator (it is $1 - P/N$).

As with the measurement of poverty, issues of timing are important in measuring labour market status. Activity status in the jobless household definition relates to the current status, and this must be borne in mind when considering the relation to household poverty, which in the ECHP is based on annual income in the prior calendar year (see Section 5.4). The link between poverty and joblessness seems to us of interest, and we recommend that a Level 2 indicator be adopted showing the proportion of people living in jobless households with an income of below 60% of the median. But a measure of poverty based on current modified income would clearly be preferable.

It may be objected that households identified as being 'jobless' according to this procedure are heterogeneous—indeed, too heterogeneous to be a meaningful category. Included are young single parents, older women who have never worked, those with disabilities and long-term health problems, and the early retired. The economic circumstances of these groups are very different. This however takes us back to the purpose of the indicator. The indicator is not being advanced as a predictor of financial poverty or as an indication of potential 'activation', but as a measure of contact with the world of work. The fact that lone parents tend to be poor and the early retired tend to be comfortably off is not in contradiction to the fact that both may lack any contact with the labour market. From this perspective, heterogeneity of the group is not an obvious drawback.

To sum up, we recommend the following.

Recommendation 21. There should be a Level 1 indicator of the proportion of people living in jobless households, as defined above, complemented by a Level 2 indicator of the proportion of people living in jobless households who are in receipt of an income below 60% of the median.

The Level 1 indicator would be accompanied by comparable figures for sub-populations, such as those in the eligible population defined above, or children. The indicator should be disaggregated by household types, since the measure of joblessness is clearly affected by the household composition of the population. Countries with more single adult households will, other things equal, tend to have a higher percentage jobless. If work were distributed randomly, say with a uniform probability of 1 in 10 of being not in work, then single (eligible)-person households would have a 1 in 10 chance of appearing, whereas two (eligible)-person households would have a 1 in 100 chance. In empirical terms, an important case is that of single-parent families. Where the sole parent, typically the mother, is not in paid work, the household is treated as jobless. This takes us back to the need to extend the concept of productive contribution.

7.4. **WORKING POOR AND LOW PAY**

The considerations set out in the previous two sections underline the heterogeneity of the circumstances of the unemployed. The employed are also a heterogeneous group. We have argued above that, while the effects of employment on poverty and social inclusion are generally positive, one must also acknowledge that not all jobs provide sufficient means of subsistence. Therefore, from a social inclusion perspective, the proportion of 'working poor' is an important indicator, i.e. the proportion of the employed aged 18–59 (or 64) who are living in households below the poverty line.

The implementation of this measure does however raise a major issue. Put simply, we have to reconcile the fact that the labour market status variable refers to the situation at the time of interview, whereas the information available in the ECHP about household income refers to the income in the previous calendar year. The person may be employed today at a generous salary but have spent much of the previous year unemployed. He may therefore be wrongly classified as working poor. This is an argument for the current modified income proposed in Section 5.4.

Suppose that current income is not available, as in the ECHP (there is a single question on total household income, but this does not provide a reliable basis for measuring poverty), and that income for the previous calendar years has to be used. Then we suggest the following procedure. We limit the analysis to those employees at the time of interview whose calendar of activities for the previous calendar year shows that they were (i) economically active for six or more months and (ii) their most frequent activity status is 'employee'. We refer to these people as 'previous year and current workers'. For this proper subset of current workers, we measure the percentage in households with incomes below 60% of the median.

People may be poor when working for different reasons: because of their household composition (number of earners and dependants), because they work part-time, or because of low hourly earnings. To shed a light on the latter issue, an indicator on low pay can complement the 'working-poor indicator'. This does however raise a number of issues of definition. These issues resemble those discussed when considering the definition of poverty, so that our treatment here can be brief; but they are not identical.

The first issue concerns the earnings measure (see Nolan and Marx 2000: 101). Is it the hourly wage? Is it the total weekly or monthly wage? Do we consider only the basic pay, or do we take total earnings including some or all of bonus payments, commission, shift premia, overtime, tips? How are periods of holiday or sickness to be treated? In order to include part-time workers, it seems desirable to take an hourly measure; and there is a case for taking total earnings in order to avoid differences across countries in payment customs (such as tips or 13-month wages). The second issue concerns the period over which earnings are measured. Are we concerned with low earnings in a single pay period? Is it annual earnings divided by months or weeks or total hours worked? Arguments can be made for some degree of averaging, but a year may miss important periods of economic stress. The third question concerns the population covered. It seems desirable to include part-time workers; and a case can be made for taking a snapshot at a particular date, including part-year workers then in work.

The final issue concerns the low-pay benchmark. There are many types of threshold for measuring the extent of low-paid employment, ranging from the earnings level of one, two, or three deciles of the earnings distribution (Gregory and Elias 1994; Sloane and Theodossiou 1996, 2000) to a percentage of median earnings (Marlier and Ponthieux 2000), or to an absolute level of pay, e.g. based on a poverty standard or a legal minimum wage. A common indicator of low pay is earnings below two-thirds of the median earnings level for a full-time employee. (Alternatively, it may be two-thirds of the mean, as in the NAPincl for Portugal.) This indicator was adopted by the CERC (1991) in its Report to the Commission, among other reasons because two-thirds of median earnings was at that time around the level of the minimum wage in a number of countries. This indicator has been selected by the OECD in the *Employment Outlook* (OECD 1996) and in *Society at a Glance* (OECD 2001*b*). The European Low-Wage Employment Research Network (LoWER 1997) has proposed this standard.

The calculation of low pay from the ECHP has been described by Marlier and Ponthieux (2000). The hourly earnings rate is obtained by dividing the current monthly earnings by the hours worked during the reference week of the interview. We propose that this be calculated for the same population as the working poor indicator. It would be possible to drop the previous year condition and hence extend the population, but this would not allow the two variables to be jointly analysed. We may for example wish to know how many of the working poor have low pay.

To conclude, we make the following recommendation.

Recommendation 22. There should be two Level 2 indicators of (a) the proportion of the 'previous year and current workers', defined as above, aged 18–59(64) who are living in households below 60% of the median (*working poor*), and (b) the proportion of the 'previous year and current workers', defined as above, aged 18–59(64) who are *low paid* in that their hourly earnings are less than two-thirds of the median hourly earnings of all previous-year and current workers.

Quality of employment is not limited to pay. Job stability is an important attribute. The European Anti-Poverty Network (2001) has proposed as an indicator the percentage of workers in stable employment, defined as six months' duration and over. We can see merits in the addition of an indicator on job precariousness, although at an EU level this will require careful definition so as to allow for different institutional arrangements in the labour markets of different member states. Quality of employment depends on the possibilities of training and the opportunities offered for personal development (Gallie 2001). It also depends on the extent of employer-provided services such as child care. A number of these aspects are covered in the NAPincls. For example, the NAPincl for Portugal proposes as an indicator the percentage of workers who have received training; the Irish NAPincl refers to differential access to training, and to levels of security of tenure in employment. We would like to see a systematic analysis of possible indicators of job quality. An important step has been taken in this direction by the European Commission (2001*b*) with a paper on investment in quality.

7.5. WITHIN-COUNTRY VARIATIONS IN UNEMPLOYMENT AND EMPLOYMENT

The Commission has proposed a specific indicator concerned with regional disparities (Commission's Structural Indicator 5), which is now based on the coefficient of variation in regional unemployment rates. However, as already discussed in Section 4.3, we believe the regional dimension to be of general concern. Regional variation is important for the labour market but also for living standards, health, housing, and other social dimensions. It is for this reason that we have proposed systematic regional breakdowns of all indicators where feasible. If this is applied to the unemployment and employment indicators proposed here, then all the ingredients for calculating the within-country variation are available. A separate indicator does not seem necessary, given the prominence that we have already accorded the regional dimension. Moreover, by considering the issue in terms of breakdowns rather than indicators of dispersion, we avoid some of the problems of normative interpretation to which we have earlier referred. A country that reduces its unemployment rate in a region where unemployment was already below average might otherwise find that its labour market performance had worsened.

8

Health, Housing, and
Wider Dimensions

In this chapter we consider indicators to cover the fields of health, housing and homelessness, functional illiteracy and innumeracy, access to essential services, financial precariousness, and social participation. These are all potentially important fields not covered by the Commission's original proposals. In each case, our interest is in indicators relevant to social inclusion. Homelessness for example is clearly a major reason for concern about social exclusion. In the case of health however it is not mortality as such that concerns us, but differential mortality according to socio-economic or other characteristics. One country may have higher mortality than another on account of dietary, smoking, or other behavioural differences, but this does not necessarily imply a problem of social inclusion within that country. Differences in life expectancy across member states are of course relevant to the social cohesion of the European Union as a whole.

8.1. HEALTH

In the area of health care and health status, the use of social indicators is relatively highly developed. Health status indicators have traditionally played a major role in assessing social progress over time and making cross-country comparisons, and a wide range of these indicators is produced by various multilateral organizations such as the World Health Organisation (WHO) and the World Bank. These most often include life expectancy at birth for men and women, infant mortality, under-5 mortality, maternal mortality, and percentage of infants with low birth weight. Life expectancy, for instance, is one of the components in the summary *Human Development Index* of the UNDP (2000), and probability of not surviving to age 60 is one of the components of its *Human Poverty Index-2* for developed countries. Specifically in a developed country context, the OECD has established an extensive health database which is regularly updated and includes measures of health status, numbers employed in health care and beds available, utilization of health services, expenditure on health, financing and remuneration, social protection with respect to health care, and some determinants of health. As far as the European Union is concerned, Eurostat regularly publishes a variety of statistics on population and demography, and has recently introduced a new publication entitled *Key Data on Health* (Eurostat 2001). This contains data for 1985–95 on population, life-styles, risks associated with environment, working conditions, leisure and traffic, health status, mortality, and health care. The regular Eurostat bulletin on what it considers 20 key indicators in the area of 'Population and Living Conditions' includes life expectancy for men and for women, and accidents at work.

This means that there already exists regular information on an unusually wide range of indicators in the area of health that can be used to make aggregate cross-country comparisons. Unfortunately, however, for the most part these are not ideally suited to capture the key aspects of health from the perspective of social exclusion, which is our central concern, as explained above. For this reason, we focus here on indicators aimed at capturing *differences* in health status or access to and utilization of health services by income or socioeconomic status, which do indeed appear highly relevant in the social inclusion context.

Health strategy indicators and targets increasingly seek to incorporate such inequalities/differentials. The World Health Organisation Regional Office for Europe, for example, in its strategy for the new century entitled *Health21*, proposed targets including a reduction in the gap in life expectancy between socioeconomic groups by at least 25%, equitable distribution of the values for major indicators of morbidity, disability, and mortality across the socioeconomic gradient, and assurance that people having special needs as a result of their health, social, or economic circumstances should be protected from exclusion and given easy access to appropriate care. To take another example, the British government's *Opportunity for All* strategy (UK Department of Social Security 1999) includes health-related progress indicators such as reducing low birth weight and hospital admission rates in designated deprived areas, drug use and smoking rates, and death rates from suicide and injury, and increasing life expectancy at age 65. It is developing indicators linked to the commitments made to narrow the gaps in mortality and morbidity between socioeconomic groups. We now look at the types of indicator that might be feasible and valuable in a European Union context, dealing first with health outcome measures and then with access to health care.

Outcome measures

Health outcomes are generally measured in terms of mortality, morbidity (sickness measured according to an agreed classification), and ability to function. The traditional source of mortality data has been administrative records, i.e. death registrations. These are the basis for infant mortality rates, one of the most widely used health indicators in international comparisons, produced by national authorities and collated by Eurostat for EU member states (see Eurostat 2001). The OECD presents infant mortality rates as a health indicator in its recent publication on Social Indicators (OECD 2001*a*). Death registrations serve as the basis for analysing death at different ages by cause, and for estimating life expectancy at birth or other ages (also employed by the OECD and more widely as a key indicator of health status). In many countries these figures have been linked to information on socioeconomic status, either from administrative records or from special surveys, providing the basis for studies of differences across socioeconomic groups in mortality. Inequalities in mortality and morbidity rates across socioeconomic groups and/or social classes have been studied more or less intensively in different EU countries (see e.g. Cavelaars 1998, and Cavelaars *et al.* 1998*a*).

The key difficulty arises in seeking to measure these differentials in a way that allows progress over time to be monitored on a consistent basis across countries. Serious problems arise in trying to harmonize the measurement of socioeconomic differences in mortality across countries and, to a lesser extent, over time. While considerable progress has been made (see e.g. Mackenbach *et al.* 1997; Kunst 1997), it is not feasible at present to construct such measures from administrative data on a comparative basis across the EU over time. It is increasingly possible to study mortality using the data collected in household panel surveys, allowing mortality to be related to economic variables such as income and wealth, as well as to socioeconomic status as measured by occupation. However, only a sufficiently large and long-running harmonized panel survey across the EU would allow in-depth comparisons across member states in socioeconomic mortality differentials. The four-year rotating panel element being considered for EU-SILC would not offer that potential. We regard the lack of evidence about mortality differentials as a particularly serious gap in the knowledge base for indicators of social inclusion. We welcome the information that Eurostat is seeking progress towards harmonized measurement of socioeconomic differences in mortality across countries from administrative sources. This should be a particularly high priority in terms of statistical capacity building.

For the present, it appears that only country aggregates relating to mortality undifferentiated by socioeconomic status, such as life expectancy or premature mortality, can be produced on a harmonized basis across countries. Individual countries can often make some assessment of how these vary by socioeconomic status, although the basis on which this can be done will differ across countries. While such a procedure fails to meet our principle that indicators should be measurable in a comparable way across member states, inequalities in life expectancy are so central to social inclusion that we feel it worth considering this approach as an interim measure while harmonization is being pursued. Concretely, one could combine taking the percentage failing to reach age 65 (premature mortality) as a Level 1 indicator, with requiring individual member states to demonstrate (as a Level 3 indicator) that reductions in premature mortality were disproportionately among lower socioeconomic groups/ the socially disadvantaged.

Registration data may also provide information on morbidity, although the extent to which registration is required may vary across member states. Household surveys provide an alternative source, obtaining information on both self-reported health and income or socioeconomic status, and these have served as the basis for studies of inequality in health status (see e.g. Van Doorslaer *et al.* 1997, Cavelaars *et al.* 1998*a,b*; Fox 1989). The European Community Household Panel contains such self-reported measures of health status and provides for categorization on the basis of harmonized measures of income and, to some extent, socioeconomic status. The indicators of health status refer to self-assessed health and to the presence of chronic conditions. There are systematic differences across countries in the way people respond when asked to assess their own health, which bear little or no relation to indicators such as life expectancy and illness rates. For example, in the 1996 wave of the ECHP, 22% of respondents (aged 16 and over) in Portugal said that their health was bad or very bad, compared with only 4% in Ireland (Eurostat 2000*a*: 112; see also Van Doorslaer and Koolman 2000). The interpretation of what constitutes a chronic illness may also be rather variable, with once again a substantially higher proportion reporting such an illness in Portugal than elsewhere.

None the less, differentials across income or socioeconomic groups are to be seen in these self-reported measures of health. These differentials could provide the basis for a common indicator in this area. Koolman and

Van Doorslaer (2000) have looked at these differentials in the ECHP for 1996. They first standardize each country to the average EU age and gender distribution; they then classify individuals according to quintiles of the distribution of equivalized disposable income of the household in which they live. The top and bottom quintile groups are then compared according to the proportions reporting themselves as being in a less than good state of health, or saying they have a chronic health problem. In the ECHP as a whole, 42% of those in their country's bottom quintile group report less than good health, compared with 28% in the top quintile group, so the ratio has an average value of 1.5. Across countries, this ratio ranges from 1.4 in Spain to 2.2 in Luxembourg. Inequality is slightly lower when the presence of a chronic condition is used as the morbidity indicator, and the ranking of countries in terms of inequality is not identical.

While cross-cultural differences in patterns of response are less of a problem when focusing on differentials within countries rather than the overall percentages reporting poor health or chronic illness across countries, they are still clearly a cause of concern. The same ratio may result from very different absolute levels of perceived ill-health. On the other hand, the ECHP does allow socioeconomic status to be measured in a harmonized way, via income (or indeed, education or occupation). This is in effect the opposite to the current situation as regards premature mortality/life expectancy, where the health indicator but not its variation by socioeconomic status can be measured in a harmonized manner.

We regard the choice between these alternatives for a Level 1 indicator of social inclusion as finely balanced, but recommend that one of them be used for the present while building the capacity to measure differentials in mortality/life expectancy by socioeconomic status in a harmonized way.

Recommendation 23. There should be a Level 1 indicator for health, the EU choosing between either (a) the percentage failing to reach age 65 (premature mortality) but with member states demonstrating (as a Level 3 indicator) that reductions in premature mortality are disproportionately among lower socioeconomic groups, or (b) the ratio of the proportions in the bottom and top quintile groups (by equivalized income) of the population aged 15 and over who classify themselves as being in a bad or very bad state of health according to the WHO definition.

It should be emphasized that we do not envisage the choice being made by individual member states; the same indicator should be used by all member states.

The indicator proposed above is a stock, rather than a flow, measure. An alternative, in the case of the second indicator, would be to consider age cohorts. This would show for example the reported health of those aged 65–74 (sample sizes permitting). Improvements would more rapidly become manifest. However, changes in such an indicator could be quite sensitive to changes in the composition of the population in certain age groups, notably as a result of immigration.

An alternative approach is to examine differentials in mortality or morbidity by geographical areas.[1] The NAPincl for the United Kingdom emphasizes the application of indicators for communities, with the goal of reducing the gap between the most deprived communities and the rest of the country. (Again, these would be affected by changes in the composition of the population.) Such a geographic approach may be seen either as a method of summarizing individual disadvantage or as embodying specific community effects on health and mortality of the kind emphasized by Wilkinson (1996). The extent to which small areas are particular slices of society, rather than a cross-section, has been examined by Berthoud (2001b), who concludes that there is considerable overlap in the income profiles of neighbourhoods. For our present purpose, the use of geographic units faces the problem of comparability across member states that we have already discussed. Such an approach seems a valuable addition to Level 3 indicators.

Mortality and morbidity information can also be combined into indicators of disability-free life expectancy. In *Society at a Glance*, (2001b) the OECD includes estimates of this sort drawn from the OECD Health Data base, collected through an international network and relating to the mid-1980s and the mid-1990s. (The WHO also produces estimates of disability-adjusted life expectancy (DALE) and focuses on this measure as a key indicator of overall population health.) These are presented with the significant qualification that these survey-based estimates are subject to serious measurement problems, largely related to cross-national differences in the definition of 'disability'; and so, while changes over time

---

[1] An example from outside the EU is the study of social inequalities in health by the New Zealand Ministry of Health (2000), which uses a small-area index of deprivation. Variation in mortality across states in the United States has been widely studied—see e.g. the study by Kaplan *et al.* (1996) on the link with income inequality.

can be analysed, they do not allow for a reliable comparison across countries—which means that this approach needs to be developed further before it can serve in an EU comparative context. In addition, from a social inclusion standpoint, it is differences in disability-adjusted life years across groups within a country that are of major interest, and much remains to be done before these can be measured in a consistent manner.

The variation in healthy life-years by socioeconomic status is important in its own right, but it is also instrumentally significant. From a social inclusion perspective, the impact that illness and disability have on ability to participate fully in the life of society is also critical. Those with a chronic illness or disability may well face severe obstacles in obtaining access to schooling, employment, independent housing, and other aspects of participation. This is difficult to capture in a comparable way across countries, given the problems we have discussed in measuring disability in a harmonized way. However, it is worth investigating the use of the EU-SILC to develop measures of the risk of poverty, employment rate, and degree of social isolation for those with disabilities compared with others in their society, focusing for example on those reporting particular types of chronic illness.

Access to health care

As far as access to and use of health services is concerned, differences in the utilization of different types of health care—e.g. hospital in-patient stays, doctor visits, specific procedures—across the income distribution or by socioeconomic group have been examined on occasion in most member states. In a comparative context, some studies have sought to compare the extent of variation across income groups in utilization of health care, notably a series of studies by Van Doorslaer, Wagstaff, *et al.* (e.g. 1992, 2000). Cross-country comparisons of differences in access to or use of health services across the income distribution have to take into account the implications of the fact that health care systems are themselves structured differently—so that, for example, certain conditions may be treated in hospital in one system and on an out-patient basis in another—and that morbidity patterns differ across countries. In a situation where health care has to be funded in part privately, financial barriers may be important. This may apply even where there is subsequent reimbursement. In a situation where there is no rationing by price, there may be rationing by waiting lists.

Failure to access care because of financial constraints is particularly salient from a social inclusion perspective, although it is difficult to measure. The WHO has recently produced a measure of fairness in financing health systems across countries, which is based on how the share of household income going on paying for health care directly or indirectly varies over the income distribution (World Health Organisation 2000). This seeks to capture an important characteristic of a country's health care system, but failure to access care will be missed. It would be possible to use existing information from surveys on health care utilization to investigate the relation to economic and social characteristics. It would also be useful to have questions in the EU-SILC on whether people had been unable, in a specified period, to obtain medical treatment either for financial reasons or because of waiting lists, distinguishing between different types of treatment or conditions. This would require asking a two-part question. First, it would be necessary to ask whether a member of the household had, during a specified period, had a serious medical condition requiring medical treatment which had not received treatment. Secondly, it would be necessary to establish the reasons why treatment had not been received. We recommend that questions be introduced into EU-SILC to serve as the basis for development of a common indicator in this area in the future.

Recommendation 24. There should be a Level 2 indicator on proportion of people unable to obtain medical treatment for financial reasons, or on account of waiting lists, during the previous 12 months.

8.2. HOUSING AND HOMELESSNESS

Housing conditions occupy a central position in poverty research and policy. Unfavourable housing conditions can contribute to social exclusion (ghettos, health problems, stress). Conversely, poverty often manifests itself in sub-standard housing conditions. The purpose of housing indicators is to provide a global and comparative picture of the housing market (macro availability of affordable and adequate housing relative to need, the latter being particularly difficult to measure) and of housing conditions, particularly in relation to poor households (quality of dwellings and the housing environment, price, security of tenure). Therefore, they must be measured in a sufficiently comparable way across member states.

It is asserted in the United Nations Habitat Agenda (UN Centre for Human Settlements 2001) that

adequate shelter means more than a roof over one's head. It also means adequate privacy; adequate space; physical accessibility; adequate security; security of tenure; structural stability and durability, adequate lighting, heating, and ventilation; adequate basic infrastructure, such as water-supply, sanitation and waste-management facilities; suitable environmental quality and health-related factors; and adequate and accessible locations with regard to work and basic facilities; all of which should be available at an affordable cost.

Besides data problems, the main difficulty with developing a limited set of indicators for measuring these aspects in a comparable way is that the concept of 'adequacy' often varies from country to country, as it depends on specific cultural, social, environmental, and economic factors, such as the climatic differences between the North and the South of Europe.

Quality

A number of countries apply standards for the quality of housing. Scotland provides an illustration. It has a statutory *Tolerable Standard*. A dwelling is considered tolerable if it

- is structurally stable (not likely to collapse);
- is substantially free from rising or penetrating damp;
- has satisfactory provision for natural and artificial lighting, for ventilation and for heating;
- has an adequate supply of drinking water available within the dwelling; has a sink provided with satisfactory supply of both hot and cold water within the dwelling;
- has a suitably located water closet available for the exclusive use of the occupants of the dwelling;
- has an effective system for the drainage and disposal of foul and surface water;
- has satisfactory facilities for the cooking of food within the dwelling;
- has satisfactory access to all external doors and outbuildings.

If any one of these criteria is not met, the dwelling is labelled as *Below Tolerable Standard*. A similar standard, referred to as the *Fitness Standard*, is applied in England and Wales. The English Fitness Standard consists of an overall assessment of the dwelling on the basis of criteria such as structural stability, state of disrepair, and dampness. (For a comparison of the English and Scottish standards, see Revell and Leather 2000: 4.)

In the Dutch Poverty Monitor (*Armoedemonitor*) (Social and Cultural Planning Office 2001), which contains a separate chapter on housing, the following qualitative indicators are applied: construction date; presence of shower/bath, insulation, central heating; size of the dwelling; double glazing; too noisy, too small; damp walls or floors, rotten window frames or floors; inadequate heating; too dark; leaking roof; residents' satisfaction with the dwelling. Most of these variables have been incorporated into the ECHP and several of them are likely to be kept in the EU-SILC. Subjective indicators (which are largely culturally determined) are less appropriate than objective indicators, such as the Eurostat Key Indicator 'dwelling with fewer than one room per household member' (overcrowded households) and 'dwelling lacking a flush toilet inside, dwelling with damp walls, ceilings and floors'.

In the National Action Plans on Social Inclusion, a variety of housing quality indicators is suggested, but there is considerable overlap. The Belgian NAPincl proposes as secondary indicators the percentage of people living in housing (i) lacking one or more of a bath or shower, running hot water, inside flush toilet, (ii) with two or more of leaking roof, inadequate heating, humidity and dampness, dilapidated doors and windows, and (iii) having less than one room per household member. It proposes as a key indicator the total percentage of the population living in housing with any one of the problems identified by these secondary indicators (i)–(iii). The French NAPincl identifies the following essential elements: bath or shower room, running hot water, inside flush toilet, adequate heating. The definition of overcrowding proposed in the French NAPincl takes account of the household composition as well as its size. The NAPincl for Finland proposes measures of inadequately equipped housing and overcrowding. The UK NAPincl includes an indicator of 'decent housing' which requires that it not only meets the fitness standard described above, but also is in a reasonable state of repair, provides a reasonable degree of heating, and has modern facilities and services.

Our conclusion is that two key elements in a housing indicator are housing quality and overcrowding. Either of these could serve as the lead indicator. There is some reason however to suppose that measures of the lack of specific amenities and dilapidation are more transparent than overcrowding measures of the kind outlined above. We therefore propose that there should be a Level 1 indicator for the proportion of people who *either* lack specified amenities (such as a bath or shower (these being alternatives), indoor flushing toilet for the sole use of household, and the ability to keep the dwelling at a suitable temperature) *or* have specified faults with the dwelling (such as leaking roof, damp walls or floors, rot in window frames or floors, inadequate daylight, noise from neighbours). There should be a Level 2 indicator based solely on overcrowding, defined in the simplest manner as having less than one room per person ('room' being appropriately defined). This is not ideal, as it fails to take account of surface area, but such information is not available for all member states.

Recommendation 25. There should be a Level 1 indicator on the proportion of people living in households that lack specified housing amenities or have specified housing faults.

Recommendation 26. There should be a Level 2 indicator on the proportion of people living in overcrowded housing.

In considering the further development of these indicators, some of the same questions arise as were discussed in chapters 5 and 6 regarding financial poverty. One significant dimension is time. The indicators proposed refer to housing circumstances at a point in time, whereas the persistence of poor housing is a particular concern. While housing circumstances may fluctuate less than incomes, there is still considerable variation. A family may be temporarily in poor accommodation while awaiting rehousing; alternatively, it may be adequately housed today but fear imminent eviction. A family may be overcrowded at the date of interview because it has relatives living with it on a temporary basis; a family may appear to have enough rooms because some of its members are temporarily absent.

Indicators regarding the *environmental quality of the housing* are less common. In the Dutch poverty monitor (Social and Cultural Planning Office 2001), reference is made to neighbours, traffic, vandalism and graffiti, being mugged or molested, facilities. The ECHP also has some data on this, and so it is likely that the EU-SILC will have such information. These aspects can be further developed, but they would then probably need to be incorporated in existing national housing surveys (if any) rather than in the EU-SILC questionnaire. If that is the route followed, then it will be important to maximize the degree of comparability across member states. In general, this seems to us an area where further research is needed and a substantial investment required in order to arrive at measures that can be used in the EU monitoring process.

Recommendation 27. A significant investment has to be made in the investigation of indicators, on a comparative basis for use in the EU monitoring process, of persons living in housing of poor environmental quality.

Affordability

Affordability is an essential prerequisite for housing. Unless a household becomes homeless or stops paying, housing costs are unavoidable expenses. In principle, for a household, housing costs are determined by price formation on the housing markets and by the choice of the household for a certain level of quality and comfort. To the extent that the element of choice is limited—by relative shortages on (segments of) the housing market, regulation of rents, etc.—housing costs reflects cost differences between households. As noted in Chapter 5, this has led the UK government to measure low incomes in terms of income after housing costs (UK Department of Social Security 2000*a*). As the level of financial difficulty of a household is determined by economic resources on the one hand and costs on the other hand, it is appropriate to give special attention to housing costs as a poverty indicator.

Belgium provides an illustration of the possible importance of this item. While income poverty remained stable in the period 1992–7, housing costs and the cost–income ratio rose considerably more for low-income households than for higher-income households (Van Dam and Geurts 2000). Such an evolution entails an increase in welfare inequality and poverty that should be registered by a set of indicators. The Dutch NAPincl refers to the issue of the acceptability of housing costs, looking at the net proportion of income spent on rent by different groups, and its trend over time (Government of the Netherlands 2001: 9).

However, indicators of the affordability of housing raise many issues. If we begin with tenants, then an indicator can be constructed on the basis of such ECHP variables as the rent (including local taxes)–income ratio. This indicator can be refined by categorizing households according to their housing burden (−10, 10–19%, 20–29%, 30–39%, 40%+). One could also determine the respective housing burdens for the poor and the non-poor, or the proportion of households whose housing ratio is in excess of a critical proportion, such as 33%. In making this calculation, it is necessary to allow for the housing allowances that may reduce the effective housing cost but on which it may be difficult to get reliable information. These allowances are typically complex and they vary considerably across member states. For owner–occupiers, the calculation of housing costs is still more complicated. Where the purchase is mortgage-financed, then one needs to know how this is split between interest and repayment of principal (the interest cost being the element relevant to this calculation, whereas the repayment of principal is in fact a saving). This is increasingly difficult as housing finance becomes more complex, and when there may be social mortgages and tax deduction. For owner–occupiers, allowance has also to be made for maintenance expenditure on the property.

The problems with measuring housing costs, and producing comparable indicators across member states, mean that we do not propose an indicator based on housing cost. In our judgement, this important subject may best be treated initially in terms of rent and mortgage payment arrears. There are institutional differences across countries that may affect the comparability of such a measure (such as the extent to which the rent of social housing is deducted from benefit payments, or housing benefit is paid direct to landlords), but these are likely to be smaller than for housing cost measures.

Recommendation 28. There should be a Level 2 indicator on the proportion of people living in households that have been in arrears on rent or mortgage payments at any time in the previous 12 months, and further work is required on the general issue of housing cost.

Security of tenure is clearly an important issue, but it is hard to translate this into internationally comparable indicators. Moreover, security-of-tenure indicators are difficult to interpret. Obviously, security of tenure is less important to young mobile households than to families with children or the elderly. The security of tenure indicators incorporated in the UN Habitat Agenda include the percentage of owners and percentage of tenants in private or social housing. These types of indicator are largely dependent on the nature of the housing markets in the various member states, some of which have a high home ownership rate, while others are characterized by extensively subsidized private or social rent sectors.

Homelessness

At a micro level, homelessness is an important indicator, and we should not miss the most vulnerable people who are at greatest risk of social exclusion. They are in a variety of circumstances. According to FEANTSA (the European Federation of National Organizations working with the Homeless), which promotes comparative research concerning homelessness in the member states, the homeless population consists of people living on the streets, those living in hostels and other temporary shelters, and people living in various types of insecure and inadequate housing. Information is not easy to obtain.

In France the National Council for Statistical Information (CNIS) decided in June 1993 that methodological research must be devoted to the issue of homelessness, and a working group was established which reported in 1996. A pilot study was conducted (Firdion and Marpsat 2000). Drawing on this experience, in 2001 INSEE carried out a survey of 4,000 people who were clients of homeless assistance programmes or users of services delivered by charities in urban areas (Brousse *et al.* 2001). The survey made use of a diary to avoid the double-counting of those making use of multiple services, but recognized that the sampling method excluded homeless people who did not make use of any service. A further part of the methodological challenge was to take account of non-French speakers and of the problems of surveying those with drug or alcohol addiction.

In other countries, reference may be made to the annual Finnish survey on homelessness, in which is identified a broad range of conditions under which homeless people may be living. It distinguishes between the following categories: persons living outdoors or in temporary shelters; persons living in night shelters or other shelters for the homeless; people living in institutions or institutional homes, either temporarily or permanently, because of lack of housing; prisoners due to be released, but lacking housing; persons living temporarily with relatives and acquaintances because of lack of housing; and members of broken-up families who are in temporary accommodation because of lack of housing. The Federal Government report on *Living Conditions in Germany: Daten und Fakten* (Bundesministerium für Arbeit und Sozialordnung 2001: 205) contains estimates of the number of homeless on an annual basis from 1994 to 1999. In Italy in 1999 the CIES launched an experimental survey of homelessness aimed at providing both quantitative and qualitative data. The survey was designed to count and interview persons in shelters and streets on the night of 14 March 2000. The exercise provided important information on the phenomenon while exposing the difficulties of this approach. (Results were summarized in Commissione di indagine sull'esclusione sociale 2000*a*: 92–5.)

Most of these data, however, are not available for comparison between member states. The ECHP (EU-SILC) does not provide such data, because the methodology excludes homeless people. The only figure that can typically be obtained nationally is the annual number of people who have called on services for the homeless; but these are affected by a number of problems including both double-counting and under-reporting. It is hard to relate such operational data to the underlying population of individuals. Efforts should therefore be made to collect comparable annual data (after agreeing on the definitions to be applied) on: the number of people living in various types of substandard and overcrowded dwellings; the number of people subjected to eviction procedures and therefore at risk of becoming homeless; the number of actual evictions; the number of people who are dependent upon public or voluntary services for the homeless; and the number of people who alternate between staying with friends or relatives, renting furnished accommodation on a short-term basis, and calling on services for the homeless. In this process, it will be important to distinguish between stock (the number of homeless) and flow measures (such as the number of evictions).

Recommendation 29. As a matter of urgency, the Commission should examine different approaches to the definition and measurement of homelessness and precarious housing in a comparable way across member states and see whether a Level 1 indicator can be developed for use in the EU monitoring process.

8.3. FUNCTIONAL LITERACY AND NUMERACY

Literacy and numeracy are of central importance in terms of ability to function within the society, both in terms of work and more broadly; and reliable information tracking their evolution over time could represent a key indicator from a social inclusion perspective. While educational attainment is the more important determinant of earnings in most countries, literacy may have either a direct impact on earnings or an indirect impact via educational attainment. (Evidence for the latter, but not the former, is found for the United States by Dougherty 2000.) Levels of numeracy have been found to have a significant direct effect on earnings in the United Kingdom (McIntosh and Vignoles 2000). Denny *et al.* (2000), using data for Ireland, Northern Ireland, and Great Britain, find a significant impact of a composite measure of literacy/numeracy, but quantitative ability has the dominant role.

The National Action Plans on Social Inclusion refer to literacy and numeracy from a national perspective. The French NAPincl cites statistics on reading difficulties measured when young people register for military service. This provides a snapshot picture. The Spanish National Action Plan on Social Inclusion presents an analysis of illiteracy among the population aged 16 and over (Government of Spain 2001: Annexe 1, pp. 15–16). The rates are considerably higher for those aged 50 and over, and one-half of the illiterate population in Spain are aged 70 or over.

The issue here is to find comparable figures across member states. One major resource is the International Adult Literacy Survey (IALS), a multi-country and multi-language assessment of adult literacy, developing scales of literacy performance to allow literacy among people with a wide range of abilities to be compared across cultures and languages. The first survey was conducted in 1994 in seven countries, while further rounds of data collection brought the total of OECD countries or regions covered by 1999 up to 19.[2] The aim is to survey nationally representative samples, and an overview of the results has recently been produced by the OECD (2000*b*). Literacy was defined by the IALS as measuring a person able to understand and employ printed information in daily life, at home, at work, and in the community. Five literacy levels were used to rank literacy along three scales: prose, document, and quantitative. Results indicated that, in all the countries and regions surveyed, at least one of every four adults failed to reach minimum literacy levels for coping with everyday life and work in a complex, advanced society, as reflected in the lowest two levels. In countries where more than one in five adults had only the lowest of the five levels of literacy (including the UK, the USA, and Ireland), the results were a source of particular unease. In all countries, there were larger skills deficits among older people than among those in their twenties and thirties, mainly because older people have a lower average educational attainment.

In any study of this kind, questions arise about the comparability of the results across countries. Concerns were expressed at an early stage of the IALS about the comparability and reliability of the data and about methodological and operational differences between the various countries. Indeed, France withdrew from the reporting stage of the study and the European Commission instigated a study of the EU dimension of

---

[2] Australia, Belgium (Flanders), Canada, the Czech Republic, Denmark, Germany, Hungary, Ireland, the Netherlands, New Zealand, Norway, Poland, Portugal, Slovenia, Finland, Sweden, Switzerland, the United Kingdom, the United States.

IALS (Carey 2000). Cultural specificity, differences in survey procedures, and criticisms of the statistical modelling techniques led Blum *et al.*
(2001), for example, to argue for 'extreme caution in interpreting results
in the light of the weaknesses of the survey'. Out of the experience with
the IALS has been developed the Adult Literacy and Lifeskills (ALL)
survey. This programme will cover prose and document literacy,
numeracy and analytical reasoning (Statistics Canada and United States
National Center for Education Statistics 1999). It is hoped to sample
around 10,000 adults in a number of countries.

To give a snapshot of literacy and numeracy as young people approach
the end of their compulsory education, the OECD has launched a new
Programme for International Student Assessment (PISA), which is a survey of students' skills and knowledge at age 15 (OECD 2000*b*). It is being
administered in 32 countries, with representation from all EU member
states. PISA covers reading literacy, numeracy, and scientific literacy. The
first assessment was undertaken in 2000, and further surveys, which will
sample between 4,000 and 10,000 students in each country, are planned
for 2003 and 2006. For a younger age group, the Progress in International
Reading Literacy Study (PIRLS) is a 40-country study measuring the
literacy achievement of fourth-grade (age 9–10) schoolchildren. This age
is chosen as reflecting the stage at which children 'move from learning to
read to reading to learn' (Campbell *et al.* 2001: 84). It is being conducted
in 2001 and will allow comparison with the earlier 1991 study of the
International Association for the Evaluation of Educational Attainment
(IEA). A comparison of PIRLS and PISA is given by Campbell *et al.*
(2001: appendix C).

There is a history of international comparisons of the mathematical
attainment of schoolchildren, dating from the IEA study, the *International
Study of Achievements in Mathematics*, of 13-year-olds in 1963–4 (Husen
1967; and see Prais 1993). A second international survey of mathematical
attainments was carried out in 1981 (Robitaille and Garden 1989), and a
further set of tests (the International Assessment of Educational Progress)
in 1990. Both of these covered some 20 countries (Prais 1993: 175, 177).
The International Study Center at Boston College has conducted the
Trends in Mathematics and Science Achievement (TIMSS), measuring
mathematics and science achievements of eighth-grade (13 and 14-year-
old) schoolchildren in 1995 (26 countries) and 1999 (38 countries).

In our view, regular monitoring of the evolution of literacy and
numeracy levels should be given a high priority, and for this purpose use
should be made where possible of the sources described above. This will

necessitate a detailed comparison of the results of different surveys. How far do they present a coherent picture over time? Use of these sources does of course face the difficulty that the coverage of the EU is not complete (for example, Belgium, Spain, Ireland, Austria, Portugal, and Finland are among countries not covered by PIRLS, and only Belgium (Flanders), England, Italy, and the Netherlands were in the 1995 TIMSSS), and our general emphasis is on making use where possible of information already supplied to Eurostat or already produced by the majority of member states for their own use. As we have stressed, a serious consideration in the design of indicators is the minimization of the burden on member states.

It is important to stress that our concern here is with social exclusion, and that, in using the existing international comparative studies, we need to consider how they can be applied to throw light on the link between lack of literacy/numeracy and social exclusion. This is relevant to the definition of the thresholds, posing the same kind of questions as asked of poverty indicators. The definitions of literacy and numeracy, like the definition of poverty, involve judgements. The IALS measure, for instance, is defined as a relative one: the standard applied in judging the capacity to understand printed information reflects the increasing complexity of life and work. But it is not clear how the questions, and the literacy levels, are to be modified over time when evaluating change in literacy. If we follow a panel of people, will we observe some people falling below the literacy threshold on account of the increasing complexity of society? Should we be using objective measures, based on the performance in comprehension tests, or subjective assessments by individuals of their capacity to cope with printed information? Should the same numeracy and literacy standards be applied to the retired (for whom questions about work performance are not relevant) as to those in the labour force? Do we want to attach particular weight to severe problems (the lowest level of literary proficiency)? (The construction of measures analogous to the poverty gap is discussed by Denny 2000.) Do we want to combine this indicator with other dimensions? For example, is a high-earning lawyer socially excluded because he cannot add up?

A major issue in terms of social exclusion is the definition of the unit of analysis. As has been pointed out by Basu and Foster, a literacy rate of $x\%$ among individuals is 'compatible with very different scenarios of the distribution of literate persons across households' (1998: 1733). If the illiterate members of society belong to households where someone else is literate, then their social functioning may be less impeded than if all members of the household are illiterate. We may want a measure of persons in 'literacy-less' households. This of course requires that data be available for all members of the household.

These questions point to the need for consideration as to how the evidence on literacy and numeracy can be used to cast light on social exclusion.

Recommendation 30. There should be investment in the development for use in the EU monitoring process of measures of literacy and numeracy, reflecting their relevance both to skill levels in the labour market and to social participation.

8.4. ACCESS TO ESSENTIAL SERVICES

Social exclusion can arise not only on account of inadequate private consumption or blockage in access to the labour market, but also because people lack access to essential public or private services. In part we have already covered these aspects. A person may be unable to receive appropriate medical treatment because the medical centre is too far away. A child may not be able to complete secondary education because the school is inaccessible. But there is also likely to be a 'bundling' of these considerations which makes it sensible to consider access to services as a separate heading. The closure of the ferry linking an island to the mainland may prevent both the grandmother from attending the stroke recovery clinic and the granddaughter from attending college. Among the services that could be covered are medical services, pharmacy, food shops, banks or financial institutions, police, fire service, education, and public transport.

The indicators of access may be either objective or subjective. The problem with objective indicators is that they are hard to specify in a way that captures the full variety of local circumstances. Distance is a highly relative matter. Perhaps the most obvious variable is the time required to travel to a particular service. This depends on the modes of transport available, which may be reasonable since transport access is one of the key ingredients. The NAPincl for France includes as an indicator the percentage living more than ten minutes' walk from public transport. On the other hand, distance and travel may not be the only barriers to access. Nor is access a simple either/or condition. The issue may be the quality of the service. There may be a local bank, but it may only open in the mornings. There may be a local hospital, but it may not be equipped for major operations. A further problem with this kind of indicator concerns the element of choice. A person may have chosen to live deep in the country, many kilometres from the nearest bank or pharmacy; but we should not consider them as deprived.

The use of subjective indicators avoids some of these problems. It is possible to ask individuals about their satisfaction or dissatisfaction with the access to specified public or private services. But this has the difficulty of interpretation that we have already noted for other indicators. There may be marked cultural differences across member states in expressed levels of satisfaction with access to essential services. This is however the best that we can suggest at this stage. This field is one where we would encourage member states to devise Level 3 indicators that can serve as a laboratory for the wider EU. In the case of essential services, it seems particularly valuable to secure the active involvement of non-governmental and grass-roots organizations in the design of possible indicators.

Recommendation 31. There should be an investigation of the possibility of constructing on a comparable basis, for use in the EU monitoring process, an index of access to private and public essential services.

8.5. FINANCIAL PRECARIOUSNESS

Income is central, but other aspects of an individual's financial situation are also very important in terms of standard of living and quality of life. In particular, the extent to which people can draw on accumulated savings or borrow to meet current spending needs or unforeseen emergencies, as opposed to being already deeply in debt so that financing that debt depletes the resources available to meet those needs, can make a very great difference to the subjective experience of a particular income level. Non-monetary indicators of living standards, of the type discussed in Section 6.3, attempt to capture the impact of broader command over resources, going beyond current income, on the items and activities people feel able to afford and thus on deprivation levels. At this point, however, we consider whether direct measures of savings and indebtedness, and of the subjective assessments by people of their own financial situation, can provide another useful element in a set of social indicators focused on social exclusion.

One possible source is administrative data on indebtedness. The Finnish NAPincl cites figures on the proportion of the population subject to debt recovery. The French NAPincl refers to administrative statistics held by the national bank. The Belgian NAPincl refers to information held by the national bank about the proportion of adults who encounter difficulties in making repayments (4.8% of the population in 2000). As is recognized by the authors, this touches only a part of the problem, and such data are very difficult to compare across countries.

Research on the wealth holdings of households and the wealth distribution has demonstrated the difficulties that have to be faced in trying to get a comprehensive picture of their assets and liabilities, particularly using household surveys. None the less, intensive efforts to do so, particularly when there is scope to over-sample those towards the top of the distribution, have had considerable success (Davies and Shorrocks 2000). In the present context the main aim is much more modest, in that our focus is on the lower reaches of the income distribution, and a complete picture of the assets and liabilities of those households is not required. Instead, the key concern is whether low-income households have some savings to draw on, to act as a buffer against emergencies and shocks, as opposed to no such capacity or indeed significant debts acting as a drain on current income. Even so, this is difficult to capture in household surveys, both because the necessary information can be hard to collect and because the underlying concept is hard to pin down.

Households can certainly be asked in surveys about their level of financial savings in various forms, such as deposits in banks and other financial institutions, and about their debts to financial and other institutions. In focusing on the capacity to draw down savings, it is liquid assets that are immediately relevant, so it may seem reasonable in this context to leave out of the picture whether the household owns its own house—by far the most important type of asset holding throughout most of the income distribution. However, owning a house greatly enhances one's capacity to borrow, which is another way of buffering financial shocks, and so a home-owner with no debt and little or no savings is in a very different position in facing even short-term financial shocks than someone with no house property. Leaving that to one side, the types of asset to be considered liquid still pose problems—stocks and shares can be readily converted into cash, but what about insurance policies, which can be cashed in but only at a significant cost in terms of forgone returns? And what about current accounts, which may not always be purely transactions balances or perceived as such by households?

Turning to debts, we can see that these are if anything even more complex. Debts may be accumulated not only by loans from financial institutions, but also by credit card debt, hire-purchase loans, and loans from moneylenders—but which debts are relevant in this context? Long-term loans such as mortgages may in some sense be regarded as the counterpart to illiquid assets such as housing, but such loans still have to be met out of current income, and they constrain capacity to borrow. And what about term loans or hire-purchase agreements over, say, three years? Short-term debt on overdrafts and credit cards are clearly relevant, but it is not always easy to distinguish the transactions element from the underlying level of debt. And what about borrowing from family or friends? The NAPincl for the Netherlands notes that 'it has proved anything but simple to estimate the number of households burdened with problematic debt' (Government of the Netherlands 2001: 8).

Detailed and reliable information on a wide range of assets and liabilities is required to get a picture of the net indebtedness or asset position of each household, even concentrating on shorter-term assets and liabilities; and having obtained such information, the implications can be difficult to tease out. At present there is no source for such information on a comparative basis across EU countries, and a comprehensive battery of questions on assets and liabilities also seems beyond the likely capacity of EU-SILC. It may then be more productive for current purposes to try to capture households' own subjective assessments of their financial situation—accepting that this type of information also has to be used with great care. A good deal of experience has been accumulated in trying to tap such assessments in household surveys, and the ECHP itself currently includes a range of questions that provide some basis for investigation of their usefulness in a comparative EU-wide context. With this range of questions, the focus also broadens from savings/debts to the way households perceive and feel about different aspects of their financial situation.

No direct question about the level of savings accumulated, or other assets, is asked in the ECHP, although in measuring income the amount received in interest or dividends is sought. As far as debts are concerned, respondents are asked whether the household has debts from hire-purchase or other loans, apart from housing and credit card debts, and whether these are a heavy financial burden. They are also asked whether housing costs are a heavy financial burden, and whether the household has been in arrears at any time in the previous 12 months on rent, mortgage, utilities, hire-purchase, or credit cards or other loans, and on hospital or medical bills. It would be possible to use this question, either combining housing arrears (see earlier recommendation) with other debts or treating separately utility bills and hire purchase debts. Another question that could help to capture financial precariousness is whether financial assistance has been received from charities. It would also be possible to make use of information on persons subject to debt recovery (as in the NAPincl for Finland), although institutional differences across countries mean that comparisons across member states are likely to be difficult.

Results produced by Eurostat bring out the complexities in interpreting and using responses to these types of question. The percentage reporting that they experienced great difficulty in 'making ends meet' varied across countries from only 2% in Germany up to 22% in Greece (Eurostat 2000*b*: 90). In each country, those below relative income poverty thresholds were much more likely than others to report such difficulty, but only a minority of the income-poor reported having great difficulty, and over half those reporting such difficulty were not income-poor. (Focusing on those persistently below the relative income thresholds for 1994–6 did not substantially widen the gap.) Very much the same pattern was seen when focusing on the percentage of households having been in arrears on utility bills or housing costs. The overall percentage reporting such financial difficulties ranged from 2% in the Netherlands up to 28% in Greece (Eurostat 2000*b*: 33), and those below relative income thresholds in each country were a good deal more likely than others to report having been in arrears. However, once again, a majority of those experiencing arrears were not income-poor, much less persistently income-poor.

The comparison between these two indicators also revealed some interesting patterns. For example, in Spain and Portugal the income-poor were much more likely to report great difficulty making ends meet than being in arrears, whereas in the UK and Belgium the opposite was the case. Comparing Ireland and the UK, the overall percentage reporting experience of arrears was similar in the two countries but the proportion reporting great difficulty making ends meet was twice as high in the UK. Across the member states, the likelihood of reporting either form of financial difficulty was related not only to income but also to both age and labour force status, tending in general to be lower among the elderly and higher among the unemployed and inactive of working age. All this points to the need for considerable caution in interpreting and using such measures of financial strain. Within countries, they do appear to be related in a systematic way to factors such as income and labour force status— indeed, analyses incorporating non-monetary indicators of deprivation show that financial strain is particularly strongly related to deprivation levels, even more than to income (Whelan *et al.* 2001). Measures of financial strain thus help to validate the notion—discussed in detail in Section 6.3—that household income can usefully be combined with such deprivation indicators to identify those most at risk of poverty and exclusion.

There are, however, two serious drawbacks to using such measures as independent indicators of social inclusion in a EU context. The first is that they cannot necessarily be interpreted in the same way across different countries. This is true both because linguistic and cultural differences can affect the way questions will be answered, and because institutional differences may influence (for example) the extent to which households can go into arrears or run up overdrafts. The second reason for caution is that many of those reporting severe strain are in the middle or even upper parts of the income distribution. This in itself is not surprising, since we are measuring a different dimension of the financial situation. Strain/burden is assessed subjectively by survey respondents relative to their own customary living standards and expectations. Households in the middle of the income distribution may feel under severe financial pressure, and indeed have objectively high levels of indebtedness. Even in the case of an indicator such as being in arrears, the overlap with other measures of poverty and exclusion will be limited. It would then be hazardous to interpret trends over time in subjectively assessed financial strain, or indicators of financial pressures such as indebtedness and arrears as reflecting the situation of those experiencing or at risk of social exclusion. A decline over time in numbers reporting great difficulty making ends meet, for example, could be achieved by an improvement in the situation of households in the middle of the distribution, leaving those towards the bottom actually worse off in relative terms. This points to considering the *intersection* of those who both have low incomes and are suffering financial strain. One could track levels of the financial strain among those otherwise identified as experiencing poverty or exclusion—below relative income poverty lines, for example—or the gap between them and the rest of the population; although, if other characteristics such as age have an influence on subjective assessments, then a way of controlling for such composition effects might be required.

At this point, further investigation is clearly needed as to how best to use the measures already available, notably in the ECHP, to monitor changes over time in a comparative context. In addition, consideration needs to be given, in designing the new instrument EU-SILC, as to whether there are other measures that would tap more directly into the financial precariousness of the households in which one is most interested from a social inclusion point of view. Our point of departure was whether households were in a position to draw on accumulated savings or borrow to meet current spending needs or unforeseen emergencies, as opposed to being already deeply in debt. It is worth considering the inclusion of a question that has been employed for example in Scandinavian surveys, which asks respondents directly whether, if they needed to, they could raise say 1,000 euro for an emergency—and if so, whether this would be by drawing down savings, borrowing from a financial institution, or getting help from family and friends. This might provide some additional information on which to track trends in the extent to which those on low incomes in particular must rely purely on those incomes, and how vulnerable they are to financial shocks. (It would also be related to access to financial services.)

Recommendation 32. There should be a Level 2 indicator of the proportion of the population living in households that would be unable in an emergency to raise a specified sum, where that sum should be related to the average monthly household income in the member state.

8.6. SOCIAL PARTICIPATION

Social participation is an aspect of social inclusion, and one that has been receiving increased attention from both researchers and policy-makers. Indeed, a central theme in the literature on social exclusion has been the emphasis on relational aspects: the damaging impact that unemployment and poverty can have in terms of social isolation, going beyond income and living standards (see e.g. Room 1995; Silver 1994; Paugam 1996). Social participation has also recently been highlighted in the context of the burgeoning literature on social capital, given impetus by the work of Putnam (2000) in the USA. It therefore seems important to consider whether indicators in this area could form a useful component of the overall set of social indicators to be used at EU level.

Social participation has long been of interest to sociologists. In addition to intensive investigation of small groups and communities, it has been measured in large-scale household surveys using a variety of questions. The latter focus for example on frequency of contact with family, neighbours, and friends, membership of clubs and voluntary societies, and participation in the activities of churches, trade unions, and political parties. Studies have looked at the relationship between participation, measured in these terms, and characteristics such as age, gender, marital status, labour force status, household income, and social class. In addition, an important focus of the recent literature on social capital has been the attempt to measure changes over time in the extent of civic participation, through formal membership of civic organizations, volunteering, and involvement in the political process, and also through participation in informal networks such as interacting with friends. (Indeed, it was the decline in a wide range of such indicators over time in the USA, highlighted by Putnam (2000), that has given much of the impetus to the interest in social capital.)

As Gallie and Paugam (2000) point out, the issue of social integration, or its converse, social isolation, has in many ways been at the heart of the concern with social exclusion. Much of the general discussion of social exclusion has been premised on the belief that there is a strong link between unemployment and social isolation, but this has not in fact been confirmed as a widespread or generalized phenomenon by empirical research. The classic interwar study of the impact of unemployment (Jahoda *et al.* 1933) did indeed suggest that unemployment led to the collapse of people's local social networks and their withdrawal from the life of their communities, and found that this could not be attributed simply to lack of income, as people stopped participating even in free activities. However, this has not been confirmed by postwar studies of unemployment. Paugam and Russell (2000), for example, used results from the first wave of the European Community Household Panel, which includes a series of questions on contact with family, friends, and neighbours and on membership of clubs, to look at the effects of unemployment on social isolation. They found no consistent evidence that unemployment was in itself an important factor in reducing people's social networks (except in the case of France), in the sense of either reducing the frequency of people's contacts with neighbours and friends, or leading them to drop out of community organizations. Indeed, in many countries the unemployed tended to be more sociable than those in permanent jobs.[3] As Gallie and Paugam conclude, this sharply contradicts theories of the effects of unemployment that were based on evidence about the interwar period.

Their findings also highlight a key broader pattern emerging from comparisons across the EU countries: patterns of sociability and

---

[3] Longitudinal analyses show this to be related to characteristics such as age and marital status.

participation in associations and other organizations vary substantially between countries, reflecting longstanding cultural differences. Levels of informal sociability are much higher in the European South than in the North, while the opposite is true for participation in formal organizations.

People in different countries thus experience unemployment or poverty in very different social contexts. While only about one-fifth of Dutch adults spoke to their neighbours on most days, for example, the corresponding figure for Italy was nearly one-half. Conversely, while about 60% of Danes participated in some type of club or organization, that figure was less than 20% in Italy. It is therefore possible that comparability across countries may, paradoxically, require the questions to differ across member states. To take a simple example, eating out in a restaurant in one country may be equivalent in another country, in terms of participation, to going to a friend's house for a meal.

Both the extent of cross-country differences in sociability and participation, and their limited relationship with income poverty, are brought out by more recent results from the ECHP produced by Eurostat (2000*a*). These show that in 1996 about 6% of adults in the EU countries covered by the survey reported infrequent (if any) contact with friends and relatives not living in the same household. However, in France, Belgium, and Portugal this figure was about 10%, whereas in Ireland, Greece, and Spain it was 2% or less (Eurostat 2000*b*: 105). Those below relative income poverty thresholds in each country did not consistently report less contact: in some countries this was the case (notably France), but in others there was little or no difference (notably the UK, Ireland, Greece, Spain, and the Netherlands).[4] Concentrating on those persistently on low income—below relative income thresholds in 1994, 1995, and 1996—did not substantially increase the distinction between poor and non-poor in terms of the percentage reporting infrequent contact. The relationship between infrequent contacts and age was considerably stronger than the relationship with income. Whelan *et al.* (2001) also use data from the first three waves of the ECHP and demonstrate the very limited relationship between persistent income poverty and both the percentage reporting that they talk to neighbours less than once a week, and the percentage meeting people outside the home less than once a week. As far as

---

[4] Furthermore, Whelan *et al.* (2001) point out that the format of these questions in France differed from elsewhere, perhaps explaining the apparently higher levels of social isolation there.

membership of clubs or organizations is concerned, they show that on average those in persistent income poverty are less likely than others to be members, but the degree of correlation is generally modest.

Comparative information on membership of groups and organizations is also available for the countries participating in the World Values Survey, and this is among the indicators of social inclusion in the set recently produced by the OECD (2001b). This covers the period around 1990 and for some countries around the mid-1990s, and shows once again the extent to which this form of participation varies across countries and, within countries, by age and gender. The distinction is also drawn between groups to which a respondent belongs, and those in which he or she is an active member. To give an example, Dutch respondents reported membership of more than two groups on average, whereas in Spain the average was less than one-half. Only a minority were active participants in each case, but the proportion active was higher in Spain so the gap between the countries was much narrower.

The other indicator presented by the OECD in this context is the proportion voting in parliamentary elections. This is based on administrative data and post-election surveys collated by the International Institute for Democracy and Electoral Assistance, allowing comparisons both across countries and over time. Some countries (such as Belgium, Greece, Italy, and Luxembourg) have compulsory voting, and there are persistent differences across countries in turnout that do not bear an obvious relationship to other aspects of societal well-being. It is therefore difficult to know how to interpret both the indicator of group membership/activity and voting in a comparative perspective, let alone variations over time.

It is certainly valuable to be able to assess the extent of social participation versus isolation in member states and its variation across groups within the population, and surveys such as the ECHP can provide a basis on which to do this. In framing indicators from a social inclusion perspective, however, this information would clearly have to be used with great care, since there are substantial differences across countries in average levels of participation, which one would be uneasy about interpreting as simply 'better' or 'worse'. Average levels of social participation thus conflict with one of the principles for social indicators we raised earlier, which was that they should have a clear and widely agreed normative content. (They may very well also fail to meet the criterion that they should be responsive to policy interventions.) The fact that in many countries little or no difference is found between the income-poor or unemployed and the rest of the population in terms of these measures of participation also raises questions. It may be that social participation is an aspect of social inclusion orthogonal to income and employment, or it may be that the measure needs to be qualified. In a sense, it is the underlying 'quality' of social networks and participation, rather than for example frequency of contacts or membership of organizations, that one would most like to capture—though even then, defining quality quickly becomes problematic. For example, for an unemployed person, contacts with other unemployed people may be perfectly satisfactory from a purely social point of view, but they will have limited value in terms of job search—so they are of lower quality only from a labour market integration perspective, not in some more general sense. Despite these complexities, it would none the less seem worthwhile to track the risk of social isolation over time. To find the best way of doing so, further investigation would seem warranted of the range of other factors one would want to control for (notably age) and how best to do so in a consistent manner across countries.

One form of participation where cross-country differences may be less salient simply because it is a very recent phenomenon is that of access to the Internet. This dimension is raised in the NAPincl for, among others, Belgium, Spain, and the United Kingdom. The global nature of the Internet may mean that its social significance transcends national boundaries. We therefore suggest that there should be further investigation of the extent to which people who wish to access the Internet are unable to do so, and whether this constitutes social exclusion.

The definition of access does however require some care. The indicator proposed by the Commission under the 'Innovation and Research' heading in its 2000 Communication on indicators (European Commission 2001a) is the number of Internet online active accounts per 100 habitants, but this covers both residential and business users. Approached from the side of households, it would be straightforward to ask in a household survey whether or not a household has an Internet connection, e.g. a modem or an Ethernet connection, together with an Internet access provider. But this cannot be directly translated into individual access. Effectively, the children may have access but not the parents. Conversely, the existence of Internet cafes and other external suppliers means that people may have access but not at home. They may well have access at work. A more appropriate question may be to ask whether an individual has access and if so whether he or she does accesses the Internet on a regular basis. Moreover, one may want to distinguish between e-mail and other Internet usage.

Any such indicator would have to be broken down by age, in view of the likely differences in use. However, we would not wish to see the indicator limited to the young, or to the working population. For the elderly, the Internet may offer a significant means of social participation, particularly when their mobility is limited. A housebound grandmother may be able to share in family life via e-mail and via the downloading of pictures of her grandchildren. Enforced exclusion from such an opportunity, by lack of skills or lack of money, may be an increasingly important concern.

Recommendation 33. There should be investigation of comparable measures, for use in the EU monitoring process, of social participation, including individual access to and usage of the Internet.

9

Coordination at the European Union Level

This book is concerned with social indicators for use as part of the EU policy of promoting social inclusion. In this chapter we consider the process by which these indicators can influence the development of the Social Agenda. This means that we now consider their relation with policy. Whereas the indicators have so far been considered as measures of performance in the social domain, for member states to make progress in combating poverty and social exclusion, they have to devise appropriate strategies. The Commission in turn has to be able to evaluate the relation between these policies and the targets set in the National Action Plans on Social Inclusion, as part of its work in preparing the Joint Report on Social Inclusion.

The first round of NAPincl will no doubt influence the subsequent consideration of social indicators, not least with regard to their practicability. At the same time, it is clear from our review of member state experience in Chapter 3 that, in a number of fields, even before the Heads of State agreements at the Lisbon and Nice summits, member states were coming to think along similar lines. Common concerns with social cohesion, associated with an increasingly common approach to the globalizing economy, are leading member states to address similar issues and to measure social progress in ways that look increasingly familiar across national boundaries. There are important differences of emphasis, and we should not exaggerate the degree of convergence in thinking, but the social policy dialogues of different member states are now sufficiently similar for there to be a fruitful common discussion. There is a great deal of scope for the cross-fertilization of knowledge.

We assume that the annual *Synthesis* report will draw extensively on the NAPincl (to be submitted every second year: 2001, 2003, . . .) and on the Commission's rich databases of statistical information for the common indicators (as already presented in Stockholm). The Commission's own synthesis of this information is, we believe, of great importance, particularly since the NAPincls are less structured than the National Action Plans on Employment. Ideally, it will (i) combine (and possibly reconcile) the information on social indicators contained in the NAPincl and the Commission's own databases; (ii) evaluate the likely impact of policy developments described by member states and their relation to the national targets set out in the NAPincl; and (iii) consider the future development of social indicators. These three elements are now discussed in turn.

9.1. USE OF INDICATORS IN NATIONAL ACTION PLANS ON SOCIAL INCLUSION AND BY THE COMMISSION

The evaluation of the National Action Plans is now a core activity of the Directorate General (DG) for Employment and Social Affairs of the Commission. The Commission will no doubt wish first to verify how far the values presented for different indicators in the NAPincl coincide with those in its database. There are therefore strong reasons to encourage member states to use EU-harmonized sources where these exist. Where member states have drawn on alternative sources, there may be differences. Member states may for instance have more up-to-date information from national sources than from the ECHP. We understand that the process of validation being adopted is similar to that for National Action Plans on Employment, with statistics in the NAPincl being checked by Eurostat and a position then agreed following written comments and bilateral meetings with each member state. As we have already stressed, we believe that the reconciliation of differing figures is a crucial task. Such reconciliation is a time-consuming process, but the process of social reporting will be credible only if EU indicators are coherent with those available nationally.

Member states have presented in their NAPincl other indicators of social inclusion, and the Commission will want to examine these, both to see what they show about the member state in question and to ask whether they can usefully be applied to the EU as a whole. Such innovations will certainly be one of the sources of ideas about new indicators to be adopted by the EU as a whole. A positive approach to such country-specific indicators will aid the acceptance of the overall process in member states.

9.2. **POLICY AND NATIONAL TARGETS**

Member states have been asked to set specific targets for social inclusion, indicating the progress expected as a result of national policies. In evaluating these plans, the Commission will have to consider (i) the likely evolution of the chosen indicators in the absence of policy changes and (ii) the impact of the national policy.

The starting point is the level of the indicator as currently reported. Realistically, delays in data availability mean that, for many social inclusion indicators, countries will be reporting on the position some years in the past. This is the first source of difficulty. Values of the indicator may have changed in the meantime even if there has been no change in policy. Social indicators are subject to a wide range of influences apart from policy. The development of poverty rates is to a large extent the result of circumstances and developments beyond the reach of social policies. Examples of such developments are socio-demographic change, such as the ageing and individualization of the population, economic growth, and employment. In other words, poverty may increase in spite of all policy efforts.

The current value of indicators may also have changed on account of policies introduced in the past. This means that the updating exercise in itself involves modelling policy. While in some cases a distinction is drawn between policy simulations and forecasting models, what is needed here is a combination of the two elements. The Commission needs to be able to update values of the indicators taking account of the changes in both external circumstances and policy parameters. This is going to require a micro-simulation model covering all member states. It requires that the model use harmonized procedures, in that it treats member states in the same way, since otherwise differences in conclusions may owe more to model construction than to real-world differences. The forecasting of 'pre-policy' values of social indicators is not easy, and the appropriate techniques will vary from one indicator to another. An example of such a model, covering the poverty rate and income distribution indicators (although not poverty persistence) is the EUROMOD model of taxes and social transfers (Immervoll *et al.* 1999; Sutherland 2000*a,b*). This allows the Commission to examine the likely impact of policy measures reported by national governments in their NAPincl. An example is the impact on household incomes of improvements in in-work benefits. Ideally, one would like to go beyond this impact calculation and consider predictions of the behavioural changes that may be induced.

The simulation of policy change is the ultimate objective, but an important intermediate step is the analysis of policy changes themselves. It is here that indicators of policy effort become important. Our focus on outputs rather than inputs has meant that we have not considered policy indicators in earlier chapters, but they come into their own when we seek to make the link between social inclusion and appropriate social strategies. A methodology can be developed that allows annual updating and international comparison of policy efforts, i.e. the input of policy, both on the macro and the micro level. In order to allow cross-national comparison, we may make use of the existing cross-national databases. These include the Commission (ECHP, Social Accounts, Digest of Statistics on Personal Protection in Europe, MISSOC), the ILO (The Cost of Social Security), the OECD (Social Expenditure database) and the US DHHS (Social Security Programs throughout the World). But the analytical tools also need to be developed. Description of benefit systems is not sufficient. Calculations have been made for model families on a comparative basis by the OECD in a number of studies and by the European Observatory on National Family Policies (Ditch *et al.* 1995*a,b*, 1996*a,b*, 1998). Such findings for model families need to be related to the observed distributions of families (as in the ECHP); the survey evidence needs in turn to be related to the aggregate spending figures.

Critics of social indicators are concerned that their adoption by the European Union will distort the pattern of social policy towards those fields covered by the indicators and away from other, equally important, areas of social concern. Cynics note that the use of performance targets by Communist planners was widely held to have distorted production systems, and that, at the level of individual remuneration, performance measures are not universally regarded as a success. We recognize that one important risk with the use of indicators for social inclusion is that they will lead national governments to design policy to achieve the numerical target to the detriment of other social goals. A country could for example redesign its transfer system to concentrate benefits on those below 60% of the median, at the expense of those just above this level. Not only would such a reaction raise issues of distributional justice, but it would also be perceived as unfair. (It may also generate a poverty trap, as the withdrawal of benefit from those above 60% of the median would mean that they gained little from additional earnings.) Alternatively, and more cynically, a country could recast its activities so that statistics record an improvement while no real change has occurred.

To this criticism we have two responses. The first is that social indicators require a degree of political commitment, and that they cannot work effectively if member states follow them according to the letter but not the spirit with which they are being introduced. By accepting the process of open coordination, member states have accepted a responsibility to take the process seriously. The Commission in turn has to be in a position to reject a National Action Plan on Social Inclusion in the (one hopes, unlikely) event that it does not consider that the plan provides a fair and reasonable picture.

The second response, which is why we raise the issue here, is that we believe that the Joint Report on Social Inclusion should consider this issue when reporting on national plans. Here again the role of the Commission is crucial. The Joint Report on Social Inclusion should place each NAPincl within the context of the whole thrust of social policy in the member state, and should indicate any situation in which it believes that the improved performance in terms of the chosen social indicators is being achieved at the expense of other social goals. While the report is 'joint' with member states, this jointness should be interpreted as involving member states as a whole, not only a series of bilateral compromises with national governments. It is the Commission's responsibility to safeguard the credibility of the process, so that it retains the confidence of EU citizens.

9.3. DEVELOPMENT OF INDICATORS AND MOBILIZING ACTORS

The development of indicators is a dynamic process. Indeed, this book is part of such a dynamic, responding to the first set of structural indicators proposed by the Commission and suggesting further developments. There are several routes by which new ideas for indicators may emerge. As already noted, member states have presented other indicators of social inclusion, and the Commission will want to examine these to see whether they can usefully be applied to the EU as a whole. The Commission itself will no doubt devote time to reflection on the development of new indicators. The Social Protection Committee and its Indicators Subgroup will also clearly play a central role in continuing these developments.

In the development of indicators, the European Union will no doubt wish to collaborate closely with international organizations engaged in this field. We have referred extensively to the work of OECD in fields such as the labour market and educational attainment and to the WHO in the field of health. Duplication of effort should be avoided, and, as far as possible, there should be adoption of common definitions. The uses of social indicators may differ, and this means that some variation in definitions is probably inevitable, but close cooperation should ensure that unnecessary differentiation is avoided.

One important reason why the indicators will need to be revisited is that the EU is in the process of enlargement. Consideration needs to be given to the implications of the entry of a new group of member states, such as any request to the accession countries to draw up National Action Plans for social inclusion. At present, issues of social inclusion do not appear to have been at the forefront of concerns in the consideration of enlargement. For example, poverty receives little attention in the annual Commission reports on the progress of applicant countries (Micklewright and Stewart 2000*b*, 2001).

The evolution of the European Union will also lead us increasingly to ask about the social cohesion of the Union as a whole. Concern about regional disparities within member states has a natural counterpart at the EU level, which is the difference in national average living standards and in 'the quality of European citizenship in all its facets', as it was put by the European Commission in its *First Report on Economic and Social Cohesion* (European Commission 1996: 46). Convergence between member states in average income per capita has long been a key focus for policy at the European level, and convergence in other dimensions is attracting increasing attention. There is a good case for the Commission being asked to provide a report on social inclusion that views the EU as a whole. A valuable model in this respect is the report on the convergence of child welfare across member states produced by UNICEF (Micklewright and Stewart 1999, 2000*a*).

Consultation

The fourth objective agreed at the Nice Council was 'to mobilize all relevant actors'. To date, the process of indicator construction has been conducted largely by the Commission and by representatives of member state governments. The Commission has made efforts to involve stake-holders, including the organization of a series of bilateral seminars on the social inclusion process, but it remains relatively little known. This has been inevitable in the first stage, but it is now important to increase still further the efforts to engage a wide range of social actors. Consultation with social partners, with non-governmental and grass-roots organizations, and with academics will not only help disseminate knowledge but also allow the indicators to be refined. It is to be hoped that member state governments will carry out such consultations, as a number have already done as part of drawing up their National Action Plans, for example, the Finnish working party held two hearings for third-sector organizations and other interest groups; the Irish government placed an advertisement in national newspapers inviting submissions and organized a Round Table at the request of the community and voluntary sectors; the Belgian NAPincl, following the model of the earlier *General Report on Poverty*, sought to carry on a dialogue with the excluded and the organizations that speak for the poor.

In these consultations, we would place particular emphasis on 'a better inclusion of the excluded in all kinds of actions, not as passive participants but as active actors' (Vranken *et al.* 2001: 5). As put by the European Anti-Poverty Network, 'the best indicators are those which gauge changes in the everyday lives of people living in poverty and social exclusion. Such indicators can only be defined through a participatory method which involves a close cooperation between them and researchers' (EAPN 2001: 3). The need for a participatory approach to the measurement of human development has long been argued by non-governmental organizations—see e.g. ATD-Quart Monde (2000) and Oxfam GB (1998), and the programmes of the ILO (Rodgers *et al.* 1995; Figueiredo and de Haan 1998). As emphasized by Bennett and Roche (2000), industrialized countries can learn from the experience of developing countries. This is especially important where government itself may be a source of social exclusion, for example, in the way in which it administers social assistance or determines access to public services.

Such an involvement of a wide range of actors at a member state level may lead to new Level 3 indicators being proposed. The process should also feed into the design of Level 1 and 2 indicators for the EU as a whole. We have for instance recommended exploration of medium-term alternatives to the relative income poverty measure. To take an example from outside the EU, the New Zealand Poverty Measurement Project (Waldegrave and Stephens 2000) has shown how a focus group methodology involving a series of meetings with low-income families can illuminate the definition of a minimum adequate level of household expenditure. As these authors recognize, there are problems in interpreting the evidence, and we have discussed some of the issues when considering subjective approaches to the measurement of poverty. Where the poverty line should be drawn is a matter to be decided by a society as a whole, but those on low income have a particular contribution to make in terms of their experience of the implications of different levels of income. A participative approach of this kind will contribute to greater transparency and hence to ensuring the legitimacy of the process.

Executive Summary and List of Recommendations

The European Union has made great progress in establishing the Internal market and achieving European Monetary Union. It is now seeking to make the same kind of progress in achieving social objectives. The methods will be different. Policy to combat poverty and social exclusion is first and foremost the responsibility of member states. But the objective is the same: to combine a dynamic economy with social inclusion and protection of the most vulnerable. As affirmed at the Stockholm European Council in March 2001, 'the fight against social exclusion is of utmost importance for the Union'. In achieving this social agenda, social indicators of national performance have a key role to play. A set of commonly agreed and defined social indicators is essential to allow the members of the Union to monitor progress towards social inclusion.

At the Lisbon European Council in March 2000, the Council adopted the strategic goal for the next decade of becoming 'the most competitive and dynamic knowledge-based economy . . . with more and better jobs and greater social cohesion'. It was agreed that the promotion of social inclusion within the overall strategy of the EU was to be achieved by an open method of coordination. This process is designed to help member states to develop their own policies, reflecting their individual national situations, to share their experience, and to review their outcomes in a transparent and comparable environment. It involves fixing guidelines for the Union, establishing indicators, and carrying out periodic monitoring.

The European Council agreed at the Nice Summit in December 2000 that member states be requested to implement two-year National Action Plans on Social Inclusion (referred to as NAPincls, to distinguish them from National Action Plans on Employment) for combating poverty and social exclusion, setting specific targets, taking into account national, regional, and local differences, and listing the indicators used to assess progress. The plans were submitted to the Commission for the first time in June 2001, and are discussed in Chapter 3. There are interesting differences between the National Action Plans, but overall there is a remarkable degree of convergence among member states in thinking and in policy.

The European Commission has been requested to monitor the implementation of the social agenda and to prepare an annual scoreboard of progress. It is invited to identify good practice and to promote its common acceptance. In the field of social inclusion, the European Commission (2000a, 2001a) has proposed an initial set of seven indicators for assessing national performance: (1) the distribution of income (ratio of share of top 20% to share of bottom 20%); (2) the share of the population below the poverty line before and after social transfers; (3) the persistence of poverty; (4) the proportion of jobless households; (5) regional disparities; (6) low education; and (7) long-term unemployment. In this book we have taken these indicators as our starting point. We have proposed a number of modifications of these indicators and suggested alternatives. We have considered other fields—notably health, housing, literacy and numeracy, and social participation.

As a basis for our analysis, we have put forward a series of principles that we feel should guide the construction of social indicators for use in monitoring national performance at the present stage of the European agenda. Of these principles, six refer to the individual indicators.

1. An indicator should identify the essence of the problem and have a clear and accepted normative interpretation.
2. An indicator should be robust and statistically validated.
3. An indicator should be responsive to effective policy interventions but not subject to manipulation.
4. An indicator should be measurable in a sufficiently comparable way across member states, and comparable as far as practicable with the standards applied internationally by the UN and the OECD.
5. An indicator should be timely and susceptible to revision.
6. The measurement of an indicator should not impose too large a burden on member states, on enterprises, or on the Union's citizens.

Of these principles, three refer to the portfolio of indicators as a whole.

1. The portfolio of indicators should be balanced across different dimensions.
2. The indicators should be mutually consistent and the weight of single indicators in the portfolio should be proportionate.
3. The portfolio of indicators should be as transparent and accessible as possible to the citizens of the European Union.

Recommendation 1 (Chapter 2). The nine principles listed above should form the basis for constructing indicators for social inclusion in the European Union.

We have considered a number of the properties of indicators. The main aim is to clarify the subsequent analysis, but we reach one conclusion that has implications for the book as a whole.

Recommendation 2 (Chapter 2). The fundamental concern when measuring social inclusion as part of the EU monitoring process is with the position of individual citizens, and statistics should in general be presented in terms of counting individuals or their circumstances (rather than households).

We have considered in detail the data required to implement the social indicators considered, taking account of the data currently available from the European Statistical System, and the potential offered by planned new sources such as the EU Statistics on Income and Living Conditions (EU-SILC). We have paid particular attention to the dangers of mismeasurement and the problems in securing comparability across member states, together with that of combining information from different sources. Consideration of the need for robustness of the indicators leads us to our third recommendation.

Recommendation 3 (Chapter 2). A systematic validation procedure has to be associated with each agreed social indicator, assessing its reliability in the light of all available sources.

In order to achieve this and the other objectives necessary to secure high-quality information, we make the following recommendation.

Recommendation 4 (Chapter 2). High priority should be given to the building of statistical capacity.

This seems to us an essential investment if the EU is to become a fully successful knowledge-based economy.

WHAT SHOULD BE THE STRUCTURE OF INDICATORS?

We endorse the proposal for three levels of indicators.

Recommendation 5 (Chapter 4). There should be three levels of indicators for use in the EU monitoring process.

- *Level 1* would consist of a restricted number of lead indicators covering the broad fields that have been considered the most important elements in leading to social exclusion.
- *Level 2* would support these lead indicators and describe other dimensions of the problem.

- *Level 3* would consist of those indicators that member states themselves decide to include in their National Action Plans on Social Inclusion, to highlight specificities in particular areas and to help interpret the Level 1 and 2 indicators.

The focus of the present book is on the common EU indicators, i.e. Levels 1 and 2. Both these levels would be commonly agreed and defined indicators, used in the future by member states in National Action Plans on Social Inclusion and by the Commission and member states in the Joint Report on Social Inclusion. They would be broken down by region, since we believe that the regional dimension is too important to be confined to a single indicator. They would be broken down by gender, since we believe that the gender dimension is of the highest priority and needs to be examined for all areas of social exclusion. They would be broken down by a number of other key relevant variables, depending on the indicator concerned and on data availability; for example, poverty rates would be given for children and for older people. While member states will be encouraged to complement the EU indicators with their own choice of indicators, it is important that the portfolio of EU indicators should command general support as a balanced representation of Europe's social concerns.

RECOMMENDATIONS FOR INDIVIDUAL INDICATORS IN THE EU MONITORING PROCESS

We begin with the measurement of the risk of poverty, which has been a longstanding concern of the European Union. In 1975 the European Council of Ministers defined the poor as those 'individuals or families whose resources are so small as to exclude them from the minimal acceptable way of life of the member state in which they live'. In concrete terms, this has come to be measured in terms of low income, and we recommend that this continue to be the starting point. It is however *only* a starting point. People below a specified income level are at risk of being unable to participate in the society in which they live, but there are other important dimensions.

Recommendation 6 (Chapter 5). The risk of financial poverty should be measured in terms of household income.

Recommendation 7 (Chapter 5). In the first stage of European indicators, the risk of financial poverty indicator at Level 1 should focus on relative poverty, the threshold being expressed in relation to the general level of incomes in the member state; in the medium term, other approaches should also be investigated.

Recommendation 8 (Chapter 5). There should be two Level 1 indicators for (risk of) financial poverty, one calculated on the basis of a threshold set at 50% of the national median equivalized income, and the other at 60% of the median; there should be Level 2 indicators set at 40% (where statistically reliable) and 70% of the median; Level 2 financial poverty information should also include the value of the 60% 'poverty line' (in purchasing power standards— PPS) for a one-person household and for a household consisting of two adults and two children. There should be a Level 2 indicator based on a poverty line fixed in real terms (i.e. uprated only for inflation) at 60% of the median at a specified date for a limited period (say about five years).

Recommendation 9 (Chapter 5). The poverty risk measure should be based on household income adjusted for differences in household size and composition by the OECD-modified equivalence scale, each household being given a weight equal to the number of household members, with the sensitivity of the results being assessed on a regular basis.

Recommendation 10 (Chapter 5). In order to be able to link income with household and individual variables, either income should be measured as 'current modified income', or countries should collect information about household and individual characteristics for the period to which the income data relate.

Recommendation 11 (Chapter 6). High importance should be attached to the measurement of the persistent (risk of) financial poverty and to the collection of appropriate data.

Recommendation 12 (Chapter 6). Level 2 indicators of persistent poverty risk should include (*a*) the percentage of persons living in households currently below 60% of the median who have been below this threshold in (at least) two of the previous three years (the persistently poor); (*b*) the percentage of persons living in households whose income when averaged over the last three years is below the average for these three years of the 60% of median threshold (the chronic poor).

Recommendation 13 (Chapter 6). As measures of the intensity of poverty, Level 2 indicators should include the mean equivalized poverty gap (with bottom-coding) and median equivalized poverty gap for poverty line set at 60% of median.

Recommendation 14 (Chapter 6). Non-monetary indicators of deprivation should where possible be included by member states at Level 3, and a significant investment should be made in developing these indicators in a comparative context for use in the EU monitoring process.

Recommendation 15 (Chapter 6). Income inequality should be measured at Level 1 by the ratio of the top and bottom quintile shares measured in terms of equivalized income, with the decile ratio and Gini coefficient (both also measured in terms of equivalized income) being included as complementary measures at Level 2.

Recommendation 16 (Chapter 7). There should be a Level 1 indicator measured as the proportion of those aged 18–24 who have only lower secondary education and are not in education or training leading to a qualification at least equivalent to upper secondary.

Recommendation 17 (Chapter 7). There should be a Level 2 indicator measured as the proportion of those aged 18–64 who have only lower secondary education or less.

Recommendation 18 (Chapter 7). A significant investment should be made in the investigation of indicators, on a comparative basis for use in the EU monitoring process, of differential access to education with a specific focus on parents' level of education and costs of education.

Recommendation 19 (Chapter 7). The overall unemployment rate and the long-term unemployment rate, measured on an ILO basis, should be Level 1 indicators.

Recommendation 20 (Chapter 7). There should be Level 2 indicators for the proportion of discouraged workers, the proportion non-employed, and the proportion in involuntary part-time work, expressed as a percentage of the total population aged 18–59 (or 64) excluding those aged 18–24 in full-time education (defined as those that are both in education and inactive).

Recommendation 21 (Chapter 7). There should be a Level 1 indicator of the proportion of people living in jobless households, as defined in Section 6.2, complemented by a Level 2 indicator of the proportion of people living in jobless households who are in receipt of an income below 60% of the median.

Recommendation 22 (Chapter 7). There should be two Level 2 indicators of (a) the proportion of the 'previous year and current workers', defined in Chapter 7, aged 18–59 (64) who are living in households below 60% of the median (the 'working poor'), and (b) the proportion of the 'previous year and current workers', defined as above, aged 18–59 (64) who are *low paid* in that their hourly earnings are less than two-thirds of the median hourly earnings of all previous year and current workers.

Recommendation 23 (Chapter 8). There should be a Level 1 indicator for health, the EU choosing between either (*a*) the percentage failing to reach age 65 (premature mortality) but with member states demonstrating (as a Level 3 indicator) that reductions in premature mortality are disproportionately among lower socioeconomic groups, or (*b*) the ratio of the proportions in the bottom and top quintile groups (by equivalized income) of the population aged 15 and over who classify themselves as in a bad or very bad state of health on the WHO definition.

Recommendation 24 (Chapter 8). There should be a Level 2 indicator on the proportion of people unable to obtain medical treatment for financial reasons, or on account of waiting lists, during the previous 12 months.

Recommendation 25 (Chapter 8). There should be a Level 1 indicator on the proportion of people living in households that lack specified housing amenities or have specified housing faults.

Recommendation 26 (Chapter 8). There should be a Level 2 indicator on the proportion of people living in overcrowded housing.

Recommendation 27 (Chapter 8). A significant investment should be made in the investigation of indicators, on a comparative basis for use in the EU monitoring process, of persons living in housing of poor environmental quality.

Recommendation 28 (Chapter 8). There should be a Level 2 indicator on the proportion of people living in households that have been in arrears on rent or mortgage payments at any time in the last 12 months, and further work is required on the general issue of housing cost.

Recommendation 29 (Chapter 8). As a matter of urgency, the Commission should examine different approaches to the definition and measurement of homelessness and precarious housing in a comparable way across member states and see whether a Level 1 indicator can be developed for use in the EU monitoring process.

Recommendation 30 (Chapter 8). There should be investment in the development for use in the EU monitoring process of measures of literacy and numeracy, reflecting their relevance both to skill levels in the labour market and to social participation.

Recommendation 31 (Chapter 8). There should be investigation of the possibility of constructing on a comparable basis, for use in the EU monitoring process, an index of access to private and public essential services.

Recommendation 32 (Chapter 8). There should be a Level 2 indicator of the proportion of the population living in households that would be unable in an emergency to raise a specified sum, where that sum should be related to the average monthly household income in the member state.

Recommendation 33 (Chapter 8). There should be investigation of comparable measures, for use in the EU monitoring process, of social participation, including individual access to and usage of the Internet.

The recommendations regarding individual indicators are summarized below.

SUMMARY OF RECOMMENDATIONS FOR INDIVIDUAL INDICATORS

Level 1

- Risk of financial poverty as measured by 50 and 60% of national median income using OECD modified equivalence scale
- Income inequality as measured by the quintile share ratio
- Proportion of those aged 18–24 who have only lower secondary education and are not in education or training leading to a qualification at least equivalent
- Overall and long-term unemployment rates measured on ILO basis
- Proportion of population living in jobless households
- Proportion failing to reach 65, *or* the ratio of those in bottom and top income quintile groups who classify their health as bad or very bad on the WHO definition
- Proportion of people living in households that lack specified housing amenities or have specified housing faults

Level 2

- Proportion of persons in households below 40% (where statistically reliable) and 70% of median income, and proportion below 60% of the median fixed in real terms at a specified date
- Value of 60% of median threshold in PPS for one- and four-person households (complementary information)

- Proportion of the population living in households that are persistently at risk of financial poverty
- Mean and median equivalized poverty gap—for 60% of median
- Income inequality as measured by the decile ratio and the Gini coefficient
- Proportion of the population aged 18–59 (64) with only lower secondary education or less
- Proportion of discouraged workers, proportion non-employed, and proportion in involuntary part-time work (as a percentage of the total population aged 18–64 excluding those in full-time education)
- Proportion of people living in jobless households with current income below 60% of the median
- Proportion of employees living in households at risk of poverty (60% median)
- Proportion of employees who are low paid
- Proportion of people unable to obtain medical treatment for financial reasons or on account of waiting lists
- Proportion of the population living in overcrowded housing
- Proportion of people living in households that have been in arrears on rent or mortgage payments
- Proportion of people living in households unable in an emergency to raise a specified sum

Both Levels 1 and 2 should be provided with breakdowns by most relevant variables, with a particular focus on disaggregation by gender and regions

Indicators for EU process to be developed

- Non-monetary indicators of deprivation
- Differential access to education
- Housing of poor environmental quality
- Housing cost
- Homelessness and precarious housing
- Literacy and numeracy
- Access to public and private essential services
- Social participation and access to Internet

Synthèse et Liste des Recommandations

OBJET DE L'OUVRAGE

L'objet du présent ouvrage est d'apporter une contribution scientifique au développement des indicateurs sociaux en tant qu'outil dans le développement de l'Agenda social de l'Union européenne. Il évalue les points forts et les points faibles des différents indicateurs concernant l'inclusion sociale en Europe ainsi que leur utilité dans la promotion de bonnes pratiques par les gouvernements des Etats membres et dans la mise à disposition d'un langage commun pour une évaluation, sur la base de critères comparables, des réalisations dans le domaine social.

Nous espérons qu'il contribuera à élargir le débat public sur la dimension sociale de l'Europe et qu'il offrira un instrument utile aux partenaires sociaux, aux organisations non gouvernementales, aux collectivités locales et autres associations de terrain, ainsi qu'à celles et ceux qui vivent en situation de pauvreté et d'exclusion sociale. Il se veut à la fois un document de synthèse et d'information constructif à une étape cruciale dans l'évolution de la dimension sociale de l'Union européenne, et un outil de référence d'une valeur durable.

Cet ouvrage a été rédigé à la demande du Gouvernement belge, dans le cadre de la Présidence belge du Conseil de l'Union européenne (01/07/01–31/12/01). Il est une initiative de M. Vande Lanotte, Vice-Premier Ministre et Ministre du Budget, de l'Intégration sociale et de l'Economie sociale, et de M. Frank Vandenbroucke, Ministre des Affaires sociales et des Pensions.

POURQUOI LES INDICATEURS SOCIAUX SONT-ILS IMPORTANTS POUR L'AGENDA SOCIAL AU SEIN DE L'UE?

L'Union européenne (UE) a fait un grand pas en avant lors de l'établissement du marché intérieur et lors de la réalisation de l'Union monétaire européenne. Il est temps maintenant de faire de même en ce qui concerne la réalisation d'objectifs sociaux. La croissance économique rend la persistance de la pauvreté et de l'exclusion encore moins acceptable.

Les méthodes seront différentes. La politique de lutte contre la pauvreté et l'exclusion sociale relève d'abord et avant tout des Etats membres (EM). Mais l'objectif est identique : il s'agit de combiner une économie dynamique avec l'inclusion sociale et la protection des plus vulnérables. Comme il a été dit au Conseil européen de Stockholm en mars 2001, «la lutte contre l'exclusion sociale revêt une importance fondamentale pour l'Union».

Dans la réalisation de cet agenda social, des indicateurs sociaux permettant d'évaluer des réalisations nationales ont un rôle clé à jouer. Un ensemble d'indicateurs sociaux convenus et définis d'un commun accord est essentiel pour permettre aux EM de suivre les progrès vers l'inclusion sociale. Le choix de cette voie devrait permettre à l'UE et ses citoyens d'avoir confiance en leur avenir.

SUR QUOI LES EM SE SONT-ILS DÉJÀ ACCORDÉS ?

Au sommet européen de Lisbonne en mars 2000, le Conseil a adopté pour les dix prochaines années l'objectif stratégique de devenir «l'économie de la connaissance la plus compétitive et la plus dynamique du monde (. . .) accompagnée d'une amélioration quantitative et qualitative de l'emploi et d'une plus grande cohésion sociale». Il a été convenu que la promotion de l'inclusion sociale dans la stratégie globale de l'UE devait être réalisée par une méthode ouverte de coordination. Ce processus a été conçu pour aider les EM à développer leurs propres politiques (reflétant leurs spécificités nationales), et pour qu'ils puissent partager leur expérience et confronter leurs résultats dans un environnement comparable et transparent. Ce processus suppose la fixation de lignes directrices pour l'Union, l'élaboration d'indicateurs et la réalisation de suivis réguliers. A Lisbonne, le Conseil a demandé à la Commission de rendre compte annuellement des indicateurs structurels des progrès des EM. A Feira, en juin 2000, il a demandé à la Commission d'assurer la cohérence nécessaire des indicateurs et d'harmoniser leur présentation. Au Sommet de Nice, en décembre 2000, les propositions de la Commission en vue de faire avancer l'Agenda social européen ont été approuvées. Un rôle important a été donné au Comité de Protection sociale (anciennement Groupe de haut Niveau sur la Protection sociale), qui a créé un Sous-Groupe chargé de développer des Indicateurs sociaux, lequel a commencé à se réunir en février 2001. Au Conseil européen de Stockholm en mars 2001, le Conseil a été invité à s'accorder, pour la fin de l'année 2001, sur des indicateurs en vue de suivre les progrès dans la lutte contre l'exclusion sociale.

EN QUOI CONSISTENT LES PLANS D'ACTION NATIONAUX SUR L'INCLUSION SOCIALE?

Le Conseil européen a, au Sommet de Nice en décembre 2000, marqué son accord pour qu'il soit demandé aux EM de mettre en œuvre des Plans d'Action nationaux sur l'Inclusion sociale (appelés PANincl pour les distinguer des Plans d'Action nationaux sur l'Emploi) afin de lutter contre la pauvreté et l'exclusion sociale. Ces plans fixent des objectifs spécifiques tenant compte des différences nationales, régionales et locales; et ils énumèrent les indicateurs utilisés pour évaluer les progrès. Ils ont été soumis à la Commission pour la première fois en juin 2001 et sont brièvement examinés au Chapitre 3.

QUEL EST LE RÔLE DE LA COMMISSION CONCERNANT LES INDICATEURS SOCIAUX?

Les indicateurs sociaux constituent un outil important dans le développement de la politique sociale. Ils nous permettent de déterminer en termes statistiques le niveau de développement social atteint dans une société donnée et l'ampleur actuelle des problèmes sociaux. Ils nous permettent d'évaluer le degré de confiance que nous pouvons avoir dans nos prestations sociales actuelles. En suivant l'évolution dans le temps, nous pouvons suivre les progrès vers la résolution de problèmes d'intérêt général.

La Commission européenne a été chargée de suivre la mise en œuvre de l'agenda social et de préparer un tableau de bord annuel des progrès réalisés. Elle est invitée à identifier les bonnes pratiques et à promouvoir leur acceptation par tous. Au Sommet de Stockholm en mars 2001, la Commission a présenté dans son premier *Rapport de synthèse* des données relatives à un premier ensemble d'indicateurs structurels provisoires, se fondant sur sa Communication relative aux Indicateurs structurels de septembre 2000. Sur la base des PANincl présentés en juin 2001, la Commission et les EM préparent un Rapport conjoint sur l'inclusion sociale.

QUELS SONT LES DOMAINES COUVERTS PAR LES INDICATEURS SOCIAUX?

Dans le domaine de l'inclusion sociale, la Commission européenne a proposé (en 2000 et 2001) un ensemble initial de sept indicateurs pour évaluer les réalisations nationales: (i) distribution des revenus (ratio des parts de revenu au sein des quintiles—revenus perçus par les 20% les plus riches comparés à ceux perçus par les 20% les plus pauvres), (ii) proportion de la population située en dessous du seuil de pauvreté avant et après versement des transferts sociaux, (iii) pauvreté persistante, (iv) proportion de ménages sans emploi (*jobless households*), (v) disparités régionales, (vi) faible niveau d'études, et (vii) chômage de longue durée. Dans le présent rapport, nous avons pris ces indicateurs comme point de départ. Nous avons proposé un certain nombre d'amendements et suggéré des alternatives. Nous avons examiné d'autres domaines, notamment le logement, la santé et la participation sociale.

QUELS SONT LES PRINCIPES QUI DEVRAIENT GUIDER LA CONSTRUCTION DES INDICATEURS SOCIAUX?

Comme base de notre analyse, nous avons avancé une série de principes qui, à notre sens, devraient guider la construction des indicateurs sociaux à utiliser afin de suivre les réalisations nationales dans la phase actuelle de l'Agenda européen. Six de ces principes se rapportent aux indicateurs individuels.

1. Un indicateur devrait saisir l'essence du problème et avoir une interprétation normative claire et reconnue.
2. Un indicateur devrait être solide et statistiquement validé.
3. Un indicateur devrait être sensible aux interventions politiques efficaces mais non sujet à manipulation.
4. Un indicateur devrait pouvoir être mesuré de manière suffisamment comparable à travers les EM et comparable dans toute la mesure du possible avec les normes appliquées internationalement par l'ONU et l'OCDE.
5. Un indicateur devrait être basé sur des données récentes et être susceptible de révision.
6. Le calcul d'un indicateur ne devrait pas constituer une charge trop importante pour les EM, les entreprises ou les citoyens de l'Union.

Trois de ces principes font référence au portefeuille d'indicateurs pris dans son ensemble.

1. Le portefeuille d'indicateurs devrait être équilibré à travers les différentes dimensions qui le composent.
2. Les indicateurs devraient être cohérents les uns par rapport aux autres et le poids de chaque indicateur au sein de l'ensemble du portefeuille devrait être proportionné.

3. Le portefeuille d'indicateurs devrait être aussi transparent et accessible que possible aux citoyens de l'UE.

Recommandation 1. Les neuf principes énumérés ci-dessus devraient constituer la base de construction des indicateurs d'inclusion sociale dans l'UE.

Nous avons examiné un certain nombre de propriétés des indicateurs. Le but principal est de clarifier l'analyse qui suit. Cependant, nous sommes arrivés à une conclusion ayant des effets sur le rapport dans son ensemble.

Recommandation 2. Le souci fondamental en ce qui concerne la mesure de l'inclusion sociale comme composante du processus de suivi au niveau de l'UE dans son ensemble porte sur la situation des citoyens individuels. Les statistiques devraient dès lors, en règle générale, être présentées en termes d'individus ou de situations dans laquelle ceux-ci se trouvent (plutôt qu'en termes de ménages).

Nous reconnaissons que les situations des ménages au sein desquels vivent les individus sont des déterminants majeurs du niveau de bien-être des individus et que les ménages peuvent être exclus socialement dans leur ensemble. Nous ne suggérons pas que les individus devraient être considérés isolément. Mais chaque personne devrait compter comme un individu à part entière.

Nous avons examiné en détail les données requises pour réaliser les indicateurs sociaux proposés, compte tenu des données actuellement disponibles au sein du *Système statistique européen* et des possibilités offertes par de nouvelles sources prévues, comme les Statistiques de l'UE sur le revenu et les conditions de vie (*EU—Statistics on Income and Living Conditions—EU-SILC*). Nous avons été particulièrement attentifs aux dangers d'erreurs de mesure et aux problèmes liés à la comparabilité entre EM. La prise en compte de la fiabilité des indicateurs nous a amenés à recommander:

Recommandation 3. Une procédure de validation systématique devrait accompagner chaque indicateur social qui sera adopté, la fiabilité de ce dernier devant être évaluée à la lumière de toutes les sources disponibles.

En vue de réaliser cette procédure ainsi que d'autres objectifs nécessaires à l'obtention d'informations de haute qualité, nous recommandons ce qui suit.

Recommandation 4. Donner une priorité élevée au développement de notre outil statistique et de notre potentiel statistique.

Cet investissement nous semble essentiel si l'Union souhaite effectivement que son économie soit basée sur la connaissance et promise au succès.

QUELLE DEVRAIT ÊTRE LA STRUCTURE DES INDICATEURS ?

Nous défendons l'idée selon laquelle les indicateurs devraient être organisés en trois niveaux distincts:

Recommandation 5. Utiliser trois niveaux d'indicateurs dans le processus de suivi de l'inclusion au niveau de l'UE.

- Le *Niveau 1* consisterait en un petit nombre d'indicateurs clés;
- Le *Niveau 2* complèterait ces indicateurs clés et décrirait d'autres dimensions du problème.

Les indicateurs clés (Niveau 1) proposés dans le présent rapport couvrent les vastes domaines qui ont été considérés comme les éléments les plus importants menant à l'exclusion sociale: *'déprivations'* matérielles, défaut d'enseignement, absence de 《rôle productif》, mauvaise santé et mauvaises conditions de logement.

Pour les Niveaux 1 et 2, les indicateurs seraient définis et acceptés d'un commun accord; ils seraient utilisés par les EM dans leurs prochains PANincl et par la Commission et les EM dans le Rapport conjoint sur l'Inclusion sociale. Ils seraient décomposés par région, parce que nous estimons que la dimension régionale est trop importante pour être confinée à un indicateur unique. Ils seraient également croisés par sexe étant donné l'importance capitale à accorder à cette dimension et la nécessité, dès lors, de l'analyser pour l'ensemble des domaines de l'exclusion sociale (il convient de rappeler que le traité d'Amsterdam a donné à l'égalité des chances entre hommes et femmes une place de premier plan). Enfin, ils seraient décomposés par toute autre variable clé pertinente—toujours, bien sûr, selon l'indicateur concerné et les données disponibles. Par exemple, les taux de pauvreté seraient donnés pour les enfants et les personnes âgées. Alors que les EM seront encouragés à compléter les indicateurs UE par des indicateurs de leur propre choix, il est important que le portefeuille d'indicateurs commun à UE puisse être soutenu dans son ensemble grâce à la représentation équilibrée qu'il donne des préoccupations sociales de l'Europe.

En outre, il y aurait des indicateurs de *Niveau 3*: ceux que les EM eux-mêmes décident d'inclure dans leur PANIncl, pour mettre en lumière des spécificités dans des secteurs particuliers et pour aider à interpréter les indicateurs de Niveaux 1 et 2.

Le présent rapport met l'accent sur les indicateurs communs de l'UE: c'est-à-dire ceux des Niveaux 1 et 2.

RECOMMANDATIONS POUR LES INDICATEURS INDIVIDUELS DANS LE PROCESSUS DE SUIVI AU NIVEAU DE L'UE DANS SON ENSEMBLE

Nous commençons par la question de la mesure du risque de pauvreté qui, depuis longtemps déjà, constitue une préoccupation de l'UE. En 1975, le Conseil européen des Ministres a défini les pauvres comme étant ⟪les individus et familles dont les ressources sont si faibles qu'ils sont exclus des modes de vie minimaux acceptables dans l'EM dans lequel ils vivent⟫. Pour qu'elle puisse devenir opérationnelle, cette notion a été mesurée de façon concrète en termes de bas revenus et nous recommandons que ceci constitue également notre point de départ. Cette recommandation n'est donc qu'un point de départ. Les personnes qui disposent d'un revenu inférieur à un seuil déterminé courent un risque de ne pas pouvoir participer pleinement à la vie de la société dans laquelle elles vivent, mais il existe également d'autres dimensions importantes.

Recommandation 6. Mesurer le risque de pauvreté monétaire (c'est-à-dire la pauvreté considérée exclusivement sous l'angle du revenu perçu par le ménage au cours de l'année de référence) sur la base du revenu du ménage.

Recommandation 7. Dans la première phase d'élaboration d'indicateurs européens, l'indicateur de (risque de) pauvreté monétaire au Niveau 1 devrait être un indicateur de pauvreté relative, en ce sens que le seuil de pauvreté devrait être exprimé en fonction du niveau général des revenus dans le pays considéré. A moyen terme, d'autres approches devraient également être examinées.

Recommandation 8. Établir deux indicateurs de Niveau 1 de (risque de) pauvreté monétaire: l'un devrait être calculé sur la base d'un seuil fixé à 50% du revenu médian national équivalisé et l'autre, sur la base d'un seuil fixé à 60% de la médiane. Pour le Niveau 2, cet indicateur devrait être calculé de façon identique mais pour des seuils fixés à 40% (si statistiquement fiable) et 70% de la médiane. L'information monétaire fournie au Niveau 2 devrait également contenir la valeur des 60% du ⟪seuil de pauvreté⟫ (exprimé en standards de pouvoir d'achat—SPA) ce, respectivement pour un ménage d'une personne et pour un ménage composé de deux adultes et deux enfants. Nous recommandons également d'inclure, parmi les indicateurs de Niveau 2, des estimations basées sur un seuil de pauvreté fixé en termes réels (c'est-à-dire augmenté uniquement à concurrence du taux d'inflation) à 60% de la médiane à un moment donné pour une période limitée (par exemple 5 ans).

Recommandation 9. Calculer le risque de pauvreté sur la base du revenu du ménage ajusté, pour tenir compte de la taille et de la composition du ménage, à l'aide de l'échelle d'équivalence modifiée de l'OCDE, et attribuer à chaque ménage un poids égal au nombre de membres qui le composent. La sensibilité des résultats à ces différents facteurs devrait être évaluée régulièrement.

Recommandation 10. Afin de pouvoir croiser le revenu avec d'autres variables relatives aux ménages et aux individus, soit le revenu devrait être mesuré en tant que 'revenu modifié courant' soit l'EM devrait collecter l'information nécessaire relative aux ménages et aux individus pour la période à laquelle se rapporte le revenu.

Recommandation 11. Accorder une grande importance à la mesure de la persistance du risque de pauvreté monétaire et à la collecte des données appropriées.

Recommandation 12. Inclure dans les indicateurs de Niveau 2 de persistance du risque de pauvreté: (a) le pourcentage de personnes vivant dans des ménages qui se situent actuellement sous le seuil de 60% de la médiane et qui ont été sous ce seuil (au moins) 2 des 3 années précédentes (les pauvres persistants), (b) le pourcentage de personnes vivant dans des ménages dont le revenu moyen au cours des trois dernières années est inférieur à la moyenne des seuils (60% de la médiane) observés pour ces trois années (les pauvres chroniques).

Recommandation 13. Comme mesures de l'intensité de la pauvreté (《poverty gap》), les indicateurs de Niveau 2 devraient inclure, calculés sur la base de montants équivalisés, l'écart moyen de pauvreté (avec recodification des valeurs les plus basses) et l'écart médian de pauvreté—ce, pour un seuil fixé à 60% de la médiane.

Recommandation 14. Des indicateurs non monétaires de 'déprivation' devraient, autant que faire se peut, être prévus par les EM au Niveau 3, et un investissement significatif devrait être fait dans le développement de ces indicateurs dans un cadre comparatif de façon à permettre leur utilisation dans le processus de suivi au niveau de l'UE.

Recommandation 15. Mesurer l'inégalité de revenus au Niveau 1 par le ratio de la part de revenu au sein du quintile inférieur et de celle au sein du quintile supérieur de revenu—celui-ci étant calculé en termes de revenu équivalent. Le ratio interdécile et l'indice de Gini (tous deux calculés aussi en termes de revenu équivalent) devraient quant à eux être inclus comme mesures complémentaires au Niveau 2.

Recommandation 16. Établir un indicateur de Niveau 1 donnant la proportion de personnes âgées de 18 à 24 ans ayant seulement un diplôme du secondaire inférieur et ne suivant pas un enseignement ou un apprentissage donnant des qualifications au moins équivalentes au secondaire supérieur.

Recommandation 17. Établir un indicateur de Niveau 2 donnant la proportion de personnes âgées de 18 à 64 ans ayant tout au plus un diplôme du secondaire inférieur.

Recommandation 18. Investir de façon significative dans la recherche d'indicateurs rendant compte du différentiel d'accès à l'enseignement, mettant un accent particulier sur le niveau scolaire des parents et sur le coût de l'enseignement. Ces indicateurs devraient être élaborés sur la base de critères comparables de façon à permettre leur utilisation dans le processus de suivi au niveau de l'UE.

Recommandation 19. Inclure dans les indicateurs de Niveau 1 le taux de chômage global et le taux de chômage de longue durée, mesurés selon les normes du BIT.

Recommandation 20. Établir des indicateurs de Niveau 2 mesurant la proportion de travailleurs découragés, la proportion de sans-emplois et la proportion de personnes travaillant involontairement à temps partiel. Ces proportions devraient être exprimées en pour cent de la population totale âgée de 18 à 59 (ou 64) ans, en excluant les personnes âgées de 18 à 24 ans qui suivent un enseignement de plein exercice (ces personnes étant définies comme celles étant à la fois aux études et inactives).

Recommandation 21. Établir un indicateur de Niveau 1 donnant la proportion de personnes vivant au sein de ménages sans emploi, comme définis dans la Section 6.2, complété par un indicateur de Niveau 2 de la proportion de personnes qui vivent au sein de ces ménages et dont le revenu du ménage se situe sous 60% de la médiane.

Recommandation 22. Établir deux indicateurs de Niveau 2 calculés comme suit: (*a*) la proportion de personnes salariées vivant au sein de ménages situés sous

60% de la médiane, parmi celles qui sont actuellement au travail et qui l'étaient également l'année précédente (comme défini dans la Section 6.4) et qui sont âgées de 18 à 59 (ou 64) ans (*travailleurs pauvres*), (*b*) la proportion de ces mêmes personnes qui ont un *faible salaire* en ce sens que leur salaire horaire est inférieur aux deux tiers du salaire horaire médian de l'ensemble des salariés ⟪qui sont actuellement au travail et qui l'étaient également l'année précédente⟫.

Recommandation 23. Établir un indicateur de Niveau 1 pour la santé, l'UE devant choisir entre (*a*) le pourcentage d'individus n'atteignant pas l'âge de 65 ans (mortalité précoce) complété par des informations fournies par les EM démontrant (par un indicateur de Niveau 3) que la diminution de la mortalité précoce est proportionnellement plus rapide parmi les groupes socio-économiques faibles ou (*b*) le rapport des proportions dans les quintiles inférieur et supérieur (par revenu équivalisé) de personnes âgées de 15 ans et plus qui s'estiment en mauvaise ou très mauvaise santé en fonction de la définition de l'OMS.

Recommandation 24. Établir un indicateur de Niveau 2 concernant la proportion d'individus n'ayant pu obtenir un traitement médical au cours des 12 derniers mois pour des raisons financières ou en raison de listes d'attente.

Recommandation 25. Établir un indicateur de Niveau 1 concernant la proportion d'individus vivant au sein d'un ménage dont le logement ne dispose pas de commodités déterminées ou présente des défauts déterminés.

Recommandation 26. Établir un indicateur de Niveau 2 concernant la proportion d'individus vivant dans des logements surpeuplés.

Recommandation 27. Investir de manière significative dans la recherche d'indicateurs relatifs aux personnes vivant dans un logement situé dans un environnement médiocre. Ces indicateurs devraient être élaborés sur la base de critères comparables de façon à permettre leur utilisation dans le processus de suivi au niveau de l'UE.

Recommandation 28. Établir un indicateur de Niveau 2 concernant la proportion d'individus vivant au sein de ménages ayant eu des arriérés de paiement dans le loyer ou le remboursement de charges d'emprunt hypothécaire au cours des 12 derniers mois; des recherches complémentaires sur la question générale du coût du logement devraient également être réalisées.

Recommandation 29. D'urgence, la Commission devrait examiner différentes approches de la définition et de la mesure de la problématique des sans-abri et du logement précaire de manière comparable entre les EM et devrait investiguer la possibilité de définir un indicateur de Niveau 1 pouvant être utilisé dans le processus de suivi au niveau de l'UE.

Recommandation 30. Afin de permettre leur utilisation dans le processus de suivi de l'UE, il conviendrait d'investir dans le développement de mesures de capacités de lecture et de calcul, qui permettraient de mettre en évidence le rapport de ces deux niveaux d'aptitudes avec le marché de l'emploi et la participation sociale.

Recommandation 31. Il conviendrait d'examiner la possibilité d'établir, sur la base de critères comparables, pour l'utiliser dans le processus de suivi de l'UE, un index de l'accès aux services privés et publics essentiels.

Recommandation 32. Établir un indicateur de Niveau 2 donnant la proportion de la population vivant au sein de ménages qui, en cas de besoins urgents, seraient incapables de rassembler une somme d'argent déterminée, cette somme devant refléter le revenu moyen d'un ménage dans l'EM considéré.

Recommandation 33. Développer des indicateurs comparables concernant la participation sociale, à utiliser dans le processus de suivi de l'UE; ceux-ci devraient inclure l'accès individuel à Internet et son usage individuel.

Les recommandations concernant les indicateurs individuels sont résumées ci-dessous.

RÉSUMÉ DES RECOMMANDATIONS POUR LES INDICATEURS INDIVIDUELS

Niveau 1

- Risque de pauvreté monétaire mesuré pour un seuil de 50% et un seuil de 60% du revenu national médian, avec le revenu ajusté au moyen de l'échelle d'équivalence modifiée de l'OCDE
- Inégalité de revenus telle que mesurée par le ratio des parts de revenu au sein des premier et cinquième quintiles de revenu
- Proportion des individus âgés de 18 à 24 ans ayant suivi uniquement un enseignement secondaire inférieur et n'étant ni aux études ni en apprentissage menant à une qualification au moins équivalente à ce niveau
- Taux de chômage global et de longue durée mesurés selon les normes du BIT
- Proportion de la population vivant au sein de ménages sans emploi (*jobless households*)

- Proportion d'individus n'atteignant pas 65 ans OU rapport des proportions d'individus appartenant aux quintiles inférieur et supérieur de revenu considérant leur état de santé comme mauvais ou très mauvais selon la définition OMS
- Proportion de personnes vivant au sein d'un ménage dont le logement ne dispose pas de commodités déterminées ou présente des défauts déterminés

Niveau 2

- Proportion de personnes vivant dans des ménages situés en dessous de 40% (si statistiquement fiable) et 70% du revenu médian et proportion située en dessous de 60% de la médiane (avec ce seuil fixé en termes réels à un moment donné)
- Valeur de 60% du seuil médian en SPA pour des ménages de 1 et de 4 personnes (information complémentaire)
- Proportion de la population vivant au sein de ménages exposés à un risque persistant de pauvreté monétaire
- Écarts moyen et médian de pauvreté—pour 60% de la médiane (*poverty gap*)
- Inégalité de revenus mesurée par le rapport interdécile (P90/P10) et l'indice de Gini
- Proportion de la population âgée de 18 à 64 ans ayant terminé tout au plus l'enseignement secondaire inférieur
- Proportion de travailleurs découragés, proportion de sans-emplois et proportion de personnes travaillant involontairement à temps partiel (en pour cent de la population totale âgée de 18 à 59 (ou 64) ans, non compris les personnes suivant un enseignement de plein exercice)
- Proportion de personnes vivant au sein de ménages sans emploi dont le revenu courant est inférieur à 60% de la médiane
- Proportion de salariés vivant au sein de ménages exposés à des risques de pauvreté (60% de la médiane)
- Proportion de salariés faiblement rémunérés
- Proportion de personnes ne pouvant obtenir un traitement médical pour des raisons financières ou en raison de listes d'attente
- Proportion de la population vivant dans des logements surpeuplés
- Proportion de personnes vivant dans un ménage ayant eu des arriérés de paiement du loyer ou de remboursement de charges hypothécaires
- Proportion de personnes vivant au sein de ménages ne pouvant, en cas d'urgence, rassembler une somme déterminée d'argent

Les Niveaux 1 et 2 devraient tous deux être fournis avec des analyses selon les variables les plus pertinentes, un accent particulier devant être mis sur la désagrégation par sexe et par région.

Indicateurs à développer pour le processus de l'UE

- Indicateurs non monétaires de 'déprivation'
- Différentiel d'accès à l'enseignement
- Logement situé dans un environnement médiocre
- Coût du logement
- Sans-abri et précarité de logement
- Capacités de lecture et de calcul
- Accès aux services essentiels publics et privés
- Participation sociale et accès à Internet

Members of the Steering Committees

Scientific Steering Committee

Chairman: Mr Yves Chassard, Bernard Brunhes International, France

Professor Jonathan Bradshaw, University of York, United Kingdom

Professor Gosta Esping-Andersen, University of Pompeu Fabra, Spain

Professor Maurizio Ferrera, University of Pavia, Italy

Professor Jean-Paul Fitoussi, President of the Observatoire Français des Conjonctures Economiques, France

Professor Duncan Gallie, Nuffield College, Oxford, United Kingdom

Professor L. J. Gunning-Schepers, University of Amsterdam, Netherlands

Professor Anton Hemerijck, University of Leyden, Netherlands

Professor John Hills, London School of Economics, United Kingdom

Professor Peter Mohler, University of Mannheim (ZUMA), Germany

Professor John Myles, Florida State University, United States

Professor Pierre Pestieau, University of Liège, Belgium

Professor Fritz Scharpf, Max Planck Institute, Germany

Professor Luc Soete, University of Maastricht, Netherlands

Professor Panos Tsakoglou, University of Athens, Greece

Professor Philippe Van Parijs, Catholic University of Louvain-la-Neuve, Belgium

Professor Jan Vranken, University of Antwerp (UFSIA), Belgium

Institutional Steering Committee

Chairman: Professor Jos Berghman, Catholic University of Leuven, Belgium

Mr Raoul Briet, Chairman of the Social Protection Committee

Professor Paolo Garonna, University of Padua (Italy) and Deputy Executive Secretary, United Nations Economic Commission for Europe (UNECE)

Ms Anna Hedborg, National Social Insurance Board, Sweden

Ms Beatrice Hertogs, European Trade Union Confederation, Belgium

Mr Ludo Horemans, President of the European Anti-Poverty Network (EAPN), Belgium

Ms Marie-Thérèse Join-Lambert, President of the National Observatory on Poverty and Social Exclusion, France

Mr Allan Larsson, Former Director General, Directorate General Employment and Social Affairs, European Commission

Ms Odile Quintin, Director General, Directorate General Employment and Social Affairs, European Commission

Mr Emmanuel Reynaud, International Labour Organisation (ILO)

Mr Peter Scherer, OECD

Mr David Stanton, Chairman of the Social Protection Committee's Sub-Group on Indicators

Mr Frank Vandenbroucke, Minister for Social Affairs and Pensions, Belgium

References

Abel-Smith, B. and Townsend, P. (1965) *The Poor and the Poorest*, Bell, London.

Anand, S. and Sen, A. K. (1997) 'Concepts of Human Development and Poverty: A Multidimensional Perspective', *Human Development Papers*, United Nations Dévelopment Programme, New York.

ATD Quart Monde (2000) 'L' Approche participative pour la mesure du développement humain et la mise en œuvre des droits de l'homme n the measurement of inequality', Montreux, September 2000.

Atkinson, A. B. (1970) 'On the Measurement of Inequality', *Journal of Economic Theory*, 2: 244–263.

—— (1998) *Poverty in Europe*, Basil Blackwell, Oxford.

—— and Micklewright, J. (1992) *Economic Transformation in Eastern Europe and the Distribution of Income*, Cambridge University Press, Cambridge.

—— and Sutherland, H. (1989) 'Inter-generational Continuities in Deprivation', in A. B. Atkinson, *Poverty and Social Security*, Harvester Wheatsheaf, Hemel Hempstead.

——, Rainwater, L. and Smeeding, T. (1995) *Income Distribution in OECD Countries*, OECD, Paris.

Baldwin, S. (1985) *The Costs of Caring*, Routledge & Kegan Paul, London.

Basu, K. and Foster, J. E. (1998) 'On Measuring Literacy', *Economic Journal*, 108: 1733–1749.

Bauer, R. (ed.) (1966) *Social Indicators*, MIT Press, Cambridge, Mass.

Beck, W., van der Maesen, L. and Walker, A. (eds.) (1997) *The Social Quality of Europe*, Kluwer, The Hague.

Becker, I. and Hauser, R. (1996) 'Einkommensverteilung und Armut in Deutschland von 1962 bis 1995', Arbeitspapier No. 9, EVS-Projekt, Universität Frankfurt am Main.

—— and Hauser, R. (2001) *Einkommensverteilung im Querschnitt und im Zeitverlauf 1973 bis 1998*, Bundesministerium für Arbeit und Sozialordnung, Bonn.

Bennett, F. and Roche, C. (2000) 'Developing Indicators: The Scope for Participatory Approaches', *New Economy*, 7: 24–28.

Berger-Schmitt, R. (2000) 'Social Cohesion as an Aspect of the Quality of Societies: Concept and Measurement', EuReporting Working Paper No. 14, ZUMA, Mannheim.

—— and Jankowitsch, B. (1999) 'Systems of Social Indicators and Social Reporting: The State of the Art', EuReporting Working Paper No. 1, ZUMA, Mannheim.

Berger-Schmitt, R. and Noll, H.-H. (2000) 'Conceptual Framework and Structure of a European System of Social Indicators', EuReporting Working Paper No. 9, ZUMA, Mannheim.

Berthoud, R. (2001a) 'A Childhood in Poverty', *New Economy*, 8: 77–81.

—— (2001b) 'Rich Place, Poor Place: An Analysis of Geographical Variations in Household Income within Britain', Institute for Social and Economic Research, University of Essex.

Blair, T. (1999) 'Beveridge Revisited: A Welfare State for the 21st Century', in R. Walker (ed.), *Ending Child Poverty*, Policy Press, London.

Blum, A., Goldstein, H. and Guerin-Pace, F. (2001) 'An Analysis of International Comparisons of Adult Literacy', *Assessment in Education*, 8: 225–246.

Bourguignon, F. and Chakravarty, S. R. (1997) 'The Measurement of Multi-dimensional Poverty', DELTA, Paris.

Bradbury, B., Jenkins, S. P. and Micklewright, J. (eds.) (2001) *The Dynamics of Child Poverty in Industrialised Countries*, Cambridge University Press, Cambridge.

Bradshaw, J. (1972) 'The Concept of Social Need', *New Society*, No. 496: 640–643.

—— (2000) 'Child Poverty in Comparative Perspective', in D. Gordon and P. Townsend (eds.), *Breadline Europe*, Policy Press, Bristol.

—— and Finch, N. (2001a) 'Core Poverty', Social Policy Research Unit, York; at http://www-users.york.ac.uk/~jrb1/.

—— and Finch, N. (2001b) 'Using Household Expenditure to Establish Poverty Thresholds', in *The Measurement of Absolute Poverty*, Report for Eurostat, Social Policy Research Unit, University of York; at http://www-users.york. ac.uk/~jrb1/.

——, Nolan, B. and Maitre, B. (2001) 'Minimum Income Standards as Poverty Thresholds', in *The Measurement of Absolute Poverty*, Report for Eurostat, Social Policy Research Unit, University of York; at http://www-users.york.ac.uk/ ~jrb1/.

Brandolini, A. and D' Alessio, G. (1998) 'Measuring Well-being in the Functioning Space', Bank of Italy, Rome.

Brousse, C., Guiot de la Rochère, B. and Massé, E. (2001) 'L'Enquête Française auprès des Sans-Domicile fréquentant les services d'hébergement et de la restauration gratuite', paper presented at Ottawa symposium on the 'Quality of Surveys'.

Bundesministerium für Arbeit und Sozialordnung (2001) *Lebenslagen in Deutschland*, Bundesministerium für Arbeit und Sozialordnung, Bonn.

Callan, T., Nolan, B., Whelan, B. J., Hannan, D. F. with Creighton, S. (1989) *Poverty, Income and Welfare in Ireland*, Paper No. 146, ESRI, Dublin.

——, Nolan, B. and Whelan, C. T. (1993) 'Resources, Deprivation and the Measurement of Poverty', *Journal of Social Policy*, 22: 141–172.

——, Nolan, B., Whelan, B. J., Whelan, C. T. and Williams, J. (1996) *Poverty in the 1990s*, Oak Tree Press, Dublin.

Campbell, J. R., Kelly, D. L., Mullis, I. V. S., Martin, M. O. and Sainsbury, M. (2001) *Progress in International Reading Literacy Study*, International Study Center, Boston College.

Cantillon, B., Marx, I. and Van den Bosch, K. (1997) 'The Challenge of Poverty and Social Exclusion', in *Towards 2000: The New Social Policy Agenda*, OECD, Paris.

——, De Lathouwer, L., Marx, I., Van Dam, R. and Van den Bosch, K. (1999*a*) 'Sociale indicatoren 1976–1997', *Belgisch Tijdschrift voor Sociale Zekerheid*, 41: 747–800.

——, De Lathouwer, L., Marx, I., Van Dam, R. and Van den Bosch, K. (1999*b*) 'Indicateurs sociaux 1976–1997', *Revue Belge de Sécurité Sociale*, 41: 713–766.

——, Van Dam, R., Van Hoorebeeck, B. and Van den Bosch, K. (2001) 'Child Poverty *à la carte*? The Effects of Measurement Period for Income on Poverty Estimates', paper for the Eight International Research Seminar of FISS on 'Issues in Social Security', Sigtuna, Sweden, 16–19 June.

Carey, S. (ed.) (2000) *Measuring Adult Literacy: The International Adult Literacy Survey in European Context*, Office for National Statistics, London.

Carley, M. (1981) *Social Measurement and Social Indicators*, Allen & Unwin, London.

CASE (2001) *Indicators of Progress: A Discussion of Approaches to Monitor the Government's Strategy to Tackle Poverty and Social Exclusion*, CASE Report No. 13, London School of Economics, London.

Cavelaars, A. E. J. M. (1998) *Cross-National Comparisons of Socio-Economic Differences in Health Indicators*, Ph.D. thesis, Erasmus University, Rotterdam.

——, Kunst, A. E., Geurts, J. J. M., Helmert, U., Lundberg, O. and Matheson, J. (1998*a*) 'Morbidity Differences by Occupational Class among Men in Seven European Countries', *International Journal of Epidemiology*, 27: 222–230.

——, Kunst, A. E., Geurts, J. J. M., Crialesi, R., Grötvedt, R. and Helmert, U. (1998*b*) 'Differences in Self-Reported Morbidity by Educational Level: A Comparison of 11 Western European Countries', *Journal of Epidemiology and Community Health*, 52: 219–227.

CERC (1991) *Les Bas Salaires dans les pays de la Communauté Economique Européene*, CERC, Paris.

Citro, C. F. and Michael, R. T. (1995) *Measuring Poverty: A New Approach*, National Academy Press, Washington, DC.

Clark, A. and Oswald, A. (1994) 'Unhappiness and Unemployment', *Economic Journal*, 104: 648–659.

Commissione di Indagine sull'esclusione Sociale (2000*a*) *Rapporto annuale sulle politiche contro la povertà e l'esclusione sociale 2000*, Istituto Poligrafico e Zecca dello Stato, Rome.

—— (2000*b*) *La Povertà delle donne in Italia*, Istituto Poligrafico e Zecca dello Stato, Rome.

Commissione di Indagine sulle Povertà e sull'Emarginazione (1997*a*) *Povertà ed istruzione*, Istituto Poligrafico e Zecca dello Stato, Rome.

Commissione di Indagine sulle Povertà e sull'Emarginazione (1997*b*) *Povertà abitativa in Italia, 1989–1993*, Istituto Poligrafico e Zecca dello Stato, Rome.

Conseil d'Analyse Economique (CAE) (2001) *Inégalités économiques*, La Documentation Française, Paris.

Cornia, A. and Danziger, S. (1998) *Child Poverty and Deprivation in the Industrialized Countries 1945–1995*, Oxford University Press, Oxford.

Cowell, F. A. (1977) *Measuring Inequality*, Philip Allan, Deddington, Oxon.

——— and Victoria-Feser, M.-P. (1996) 'Poverty Measurement with Contaminated Data: A Robust Approach', *European Economic Review*, 40: 1761–1771.

da Costa, A. (1994) 'The Measurement of Poverty in Portugal', *Journal of European Social Policy*, 4: 95–115.

Davies, J. and Shorrocks, A. F. (2000) 'The Distribution of Wealth', in A. B. Atkinson and F. Bourguignon (eds.), *Handbook of Income Distribution*, North-Holland, Amsterdam.

De Beer, P. (2001) *Over werken in de post-industriële samenleving*, Sociaal-Cultureel Planbureau, The Hague.

De Lathouwer, L. and Bogaerts, K. (2000) *Schorsingsbeleid in de Werkloosheidsze-kering en Herintrede op de Arbeidsmarkt*, Federale Diensten voor Wetenschappe-lijke, Technische en Culturele Aangelegenheden, Brussels.

Deleeck, H., Cantillon, B., De Lathouwer, L., Van den Bosch, K. and Wyns, M. (1986*a*) 'Indicateurs de la sécurité sociale 1976–1985 (résultats globaux)', *Revue Belge de Sécurité Sociale*, annexe au 4–5.

———, Cantillon, B., De Lathouwer, L., Van den Bosch, K. and Wyns, M. (1986*b*), *Indicators of Social Security (General Results) 1976–1985*, Centre for Social Policy, University of Antwerp, Antwerp.

———, Cantillon, B., Meulemans, B. and Van den Bosch, K. (1991*a*) 'Sociale indicatoren van de sociale zekerheid 1985–1988', *Belgisch Tijdschrift voor Sociale Zekerheid*, 10–11–12: 711–761.

———, Cantillon, B., Meulemans, B. and Van den Bosch, K. (1991*b*) 'Indicateurs sociaux de la sécurité sociale 1985–1988', *Revue Belge de Sécurité Sociale*, 10–11–12: 689–756.

———, Van den Bosch, K. and Lathouwer, L. (1992) *Poverty and the Adequacy of Social Security in the EC*, Avebury, Aldershot.

Delors, J. (1971) *Les Indicateurs sociaux*, Futuribles, Paris.

De Neufville, J. I. (1975) *Social Indicators and Public Policy*, Elsevier, Amsterdam.

Denny, K. J. (2000) 'New Methods for Comparing Literacy across Populations', Institute for Fiscal Studies Working Paper No. W00/7.

———, Harmon, C. P. and Redmond, S. (2000) 'Functional Literacy, Educa-tional Attainment and Earnings', Institute for Fiscal Studies Working Paper No. W00/9.

De Witte, H. (1992) *Tussen optimisten en teruggetrokkenen: een empirisch onderzoek naar het psycho-sociaal profiel van langdurige werklozen en deelnemers aan de Weer-Werkactie in Vlaanderen*, HIVA, Leuven.

Dirven, H.-J. and Berghman, J. (1992) 'The Evolution of Income Poverty in the Netherlands', IVA, Tilburg.

De Witte, H. (2000) 'Houdingen tegenover arbeid in België op de drempel van de eenentwintigste eeuw', in K. Dobbelaere and M. Elchardus (eds.), *Verloren zekerheid: de Belgen en hun waarden, overtuigingen en houdingen*, Koning Boudewijnstichting, Tielt.

Ditch, J., Barnes, H., Bradshaw, J., Commaille, J. and Eardley, T. (1995*a*) *A Synthesis of National Family Policies 1994*, Vol. 1, European Observatory on National Family Policies, Social Policy Research Unit, York.

——, Barnes, H., Bradshaw, J., Commaille, J. and Eardley, T. (1995*b*), *Developments in National Family Policies in 1994*, Vol. 2, European Observatory on National Family Policies, Social Policy Research Unit, York.

——, Barnes, H. and Bradshaw, J. (1996*a*) *A Synthesis of National Family Policies 1995*, Vol. 1, European Observatory on National Family Policies, Social Policy Research Unit, York.

——, Barnes, H. and Bradshaw, J. (1996*b*) *Developments in National Family Policies in 1995*, Vol. 2, European Observatory on National Family Policies, Social Policy Research Unit, York.

——, Barnes, H. and Bradshaw, J. (1998) *A Synthesis of National Family Policies 1996*, Vol. 1, European Observatory on National Family Policies, Social Policy Research Unit, York.

Dougherty, C. (2000) 'Numeracy, Literacy, and Earnings', Centre for Economic Performance Discussion Paper No. 478, London School of Economics.

Durkheim, E. (1893) *The Division of Labour in Society*, Free Press, Glencoe, Ill., 1933.

Ebert, U. (1997) 'Social Welfare when Needs Differ: An Axiomatic Approach', *Economica*, 64: 233–244.

Erikson, R. (1993) 'Descriptions of Inequality: The Swedish Approach to Welfare Research', in M. C. Nussbaum and A. Sen (eds.), *The Quality of Life*, Clarendon Press, Oxford.

—— and Åberg, R. (eds.) (1987) *Welfare in Transition*, Clarendon Press, Oxford.

—— and Uusitalo, H. (1987) 'The Scandinavian Approach to Welfare Research', in R. Erikson, E. J. Hansen, S. Ringen and H. Uusiatalo (eds.), *The Scandinavian Model: Welfare States and Welfare Research*, M. E. Sharpe, Armonck, NY.

European Anti-Poverty Network (EAPN) (2001) *The European Strategy for Combating Poverty and Social Exclusion: EAPN Proposals for Evaluation, Monitoring and Indicators*, EAPN, Brussels.

European Commission (1981) *Final Report on the First Programme of Pilot Schemes and Studies to Combat Poverty*, COM(81), 769 (final), Brussels.

—— (1985) 'On Specific Community Action to Combat Poverty' (Council Decision of 19 December 1984), 85/8/EEC, *Official Journal of the EEC*, 2/24.

—— (1989) *The Fight against Poverty: Interim Report on the Second European Poverty Programme*, Social Europe, Supplement 2/89.

European Commission (1991) *Final Report on the Second European Poverty Programme 1985–1989*, Brussels.

—— (1992) *Toward a Europe of Solidarity: Intensifying the Fight against Social Exclusion, Fostering Integration*, Communication from the Commission, Brussels.

—— (1996) *First Report on Economic and Social Cohesion*, Brussels.

—— (1998) *A Guide to Gender Impact Assessment: Equality between Women and Men*, Office for Official Publications of the European Communities, Luxembourg.

—— (2000*a*) 'Structural Indicators', Communication from the Commission, COM (2000), 594 (final).

—— (2000*b*) 'Proposal for a Decision of the European Parliament and of the Council Establishing a Programme of Community Action to Encourage Cooperation between Member States to Combat Social Exclusion', COM (2000), 368 (final).

—— (2000*c*) *Employment in Europe*, Office for Official Publications of the European Communities, Luxembourg.

—— (2001*a*) 'Structural Indicators, Annex 2 to the Stockholm Report', Communication from the Commission, COM (2001), 79 (final/2).

—— (2001*b*) 'Employment and Social Policies: A Framework for Investing in Quality', Communication from the Commission.

Eurostat (1999) *European Community Household Panel* (ECHP): *Selected Indicators from the 1995 Wave*, Office for Official Publications of the European Communities, Luxembourg.

—— (2000*a*) *The Social Situation in the European Union*, Office for Official Publications of the European Communities, Luxembourg.

—— (2000*b*) *Income, Poverty and Social Exclusion in Member States of the European Union*, Office for Official Publications of the European Communities, Luxembourg.

—— (2001) *Key Data on Health 2000*, Office for Official Publications of the European Communities, Luxembourg.

Eurostat Task Force (1998) 'Recommendations on Social Exclusion and Poverty Statistics', Paper presented to the 26–27 Nov. 1998 meeting of the EU Statistical Programme Committee.

Expert Group on Household Income Statistics (Canberra Group) (2001) *Final Report and Recommendations*, Ottawa.

Figueiredo, J. B. and de Haan, A. (1998) *Social Exclusion: An ILO Perspective*, ILO, Geneva.

Firdion, J. M. and Marpsat, M. (2000) 'La Rue et le foyer', *Travaux et Documents*, INED No. 144.

Fisher, G. R. (1992) 'The Development and History of the Poverty Thresholds', *Social Security Bulletin*, 55: 3–14.

Fondation Roi Baudouin (1994) *Rapport Général sur la Pauvreté*, Pauwels S.A., Eeklo.

Förster, M. (2000) 'Trends and Driving Factors in Income Distribution and Poverty in the OECD Area', Labour Market and Social Policy Occasional Papers No. 42, OECD, Paris.

——, Redl, J., Tentschert, U. and Till, M. (2001) *Dimensions of Poverty in Austria in the Late 1990s*, European Centre, Vienna.

Foster, J. E., Greer, J. and Thorbecke, E. (1984) 'A Class of Decomposable Poverty Measures', *Econometrica*, 52: 761–766.

Fox, A. J. (1989) *Health Inequalities in European Countries*, Gower, Aldershot.

Friedman, M. (1957) *A Theory of the Consumption Function*, Princeton University Press, Princeton.

Gallie, D. (1999) 'Unemployment and Social Exclusion in the European Union', *European Societies*, 1: 139–167.

—— (2001) 'Working Life, Social Participation and Welfare', in G. Esping-Andersen, D. Gallie, A. Hemerijck and J. Myles, *A New Welfare State Architecture for Europe?* Forthcoming.

—— and Alm, S. (2000) 'Unemployment, Gender, and Attitudes to Work', in D. Gallie and S. Paugam (eds.), *Welfare Regimes and the Experience of Unemployment in Europe*, Oxford University Press, Oxford.

—— and Paugam, S. (eds.) (2000) *Welfare Regimes and the Experiences of Unemployment in Europe*, Oxford University Press, Oxford.

—— and Russell, H. (1998) 'Unemployment and Life Satisfaction: A Cross-Cultural Comparison', *European Journal of Sociology*, 2: 248–280.

Gemeenschappelijke Gemeenschapscommissie voor Brussel-Hoofstad (1993–2000) *Rapport over de staat van armoede in het Brusselse Hoofdstedelijk Gewest*, Gemeenschappelijke Gemeenschapscommissie voor Brussel-Hoofstad, Brussels.

Goldstein, H. and Spiegelhalter, D. J. (1996) 'League Tables and their Limitations: Statistical Issues in Comparisons of Institutional Performance', *Journal of the Royal Statistical Society*, Series A, 159: 385–443.

Gordon, D. and Townsend, P. (eds.) (2000) *Breadline Europe*, Policy Press, Bristol.

——, Adelman, A., Ashworth, K., Bradshaw, J., Levitas, R., Middleton, S., Pantazis, C., Patsios, D., Payne, S., Townsend, P. and Williams, J. (2000) *Poverty and Social Exclusion in Britain*, Joseph Rowntree Foundation, York.

Government of Belgium (2001) *Plan d'Action National Inclusion Sociale*, EU website, europa.eu.int/comm./employment social/news/2001/jun/napsincl2001 en.html.

Government of Denmark (2001) *Denmark's National Action Plan to Combat Poverty and Social Exclusion (NAPincl) 2001/2003*, EU website, europa.eu.int/comm./ employment social/news/2001/jun/napsincl2001 en.html.

Government of Federal Republic of Germany (2001) *National Action Plan to Combat Poverty and Social Exclusion (NAPincl) 2001–2003*, EU website, europa.eu.int/comm./employment social/news/2001/jun/napsincl2001 en.html.

Government of Finland (2001) *National Action Plan against Poverty and Social Exclusion*, EU website, europa.eu.int/comm./employment social/news/2001/jun/napsincl2001 en.html.

Government of France (2001) *Plan national d'action français contre la pauvreté et l'exclusion sociale*, EU website, europa.eu.int/comm./employment social/news/2001/jun/napsincl2001 en.html.

Government of Greece (2001) *National Action Plan for Social Inclusion*, EU website, europa.eu.int/comm./employment social/news/2001/jun/napsincl2001 en.html.

Government of Ireland (2001) *National Action Plan against Poverty and Social Exclusion (NAPincl) 2001–2003*, EU website europa.eu.int/comm./employment social/news/2001/jun/napsincl2001 en.html.

Government of Italy (2001) *Piano nazionale per l'inclusione 2001*, EU website, europa.eu.int/comm./employment social/news/2001/jun/napsincl2001 en.html.

Government of the Netherlands (2001) *Dutch National Action Plan against Poverty and Social Exclusion*, EU website, europa.eu.int/comm./employment social/news/2001/jun/napsincl2001 en.html.

Government of Portugal (2001) *Plan National d'Action pour l'Inclusion*, EU website, europa.eu.int/comm./employment social/news/2001/jun/napsincl2001 en.html.

Government of Republic of Austria (2001) *National Action Plan to Combat Poverty and Social Exclusion*, EU website, europa.eu.int/comm./employment social/news/2001/jun/napsincl2001 en.html.

Government of Spain (2001) *Plan National d'Action du Royaume d'Espagne pour l'Inclusion Sociale juin 2001–juin 2003*, EU website, europa.eu.int/comm./employment social/news/2001/jun/napsincl2001 en.html.

Government of Sweden (2001) *Sweden's Action Plan against Poverty and Social Exclusion*, EU website, europa.eu.int/comm./employment social/news/2001/jun/napsincl2001 en.html.

Government of the United Kingdom (2001) *United Kingdom National Action Plan on Social Inclusion 2001–2003*, EU website, europa.eu.int/comm./employment social/news/2001/jun/napsincl2001 en.html.

Grande-Duché de Luxembourg (2001) *Plan National d'Action pour L'Inclusion Sociale*, EU website, europa.eu.int/comm./employment social/news/2001/jun/napsincl2001 en.html.

Gregg, P. and Wadsworth, J. (1996) 'More Work in Fewer Households?' in J. Hills (ed.), *New Inequalities: The Changing Distribution of Income and Wealth in the United Kingdom*, Cambridge University Press, Cambridge.

Gregory, M. and Elias, P. (1994) 'Earnings Transitions of the Low-paid in Britain, 1976–91: A Longitudinal Study', *International Journal of Manpower*, 15: 170–188.

Gustafsson, B. (2000) 'Poverty in Sweden: Changes 1975–1995, Profile and Dynamics', in B. Gustafsson and P. J. Pedersen (eds.), *Poverty and Low Income in the Nordic Countries*, Ashgate, Aldershot.

Hagenaars, A., de Vos, K. and Zaidi, A. (1994) *Poverty Statistics in the Late 1980s*, Eurostat, Luxembourg.

Halleröd, B. (1995) 'The Truly Poor: Direct and Indirect Consensual Measurement of Poverty in Sweden', *Journal of European Social Policy*, 5: 111–129.

Hauser, R., Nolan, B., Morsdorf, C. and Strengmann-Kuhn, W. (2000a) 'Unemployment and Poverty: Change over Time', in D. Gallie and S. Paugam (eds.), *Welfare Regimes and the Experience of Unemployment in Europe*, Oxford University Press, Oxford.

——, Nolan, B. and Zoyem, J. P. (2000b) 'The Changing Effects of Social Protection on Poverty', in D. Gallie and S. Paugam (eds.), *Welfare Regimes and the Experience of Unemployment in Europe*, Oxford University Press, Oxford.

Hoff, S. and Jehoel-Gijsbers, G. (1998) *Een bestaan zonder baan*, SCP-Cahier 150, SCP/Elsevier bedrijfsinformatie, Rijswijk and The Hague.

Howarth, C., Kenway, P., Palmer, G. and Street, C. (1998) *Monitoring Poverty and Social Exclusion: Labour's Inheritance*, Joseph Rowntree Foundation, York.

——, Kenway, P., Palmer, G. and Miorelli, R. (1999) *Monitoring Poverty and Social Exclusion 1999*, Joseph Rowntree Foundation, York.

Husen, T. (ed.) (1967) *International Study of Achievement in Mathematics*, Almquist & Wiksell, Stockholm.

Immervoll, H. and O'Donoghue, C. (2001) 'Imputation of Gross Amounts from Net Incomes in Household Surveys: An Application Using EUROMOD', EUROMOD Working Paper No. EM1/01.

——, O'Donoghue, C. and Sutherland, H. (1999) 'An Introduction to EUROMOD', EUROMOD Working Paper No. EM0/99.

ISTAT (2000) 'Povertà in Italia 1999', *Note rapide*, 5, No. 5.

Jahoda, M., Lazarsfeld, and Zeisel, H. (1933) *Marienthal: The Sociography of an Unemployed Community*, Tavistock, London, 1972.

Jäntti, M. and Ritakallio, V.-M. (2000) 'Income Poverty in Finland 1971–1995', in B. Gustafsson and P. J. Pedersen (eds.), *Poverty and Low Income in the Nordic Countries*, Ashgate, Aldershot.

Jenkins, S. P. (1991) 'Poverty Measurement and the Within-household Distribution: Agenda for Action', *Journal of Social Policy*, 20: 457–483.

Johansson, S. (1973) 'The Level of Living Survey: A Presentation', *Acta Sociologica*, 16: 211–219.

Kaplan, G., Pamuk, E. R., Lynch, J. M., Cohen, R. D. and Balfour, J. L. (1996) 'Inequality in Income and Mortality in the United States: Analysis of Mortality and Potential Pathways', *British Medical Journal*, 312: 999–1003.

Klasen, S. (1999) 'Social Exclusion, Children and Education: Conceptual and Measurement Issues', University of Munich.

Koning Boudewijnstichting (1994) *Algemeen verslag over de armoede*, Koning Boudewijnstichting, Brussels.

Koolman, X. and Van Doorslaer, E. (2000) 'Inequalities in Self-Reported Health and Utilisation of Health Care in European Union Countries', mimeo, Erasmus University, Rotterdam.

Kunst, A. (1997) 'Cross-national Comparisons of Socio-economic Differences in Mortality', thesis, Erasmus University, Rotterdam.

Layte, R., Nolan, B. and Whelan, C. T. (2000) 'Targeting Poverty: Lessons from Monitoring Ireland's National Anti-poverty Strategy', *Journal of Social Policy*, 29: 553–575.

——, Maitre, B., Nolan, B. and Whelan, C. T. (2000*a*) 'Explaining Deprivation in the European Union', *Acta Sociologica*, 44(2): 105–122.

——, Maitre, B., Nolan, B. and Whelan, C. T. (2000*b*) 'Persistent and Consistent Poverty: An Analysis of the First Two Waves of the European Community Household Panel Survey', *Review of Income and Wealth*, Series 47, 4.

Leisering, L. and Leibfried, S. (1999) *Time and Poverty in Western Welfare States*, Cambridge University Press, Cambridge.

Levecque, K. and Vranken, J. (2000) 'La Valorisation des banques de données socio-economiques dans l'étude de la pauvreté et de l'exclusion sociale', *Revue Belge de la Sécurité Sociale*, 42: 193–214.

Lollivier, S. and Verger, D. (1997) 'Pauvreté d'existence, monétaire ou subjective sont distinctes', *Economie et Statistique*, 308–9–10: 113–42.

LoWER (European Low-Wage Employment Research Network) (1997) 'Statistical Data available on Low-Wage Employment in the European Union and its Member States', Special Report, LoWER, Groningen.

Mack, J. and Lansley, S. (1985) *Poor Britain*, Allen & Unwin, London.

Mackenbach, J., Kunst, A., Cavelaars, E., Groenhof, F., Geurts, J. *et al.* (1997) 'Socioeconomic Inequalities in Morbidity and Mortality in Western Europe', *The Lancet*, 349: 1655–1659.

MacRae, D. Jr (1985) *Policy Indicators: Links between Social Science and Public Debate*, University of North Carolina Press, Chapel Hill, NC.

Marlier, E. (1999) 'Dynamic Measures of Economic Activity and Unemployment: 1 and 2', *Statistics in Focus*, Theme 3, 17 and 18/1999.

—— and Cohen-Solal, M. (2000) 'Social Benefits and their Redistributive Effects', *Statistics in Focus*, Theme 3, 9/2000.

—— and Ponthieux, S. (2000) 'Low-Wage Employees in EU Countries', *Statistics in Focus*, Theme 3, 11/2000.

Marx, I. and Verbist, G. (1999) 'Low-Paid Work and Poverty: A Cross-Country Perspective', in M. Gregory, W. Salverda and S. Bazen (eds.), *Low-Wage Employment in Europe*, Edward Elgar, Cheltenham, Glos.

McGregor, P. L. and Borooah, V. K. (1992) 'Is Low Spending or Low Income a Better Indicator of Whether a Household is Poor', *Journal of Social Policy*, 21: 53–69.

McIntosh, S. and Vignoles, A. (2000) 'Measuring and Assessing the Impact of Basic Skills on Labour Market Outcomes', Centre for the Economics of Education Discussion Paper No. 6, London School of Economics.

Mejer, L. and Linden, G. (2000) 'Persistent Income Poverty and Social Exclusion in the European Union', *Statistics in Focus*, Theme 3, 13/2000.

Mejer, L. and Siermann, C. (2000) 'Income Poverty in the European Union: Children, Gender and Poverty Gaps', *Statistics in Focus*, Theme 3, 12/2000.

Micklewright, J. (2001) 'Should the UK Government Measure Poverty and Social Exclusion with a Composite Index?' in CASE, *Indicators of Progress: A Discussion of Approaches to Monitor the Government's Strategy to Tackle Poverty and Social Exclusion*, CASE Report No. 13, London School of Economics.

—— and Stewart, K. (1999) 'Is the Well-being of Children Converging in the European Union?', *Economic Journal*, 109: F692–F714.

—— and Stewart, K. (2000a) *The Welfare of Europe's Children*, Policy Press, Bristol.

—— and Stewart, K. (2000b) 'Child Well-Being in the EU and Enlargement to the East', in K. Vleminckx and T. Smeeding (eds.), *Child Well-being, Child Poverty and Child Policy in Modern Nations*, Policy Press, Bristol.

—— and Stewart, K. (2001) 'Poverty and Social Exclusion in Europe', *New Economy*, 8: 104–109.

Ministère de la Région Wallonne (2001) *Premier Rapport sur la Cohesion Sociale en Région Wallonne*, Direction Interdépartmentale de l'Integration Sociale, Jambes.

Ministry of Economic Affairs (2000) *Familier og Indkomster*, Ministry of Economic Affairs, Copenhagen.

MISSOC (various years) *Social Protection in the Member States of the Union*, DG-V, Brussels.

Muffels, R., Kapteyn, A. and Berghman, J. (1990) *Poverty in the Netherlands*, VUGA,'s-Gravenhage.

——, Berghman, J. and Dirven, H.-J. (1992) 'A Multi-Method Approach to Monitor the Evolution of Poverty', *Journal of European Social Policy*, 2: 193–213.

National Anti-Poverty Strategy (1997) *Sharing in Progress*, Stationery Office, Dublin.

New Zealand Ministry of Health (2000) *Social Inequalities in Health: New Zealand 1999*, Ministry of Health, Wellington.

Noble, M. and Smith, G. (1996) 'Two Nations? Changing Patterns of Income and Wealth in Two Contrasting Areas', in J. Hills (ed.), *New Inequalities*, Cambridge University Press, Cambridge.

Nolan, B. and Callan, T. (eds.), (1994) *Poverty and Policy in Ireland*, Gill & Macmillan, Dublin.

—— and Marx, I. (2000) 'Low Pay and Household Poverty', in M. Gregory, W. Salverda and S. Bazen (eds.), *Labour Market Inequalities. Problems and Policies of Low-Wage Employment in International Perspective*. Oxford University Press, Oxford.

—— and Whelan, C. T. (1996a) *Resources, Deprivation, and Poverty*, Clarendon Press, Oxford.

—— and Whelan, C. T. (1996b) 'Measuring Poverty using Income and Deprivation Indicators: Alternative Approaches', *Journal of European Social Policy*, 6: 225–240.

Nolan, B., O'Connell, P. J. and Whelan, C. T. (2000) *Bust to Boom: The Irish Experience of Growth and Inequality*, Institute of Public Administration, Dublin.

Observatoire National de la Pauvreté et de l'Exclusion Sociale (2000) *Travaux de l'Observatoire national de la pauvreté et de l'exclusion sociale*, La Documentation Française, Paris.

Observatoire Social Européen (2001) *Les Indicateurs monétaires et non-monétaires de pauvreté et de l'exclusion sociale dans l'Union européene*.

OECD (1982) *Social Indicators*, OECD, Paris.

—— (1983) *Employment Outlook*, OECD, Paris.

—— (1986) *Living Conditions in OECD Countries*, OECD, Paris.

—— (1987) *Employment Outlook*, OECD, Paris.

—— (1990) *Employment Outlook*, OECD, Paris.

—— (1993) *Employment Outlook*, OECD, Paris.

—— (1994a) *Employment Outlook*, OECD, Paris.

—— (1994b) *The Jobs Study*, OECD, Paris.

—— (1995) *Employment Outlook*, OECD, Paris.

—— (1996) *Employment Outlook*, OECD, Paris.

—— (1997) *Education at a Glance*, OECD, Paris.

—— (1998) *Employment Outlook*, OECD, Paris

—— (2000a) *Education at a Glance*, OECD, Paris.

—— (2000b) *Measuring Student Knowledge and Skills: A New Framework for Assessment*, OECD, Paris.

—— (2001a) *Employment Outlook*, OECD, Paris.

—— (2001b) *Society at a Glance: OECD Social Indicators*, OECD, Paris.

Oxfam, G. B. (1998) 'Participatory and Qualitative Indicators and Success Measures', Memorandum to the Select Committee on Social Security.

Oxley, H., Burniaux, J.-M., Dang, T.-T. and d'Ercole, M. M. (1997) 'Income Distribution and Poverty in 13 OECD Countries', *OECD Economic* Studies, No. 29: 55–94.

Paugam, S. (1996) *L'Exclusion: l'état des savoirs*, La Découverte, Paris.

—— and Russell, H. (2000) 'The Effects of Employment Precarity and Unemployment on Social Isolation', in D. Gallie and S. Paugam (eds.), *Welfare Regimes and the Experience of Unemployment in Europe*, Oxford University Press, Oxford.

Pedersen, P. J. and Smith, N. (2000) 'Low Incomes in Denmark 1980–1995', in B. Gustafsson and P. J. Pedersen (eds.), *Poverty and Low Income in the Nordic Countries*, Ashgate, Aldershot.

Pen, J. (1971) *Income Distribution*, Allen Lane the Penguin Press, London.

Pollet, I., De Weerdt, Y., Van Hootegem, G. and De Witte, H. (2000) *Pizzas, software en jobs? Laaggeschoold en dienstverlenend: met hoeveel zijn ze, wat doen ze?* HIVA, Leuven.

Prais, S. J. (1993) 'Economic Performance and Education: The Nature of Britain's Deficiencies', *Proceedings of the British Academy*, 84: 151–207.

Putnam, R. (2000) *Bowling Alone*, Harvard University Press, Cambridge, Mass.

Rendall, M. and Speare, A. (1993) 'Comparing Economic Well-Being among Elderly Americans', *Review of Income and Wealth*, 39: 1–21.

Revell, K. and Leather, P. (2000) *The State of UK Housing*, 2nd edn, Policy Press, Bristol.

Ringen, S. (1988) 'Direct and Indirect Measures of Poverty', *Journal of Social Policy*, 17: 351–365.

Robitaille, D. F. and Garden, R. A. (eds.) (1989) *The IEA Study of Mathematics*, Pergamon, Oxford.

Rodgers, G., Gore, C. and Figueiredo, J. B. (1995) *Social Exclusion: Rhetoric, Reality, Responses*, ILO, Geneva.

Room, G. (ed.) (1995) *Beyond the Threshold*, Policy Press, Bristol.

Rothenbacher, F. (1998) 'European Scientific Socio-Economic Reporting: State and Possibilities of Development', *Social Indicators Research*, 43: 291–328.

Rowntree, B. S. (1901) *Poverty: A Study of Town Life*, Longmans, London.

Ruggles, P. (1990) *Drawing the Line: Alternative Poverty Measures and their Implications for Public Policy*, Urban Institute Press, Washington, DC.

—— and Williams, R. (1989) 'Longitudinal Measures of Poverty: Accounting for Income and Assets over Time', *Review of Income and Wealth*, 35: 225–244.

Ruiz-Castillo, J. (1987) *La Medición de la Pobreza y de la Desigualdad en España, 1980–81*, Estudios Económicos, Banco de España, No. 42.

Saraceno, C. (ed.) (2002) *Social Assistance Dynamics in European Countries*, Policy Press, Bristol.

Schuyt, C. (1995) *Tegendraadse werkingen: sociologische opstellen over de onvooorziene gevolgen van verzorging en verzekering*, Amsterdam University Press, Amsterdam.

Sen, A. K. (1974) 'Informational Bases of Alternative Welfare Approaches', *Journal of Public Economics*, 3: 387–403.

—— (1976) 'Poverty: An Ordinal Approach to Measurement', *Econometrica*, 44: 219–231.

—— (1985) *Commodities and Capabilities*, North-Holland, Amsterdam.

—— (1999) *Development as Freedom*, Oxford University Press, Oxford.

—— and Foster, J. (1997) *On Economic Inequality*, 2nd edn, Clarendon Press, Oxford.

Seymour, J. (2000) *Poverty in Plenty: A Human Development Report for the UK*, Earthscan, London.

Silver, H. (1994) 'Social Exclusion and Solidarity: Three Paradigms', *International Labour Review*, 133: 531–578.

Sinfield, A. (1981) *What Unemployment Means*, Martin Robertson, Oxford.

Sloane, P. and Theodossiou, I. (1996) 'Earnings Mobility, Family Income and Low Pay', *Economic Journal*, 106: 657–666.

—— and Theodossiou, I. (1998) 'An Econometric Analysis of Low Pay and Earnings Mobility in Britain', in R. Asplund, P. Sloane and I. Theodossiou (eds.), *Low Pay and Earnings Mobility in Europe*, Edward Elgar, Aldershot.

Sloane, P. and Theodossiou, I. (2000) 'Earnings Mobility of the Low Paid', in M. Gregory, W. Salverda and S. Bazen (eds.), *Labour Market Inequalities: Problems and Policies of Low-Wage Employment in International Perspective*, Oxford University Press, Oxford.

Smeeding, T. and Weinberg, D. (2001) 'Toward a Uniform Definition of House-hold Income', *Review of Income and Wealth*, 47: 1–24.

Social and Cultural Planning Office (SCP) (2001) *Armoedemonitor*, SCP, The Hague.

Standing, G. (1999) *Global Labour Flexibility: Seeking Distributive Justice*, Macmillan, London.

Statistics Canada and United States National Center for Education Statistics (1999) 'Adult Literacy and Lifeskills Survey International Planning Report', Discussion Paper at a meeting, 23–24 September, Luxembourg.

Steedman, H. (1999) 'Measuring the Quality of Educational Outputs: Some Unresolved Problems', in R. Alexander, A. R. Broadfoot and D. Phillips (eds.), *Learning from Comparing: New Directions in Comparative Educational Research*, Vol. 1, Symposium Books, Oxford.

—— and McIntosh, S. (2001) 'Measuring Low Skills in Europe: How Useful is the ISCED Framework?' *Oxford Economic Papers*, 53: 564–581.

Strauss, J. and Thomas, D. (1996) 'Measurement and Mismeasurement of Social Indicators', *American Economic Review*, Papers and Proceedings, 86: 30–34.

Sutherland, H. (1997) 'Women, Men and the Redistribution of Income', *Fiscal Studies*, 18: 1–22.

—— (2000*a*) 'EUROMOD', in A. Gupta and V. Kapur (eds.), *Microsimulation in Government Policy and Forecasting*, North-Holland, Amsterdam.

—— (2000*b*) 'EUROMOD', *Transfer*, 6: 312–316.

Townsend, P. (1979) *Poverty in the United Kingdom*, Allen Lane, Harmondsworth.

Tsakloglou, P. (1990) 'Aspects of Poverty in Greece', *Review of Income and Wealth*, 36: 381–402.

—— and Panopoulou, G. (1998) 'Who Are the Poor in Greece?' *Journal of European Social Policy*, 8: 213–236.

UK Department of Social Security (1996*a*) *Households below Average Income: Methodological Review*, Analytical Services Division, London.

—— (1996*b*) *Social Assistance in OECD Countries*, HMSO, London.

—— (1999) *Opportunity for All*, HMSO, London.

—— (2000*a*) *Opportunity for All: One Year On*, HMSO, London.

—— (2000*b*) *Households Below Average Income: 1994/5 to 1998/9*, Corporate Document Services, Leeds.

UN Centre for Human Settlements (2001) *The Habitat Agenda*, UNCHS website, www.unchs.org/unchs/english/hagenda/index.htm.

UNDP (2000) *Human Development Report 2000*, Oxford University Press, Oxford.

UNICEF (2000) *A League Table of Child Poverty in Rich Nations*, UNICEF, Florence.

US Department of Health, Education, and Welfare (1969) *Toward a Social Report*, US Government printing Office, Washington, DC.

Van Dam, R. and Geurts, V. (2000) *De bewoners van gesubsidieerde en nietgesubsidieerde woningen in Vlaanderen: profiel, woningkwaliteit en betaalbaarheid*, Berichten/UFSIA, Centrum voor Sociaal Beleid, Antwerp.

Van den Bosch, K. (1998) 'Poverty and Assets in Belgium', *Review of Income and Wealth*, 44: 215–228.

—— (2001) *Identifying the Poor, Using Subjective and Consensual Measures*, Ashgate, Aldershot.

Van Doorslaer, E. and Koolman, X. (2000) 'Income-related Inequalities in Health in Europe: Evidence from the European Community Household Panel', Working Paper, Department of Health Policy and Management, Erasmus University, Rotterdam.

——, Wagstaff, A. *et al.* (1992) 'Equity in the Delivery of Health Care: Some International Comparisons', *Journal of Health Economics*, 11: 389–411.

——, Wagstaff, A., Bleichrodt, H. *et al.* (1997) 'Income-related Inequalities in Health: Some International Comparisons', *Journal of Health Economics*, 16: 93–112.

——, Wagstaff, A. *et al.* (2000) 'Equity in the Delivery of Health Care in Europe and the US', *Journal of Health Economics*, 19: 553–583.

van Praag, B. M. S. and Kapteyn, A. (1994) 'How Sensible is the Leyden Individual Welfare Function of Income? A Reply', *European Economic Review*, 38: 1817–1825.

——, Hagenaars, A. J. and van Weeren, H. (1982) 'Poverty in Europe', *Review of Income and Wealth*, 28: 345–359.

Veit-Wilson, J. H. (1998) *Setting Adequacy Standards*, Policy Press, Bristol.

Vleminckx, K. and Smeeding, T. (eds.) (2000) *Child Well-being, Child Poverty and Child Policy in Modern Nations*, Policy Press, Bristol.

Vogel, J. (1997a) 'Social Indicators: A Swedish Perspective', *Journal of Public Policy*, 9: 439–444.

—— (1997b) 'The Future Direction of Social Indicator Research', *Social Indicators Research*, 42: 103–116.

Voges, W. (2001) 'Inclusion or Exclusion via Minimum Income Support Policy?' Centre for Social Policy Research, Bremen.

Vranken, J. and Geldof, D. (1992) *Armoede en sociale uitsluiting: Jaarboek 1991*, Acco, Leuven/Amersfoort.

—— and Geldof, D. (1993) *Armoede en sociale uitsluiting: Jaarboek 1992–1993*, Acco, Leuven/Amersfoort.

——, Geldof, D. and Van Menxel, G. (1994) *Armoede en sociale uitsluiting: Jaarboek 1994*, Acco, Leuven/Amersfoort.

——, Geldof, D. and Van Menxel, G. (1995) *Armoede en sociale uitsluiting: Jaarboek 1995*, Acco, Leuven/Amersfoort.

——, Geldof, D. and Van Menxel, G. (1996) *Armoede en sociale uitsluiting: Jaarboek 1996*, Acco, Leuven/Amersfoort.

——, Geldof, D. and Van Menxel, G. (1997) *Armoede en sociale uitsluiting: Jaarboek 1997*, Acco, Leuven/Amersfoort.

——, Adiaenssens, S. and Block, T. (1998*a*) 'Valorisatie federale sociaal-economische databanken: armoede en sociale uitsluiting', UFSIA, Antwerp.

——, Geldof, D. and Van Menxel, G. (1998*b*) *Armoede en sociale uitsluiting: Jaarboek 1998*, Acco, Leuven/Amersfoort.

——, Geldof, D. and Van Menxel, G. (eds.) (1999) *Armoede en sociale uitsluiting: Jaarboek 1999*, Acco, Leuven/Amersfoort.

—— et al. (eds.) (2000) *Armoede en sociale uitsluiting: Jaarboek 2000*, Acco, Leuven/Leusden.

——, De Keulenaer, F., Estivill, J., Aiguabella, J., Breuer, W. and Sellin, C. (2001) *Towards a Policy-Relevant European Database on Forms of Social Exclusion*, UFSIA, Antwerp.

Waldegrave, C. and Stephens, B. (2000) 'Poverty: The Litmus Test of Social and Economic Policy Failure', Second Biennial Aotearoa New Zealand International Development Studies Network (DEVNET) Conference.

Wagstaff, A. (2000) 'Measuring Equity in Health Care Financing: Reflections and Alternatives to WHO's Fairness in Financing Index', Policy Research Working Paper No. 2550, World Bank, Washington DC.

Whelan, C. T., Layte, R., Maitre, B. and Nolan, B. (2001) 'Persistent Income Poverty and Deprivation in the European Union', European Panel Analysis Group Working Paper No. 17, Institute for Social and Economic Research, University of Essex, Wivenhoe.

Wilkinson, R. G. (1996) *Unhealthy Societies: The Afflictions of Inequality*, Routledge, London.

Wolff, E. (1990) 'Wealth Holdings and Poverty Status in the US', *Review of Income and Wealth*, 36: 143–165.

Wolfson, M. and Evans, J. M. (1989) *Statistics Canada's Low Income Cut-Offs*, Research Paper Series, Statistics Canada, Ottawa.

World Bank (1996) *Social Indicators of Development 1996*, Johns Hopkins University Press, Baltimore.

—— (2001) *World Development Report 2000/2001 Attacking Poverty*, Oxford University Press, Oxford.

World Health Organisation (2000), *The World Health Report 2000 Health Systems: Improving Performance*, WHO, Geneva.

Zaidi, A. and de Vos, K. (2001) 'Trends in Consumption-Based Poverty and Inequality in the European Union during the 1980s', *Journal of Population Economics*, 14: 367–390.

Author Index

Subject Index